In the service of the company

Letters of Sir Edward Parry, Commissioner to the Australian Agricultural Company

Volume II: June 1832 – March 1834

Edited by Dr Pennie Pemberton

E PRESS

Published by ANU E Press
The Australian National University
Canberra ACT 0200, Australia
Email: anuepress@anu.edu.au
Web: http://epress.anu.edu.au

Previously published by the Noel Butlin Archives Centre
The Australian National University

National Library of Australia
Cataloguing-in-Publication data:
Parry, William Edward, Sir, 1790-1855.
In the service of the company: letters of Sir Edward Parry,
Commissioner to the Australian Agricultural Company.
Volume II, June 1832-March 1834.

Includes index.
ISBN 0 7315 4634 2

1. Parry, William Edward, Sir, 1790-1855 - Correspondence.
2. Australian Agricultural Company.
3. Pioneers - Australia - Correspondence. I. Australian National University. Noel Butlin Archives Centre. II. Title.

994.4202

All rights reserved. No part of this publication may be reproduced, stored in a retrieval system or transmitted in any form or by any means, electronic, mechanical, photocopying or otherwise, without the prior permission of the publisher.

Cover: Tahlee House, 1830: Sir Edward Parry's residence at Carrington, Port Stephens. Work on the house commenced in 1826. The south west (left hand) wing was completed in April 1831. The north east (right hand wing) was not built. [Noel Butlin Archives Centre, Australian Agricultural Company, Deposit 1, Plan 11]

Designed by Green Words & Images (GWi)
Cover design by Brendon McKinley

Transcribed and edited by the Noel Butlin Archives Centre, The Australian National University, Canberra ACT 0200

First edition © 2003 The Australian National University
This edition © 2004 ANU E Press

CONTENTS

Acknowledgements	ii
Preface by Professor Alan Atkinson	iii
Introduction by Dr Pennie Pemberton	v
Note on transcription	x
List of maps and illustrations	xi
1832, letters No 637 - 764	1
1833, letters No 765 - 1,048	91
1834, letters No 1,049 - 1,107	231
Index	257

ACKNOWLEDGEMENTS

The project to transcribe this volume has been undertaken to enhance the accessibility of an item significant for the history of business in Australia. It has been a real team effort. Sir Edward Parry's letter books were deposited with the Noel Butlin Archives Centre (then The Australian National University Archives of Business and Labour) by the Australian Agricultural Company in 1956, and this volume is now published with the Company's approval. We would like to thank Kim Morris of Art & Archival Pty Ltd for conservation work. We are most grateful to the Thyne Reid Charitable Trusts for a grant towards the conservation and transcription of these letter books. In this connection, we would also like to thank Bruno Yvanovich of the ANU Development Office for his assistance. The original transcription of the faded, heavily abbreviated handwriting was undertaken with enthusiasm by Sandra Coupard. Subsequent editing and proofreading was carried out by Chelsey Bell, Emma Jolley, Mary Paton and Pennie Pemberton. Barry Howarth provided the detailed index, and Winfred Mumford drew the maps from originals held by the Noel Butlin Archives Centre and State Records New South Wales. Maven Online Media scanned the images. Members of the Centre's staff, led by Emma Jolley with assistance from Tatiana Antsoupova, Mary Paton and Deirdre Ward, administered the project. Finally, we are indebted to Professor Alan Atkinson, School of Classics History & Religion, University of New England, for writing the preface.

Dr Sigrid McCausland
The Australian National University Archives Program
October 2003

PREFACE

The Australian Agricultural Company occupies a strange, half-way position in the story of Australian settlement. On the one hand it was just another large sample of free enterprise, similar to any number of others which have characterised Australia since the 1820s. On the other hand the Company's early aspirations and experience cast a distinctive, sideways light on the whole business of colonisation.

Increasingly, towards the end of the twentieth century, Australian historians have been preoccupied with the story of the nation. A hopeful and enlightening move this may be in many ways. But we lose a little as well. In the first place, a concern with the nation as such means less interest in the way in which the various colonies began and evolved, each in its own right – their fundamental ideals, their methods of government and so forth. Even the foundations of democracy and of mass education during the second half of mid-nineteenth century seem less important now because they were colonial rather than national achievements.

In these circumstances it may be even more difficult to appreciate the significance of the Australian Agricultural Company as a colonising effort. Founded by an Act of the British Parliament in 1824 the Company followed very deliberately in the steps of those great chartered enterprises which had sent English capital and labour to several parts of North America – to Virginia, Pennsylvania, Massachusetts and Georgia – when that continent was, from an English perspective, a "wilderness". But the A. A. Company itself set a precedent. It was one of several such enterprises designed for the frontier of settlement in Europe's antipodes. The Van Diemen's Land Company followed almost immediately. Both the A. A. Company and the V. D. L. Company took very large grants of land and their acreage made it hard for them to position themselves anywhere but at a distance from the colonial capitals. But there was a virtue also in isolation. Both were to be mini-colonies in their own right, subject to the governors in Sydney and in Hobart but ruled as well from board-rooms in London.

Some of the founders of settlement at Swan River, in Western Australia, hoped to use the same model. This scheme came unstuck, but its failure did not prevent the foundation of the South Australian Company as an essential part of the project at St Vincent Gulf in the mid 1830s – the "province" of South Australia. There too there was a peculiar tension, for a time, between the company's little principality on Kangaroo Island and the governor in Adelaide. Finally, across the Tasman, the New Zealand Company was profoundly important in the settlement of New Zealand during the 1840s.

In each case the tug of war was not only one of rival authorities. It was also a matter of varying idealism. It would be wrong to be too starry-eyed about the altruistic hopes of the Australian Agricultural Company. As with all these enterprises, the main point was to make money. To some extent high-mindedness was a disguise, taken up in order to win friends in Parliament and to put as much pressure as possible on the Colonial Office in the argument for Crown land and convict labour. But there certainly was an understanding that the Company represented something unprecedented in the colonisation of the Australian mainland. It was designed to create in this country a new kind of workforce, and thus a new kind of population – moral, orderly and intelligent. It was a striking symptom of the kind of ambition which was now focussed on this part of the world. This was a chartered company backed by large official promises. It represented one aspect of a powerful combination of free and state enterprise, a combination characteristic of the period which followed the Napoleonic wars and one which may be too little understood in Australian history. Here, in some ways, was a curious echo of eighteenth-century mercantilism. But here too was the beginning of that tradition, so important for Australia, which made officialdom itself into something of an entrepreneur.

The Australian Agricultural Company thus offered an unusual challenge to the government in Sydney. The local committee which managed in the first years was the most powerful body which had ever existed in the colony, outside government. The commissioners who took over from the committee from 1829 were also important men, though as the colony expanded they became gradually less obvious in the overall scheme of things. Sir Edward Parry, the first commissioner, was a particularly striking figure, a gentleman of title, certain of his own importance, highly intelligent and determined to make the Company a moral enterprise – a beacon of high-minded paternalism for the colony at large.

In some ways then, the early records of the Australian Agricultural Company have an importance for historians similar to *Historical Records of New South Wales* and the *Historical Records of Australia*. They do not have the same far-ranging significance, but as a core of official data they tell a similar story of order imposed and of idealism both realised and disappointed. In reading one by one the governor's despatches, as they appear in *HRNSW* and *HRA*, it is possible to trace the unfolding of personality among leading figures as well as catching a little at least of the cross-currents of lesser lives. The same can be done with the records reproduced here.

This was government in the bush. The Company's ambivalent character is frequently obvious – money-making is often overlaid in these documents with a sense of some larger purpose, or at least some larger dignity. In that way the official records of the Company not only say something about the early possibilities of government in Australia but also about the early possibilities of capitalism.

Professor Alan Atkinson
University of New England

INTRODUCTION

The Australian Agricultural Company was formed in London in April 1824 to raise fine woolled sheep on a Crown Grant in the Colony of New South Wales. The labour-force was to consist mainly of assigned convicts, but the Company was to send out overseers, shepherds, mechanics and other servants, together with a supply of pure-bred Merino sheep, cattle and horses.

The first Company 'Establishment' sailed from England in June 1825 on the *York* and the *Brothers* – under the direction of the Company's Agent, Robert Dawson. Dawson was to be supported in his endeavours by a Colonial Committee of Management composed of local shareholders. In the event, the members of the Committee were James Macarthur, Dr James Bowman and Hannibal Hawkins McArthur.

Soon after his arrival, in early 1826, Dawson made the decision to take up the whole of the Company's one million acre grant between Port Stephens and the Manning River. The next two years were occupied with exploration and the establishment of the Company Settlement at Carrabean (later Carrington) on the northern shore of Port Stephens, No 1 Farm (near Carrington), No 2 Farm (Stroud), and a chain of sheep stations north towards the out station at Gloucester.

Meanwhile, in London, the Company had been prevailed on to take over the coal mines at Newcastle NSW. The Mining Establishment, under John Henderson, arrived aboard the *Australia* in November 1826. Through various misunderstandings between the Company, the Company's Colonial Committee, the 'Home Government' (London) and the 'Local' Government' (NSW), the matter did not proceed, the differences being referred back to London for resolution.

Robert Dawson was dismissed by the Colonial Committee in April 1828. When the news was received in London, the Directors sought to appoint an authoritative Commissioner who could manage their operations without an advisory Colonial Committee. Their choice was Captain William Edward Parry RN (1790-1855), then Hydrographer Royal. In 1829 he and John Franklin were knighted in recognition of their naval expeditions between 1817 and 1825 in the Canadian Arctic in search of the North West Passage.

Sir Edward Parry and his wife Isabella (née Stanley) arrived in New South Wales in December 1829 aboard the *William*. His brief was to restore and maintain due order in the Company's establishments; to review the situation of the Company's million acre Grant on the northern shores of Port Stephens and arrange an exchange of lands if necessary; and to negotiate further with the Colonial Government over the management of coal mines. By the time this volume opens, some matters had been resolved.

The Land Grant
It had been agreed that that the eastern part of the Port Stephens Estate (around the Great Lakes) should be returned to the Crown and an area equivalent in size should be taken in another elsewhere. The selection of this new location took up a good deal of Parry's time, as will be seen from the number of letters dedicated to the subject.

The Coal Mines at Newcastle
By mid 1832, the Company's mine (A Pit) at Newcastle had been in regular operation for six months. In part to compensate the Company for the expense of the extended negotiations, the Home Government had agreed to a thirty one year monopoly for the Company's coal mining operations.

The questions which remain to be resolved, and covered by these letters, include the price at which coal was to be sold to the Government and the area and location of the 2,000 acre land grant at Newcastle.

The Company's Establishment

Officers
Under Parry as Commissioner – based at Tahlee, near Carrington – the Company's Establishment at Port Stephens was divided into departments: Accounts (Accountant J E Ebsworth), Flocks (Superintendent Charles Hall), Cattle, Stud and Agriculture (Superintendent Henry Hall), and Works (Superintendent Thomas Lindsay Ebsworth). The Coal Establishment in Newcastle consisted of John Henderson (Colliery Manager), William Croasdill (Accountant) and James Steel (Engineer). Other officers included the Surgeon and Botanist, Dr James Edward Stacy, the Surveyors John Armstrong and Henry Dangar, and Parry's private secretary, Henry Darch.

Indentured Servants
Most of the overseers, and some of the shepherds and mechanics were originally recruited in Europe: England, Scotland and Germany. They were collectively known as the 'indented servants', from the 'indentures' or contracts they had signed to serve the Company for a fixed period, usually seven years. By early 1832 many of these contracts were coming up for renewal or cancellation.

Convicts/Assigned Servants
Most of the Company's shepherds, stockmen and labourers, were convicts otherwise termed 'assigned servants'. Convicts had either a fixed term sentence, usually seven or fourteen years, or Life. Others employees in this general category included:

- Ticket of leave men, that is convicts holding a 'ticket' entitling them a degree of freedom of occupation and lodging within a nominated district (such as Port Stephens) before the end of their sentence or obtaining a pardon, or

- Emancipists, that is former convicts whose terms had expired or who had obtained a pardon.

Obtaining sufficient numbers of convicts was a constant battle for the Company: the Board for the Assignment of Servants never had sufficient newcomers to meet the increasing demand; nor even to replace those whose sentences were completed.

The indentured servants and emancipists were also generally categorised as 'Free' (F), the assigned servants and ticket-of-leave men as 'Convict' (C).

Military Establishment
Although appointed justices of the peace, neither Sir Edward Parry, nor Edward Ebsworth could act in cases concerning Company servants, free or convict. These were matters for the Resident Magistrate, Captain Moffatt, who headed the small military police establishment based at Port Stephens. The maintenance of the police establishment, the responsibility for payment of salaries and wages, and relations with the Company's own convict constables, were frequently the subject of correspondence.

Company Chaplain
Sir Edward Parry actively sought the support of the Directors in the appointment of a Chaplain. In the meantime he personally conducted the Sunday services, baptisms and funerals at Port Stephens, arranging occasional visits by the Archdeacon and other clergy whenever possible. The appointment of Charles Price, a Congregational minister, as Chaplain caused some controversy amongst the Company's Officers, and invoked the disapproval of the Archdeacon, William Grant Broughton.

Colonial Shareholders
The Company's capital stock was divided into 10,000 shares, each to a nominal value of £100. As additional monies were needed, 'calls' were made on the shareholders. By 1832, thirteen calls had been made, totalling £23 per £100 share.

Two hundred shares had been reserved for offer to colonial shareholders, and the Commissioner was responsible for arranging the collection of the calls as they came due. By mid 1832, several of the original colonial shareholders had died (eg John Piper, John Oxley and Robert Campbell); others had transferred responsibility for call payments to their English agents (eg Alexander Berry, Thomas Icely and Matthew Hindson, William Walker and the Macarthurs). Most of the remainder forfeited their shares through non-payment in 1834.

Sales and Stores
As far as possible, the Company sought to be self-contained. Annually, stores from colliery machinery to slop clothing, shoes and wool bales were dispatched from London on requisition.

At Port Stephens the Company attempted to raise its own grain and tobacco for rations – and such things as pit props for Newcastle. However, such self-sufficiency was never completely possible – and it was necessary to advertise for tenders of wheat and other staples; the sale of horses and cattle at the Maitland sales; and the services of the Company's stallions.

The Company's wool clip was intended for the London auction houses. From the first it was necessary to advertise for additional shearers, and for transport to convey the wool from Port Stephens to Sydney and thence to England. Many of these matters were handled through the Company's agents in Sydney, the merchant house of George Bunn & Co.

The Company cutter *Lambton* (62 tons) had been purchased in from the New Zealand Company in March 1827. Under her master, James Corlette, she plied between Sydney and Port Stephens, occasionally via Newcastle. However, as a sailing ship, she could be unreliable in unfavourable weather.

After the establishment of the regular steamship service between Sydney and Maitland/Morpeth, Sir Edward Parry frequently used it for the prompt dispatch of mail, or to travel himself, especially when visiting Newcastle – riding from Tahlee to 'Kinross', James Graham's grant at the confluence of the Hunter and Williams Rivers – just below Raymond Terrace, where he boarded the steamer.

In 1834, on the completion of his term, Sir Edward Parry with his family returned to London aboard the *Persian*. He was succeeded as the Company's Commissioner by Lieutenant Colonel Henry Dumaresq.

The Archives of the Australian Agricultural Company
The extensive archives of the Australian Agricultural Company, including the records of both the London and Australian head offices, have been deposited with the Noel Butlin Archives Centre (formerly the ANU Archives of Business and Labour) since 1955.

Sir Edward Parry's correspondence and record keeping as Commissioner to the Australian Agricultural Company was voluminous. In addition to the letters contained in these letterbooks, he wrote lengthy formal, usually monthly, Despatches to the Directors in England [NBAC reference 78/1], kept a Demi-Official Letter Book ([NBAC reference 1/2B] also to be transcribed), Order Books (of instructions to the Company's Officers, Indentured and Assigned Servants), and an official journal or diary (the diary is held by the Mitchell Library, State Library of New South Wales).

The copies of Sir Edward's letters written for recipients in New South Wales are contained in two leather-bound volumes, 36.5 x 23.5 cm (14" x 9"), containing 300 pages, feint-ruled [NBAC reference 1/38/1-2]. The first volume covers the period 1829-1832, the second – this volume – the period

1832-1834. As the second volume was both easier to read and needed of less conservation work, it was transcribed first. Work on the first volume is now in hand.

It would seem, from internal evidence, that Sir Edward (or J. Edward Ebsworth in Parry's absence) would write the final draft of a letter into copybook or amend an existing letter in pencil, from which Parry's Secretary, Henry Darch, would write the final version 'in a fair hand'. Some entries are merely instructions for the completion of standard letters, such as those to the Board of Assignment of Servants [eg Letter 650]

Dr Pennie Pemberton
Noel Butlin Archives Centre

NOTE ON TRANSCRIPTION

All the letters are heavily – and inconsistently – abbreviated, with the frequent use of superscript letters. For ease of consultation, the following editorial changes have been made:

(1) Some spelling has been standardised but some frequently used words have been left in their original form: eg Honorable, advertizement, favorable and expences

(2) All given names have been extended: Jno. to John; Geo. to George; D^l to Daniel; Ben^{jm} to Benjamin. Also Aus^n to Australian, Comm^{sy} to Commissary &c.

(3) ultimo, instant and proximo have been extended.

(4) The names of newspapers and ships have been italicised.

(5) Single inverted commas have been used for the names of horses, eg. 'Cleveland'.

(6) Double invested commas " " have been used only for reported speech.

(7) Abbreviations such as TL or TofL (Ticket of Leave); H. M. (His Majesty); H. E.(His Excellency [The Governor]) have been extended as sense required.

(8) The capitalisation is erratic and has generally been left as in the original.

(9) Additional punctuation – usually dashes – has been removed.

(10) Place names have been left as spelled (see index for modern version). Surnames have been 'corrected' only if spelt incorrectly in one place and not another.

(11) Sums of money and weights have been written in a standardised form.

(12) Paragraph numbering has been retained in (semi-) official letters.

(13) The usual method of referring to convicts (by their ship and sentence) has been retained, eg Thomas Cooper, *Lord Melville*, Life.

(14) Letter numbers, in square brackets, have been added for letters unnumbered in the original.

(15) All letters are signed by Sir Edward Parry unless otherwise noted.

LIST OF MAPS AND ILLUSTRATIONS

Map 1: xii
Places mentioned in the text.

Map 2: 60
The proposed Newcastle Coal Grant
as discussed in Letter No. 721 – based on AO Map 6268,
State Records of NSW.

Map 3A: 87
The Company locations.

Maps 3B and 3C: 87
Locations discussed in Letter No. 764,
22 December 1832 – based on AO Map 3362,
State Records NSW.

Illustration 1: 33
Sydney Herald, 23 August 1832 (Letter No. 687a)

Illustration 2: 49
Sydney Herald, 4 October 1832 (Letter No. 706a)

Illustration 3: 90
Australian Agricultural Company Annual and Half Yearly Reports
1824-1849 [Noel Butlin Archives Centre,
Australian Agricultural Company, Deposit Z173, Box 11]

Illustration 4: 169
Sydney Herald, 19 September 1833 (Letter No. 940c)

Illustration 5: 169
Sydney Herald, 19 September 1833 (Letter No. 940d)

Illustration 6: 210
Sydney Herald, 2 December 1833 (Letter No. 1,011a)

Illustration 7: 239
Letter No. 465

Map 1:
Places mentioned in the text. *Modern place names are shown in bold type*

letters 1832

Letter No. 637

Parramatta
4th June 1832

Major Mitchell
Surveyor General

Sir,
    With reference to the discussion which took place this day at Government House, relative to the Lands which I had selected for the A. A. Company, & to the Instructions which you intimated your intention of drawing up immediately for Mr White.
    I beg leave to suggest to you that it will probably be a saving of time not to commence any examination on the North Eastern side of Peel's River until the Range on the South Western side, which you propose to me as the Boundary, be accurately surveyed, & the actual Area included between that Range & the River be determined.
    I suggest this as the first point to be ascertained, because, from the knowledge which we do already possess of the position of the Range, I do not think it at all probable that I shall accede to the proposal of its forming the Boundary in question. In this case, it is obvious that an examination of the opposite or North Eastern side of the River would be only time thrown away.
    I beg leave to add that Mr Dangar & his Party will be ready to meet Mr White at Newcastle any day after the 20th instant; & to avoid the necessity of any further arrangement between us, I request you will direct that notice be given to me at Port Stephens, when the day is fixed for Mr White to be at Newcastle.
    As, however, I remain in till next Friday afternoon, perhaps it may be in your power to name the day of their meeting, before I return to Port Stephens.

Letter No. 638

Sydney
8th June 1832

Honorable Colonial Secretary
Sydney

Sir,
    The Prisoner of the Crown named in the Margin having obtained a Ticket of Leave for the District of Sydney being desirous of entering the service of

Charles Hancock, Malabar 1, Life

the A. A. Company, I request on behalf of this man that his Ticket of Leave may be altered to the District of Port Stephens.

Letter No. 639

Sydney
8th June 1832

Honorable The Colonial Secretary
Sydney

Sir,
    In consequence of the difficulty of obtaining Mechanics for completing the Buildings, intended to be erected at the Coal Works of the A. A. Company at Newcastle.
    I request you will obtain for me the permission of His Excellency the Governor to occupy, as the residence of the Company's Servants, the Workshops in the Lumber Yards at that place, until the necessary accommodation can be procured.

Letter No. 640

Sydney
9th June 1832

The Editor of the *Sydney Monitor*

Sir,
    I request you will, in future, cause One Copy of the *Sydney Monitor* to be sent to me, through the Post Office, on account of the Australian Agricultural Company, and that you will direct the Account for the same to be transmitted to me as soon as possible after the expiration of each quarter.

Letter No. 641

Sydney
9th June 1832

Honorable Colonial Secretary

Sir,
    Mr Richard Stubbs, the storekeeper at Port Stephens having informed me that he has applied to the Governor to be allowed the indulgence of a Free licence for one of the two Public Houses kept by him on the Estate of the A. A. Company, and requested me to certify the correctness of his Statement.

I beg leave to acquaint you for the information of His Excellency that I do not think Mr Stubbs can derive an adequate profit from the maintenance of this accommodation to the Company's Servants and Travellers passing thro' the Estate if he has to pay for two licences. And on this account, as well as from Mr Stubbs' high character, I have no hesitation in recommending his Application to the favorable consideration of His Excellency.

Letter No. 642

Sydney
9th June 1832

Honorable Colonial Secretary

Sir,
　　Mr Edward W. Lord having applied to me for the Transfer of the Prisoner of the Crown first named in the margin to his service in the room of the other Prisoner named in the margin whom he wishes to transfer to the A. A. Company, I beg to acquaint you that I have no objection to this exchange & I request His Excellency's permission for this purpose.

Thomas Cooper,
Lord Melville,
Life

Robert Whalin,
Captain Cook,
7 years

[Letter No. 642a]

The following <u>Advertizement</u> was this day (9th June 1832)
Transmitted to the
Sydney Gazette
Sydney Herald
Sydney Monitor
The Australian

Notice

In order to obviate the inconveniences which are represented to arise occasionally from Cash payments being required for Coals at the Works of the Australian Agricultural Company at Newcastle I hereby give notice that in future, all payments for Coals may be made into the Bank of Australia as a deposit on account of the Australian Agricultural Company – and the Bank Deposit Receipt will be received at the Works as payment.

Sydney
9th June 1832
W. E. Parry. Commissioner to the A. A. Company

Letter No. 643

Port Stephens
11th June 1832

Principal Superintendent of Convicts

Sir,

John Waters,
Florentia,
14 years

The Prisoner named in the margin an Assigned Servant of the A. A. Company having been sentenced, at the Sydney Quarter Sessions in January last, to an Iron Gang for Six Months, and his Sentence being just now about to expire, I request you will give directions for his being returned without delay to his Employers, his Services being very much required.

Letter No. 644

Port Stephens
11th June 1832

Captain Moffatt J.P.
Resident Magistrate
Port Stephens

Sir,

1. Having failed in my Endeavours during more than Two Years past, to obtain for the Establishment of the A. A. Company on this Estate, Civil Protection at the Public Expense, proportionate to the Protection afforded to Settlers in other Districts of the Colony.

2. It now becomes my Duty under my Instructions from the Court of Directors of the Company, to make such Reductions in the Expense of their present Police Department, as may accord with similar Reductions now making in the other Departments of their Establishment.

3. I therefore beg to acquaint you that in pursuance of these Instructions it is my intention to fix the number & allowances of the Company's Police Establishment, as follows after the 30th instant.

Resident Magistrate	Salary £50 per Annum with a Residence & the other advantages for himself & Family of Fuel, Dairy Produce, Medicines, Medical Attendance. Free conveyance in the *Lambton* of Stores for his own Private use, and the run of the Company's Paddocks for his Horses (if Geldings).
One Free Constable	Salary 2/6 per day with a Residence & the other advantages for himself & family of Fuel, Dairy Produce, Medicines & Medical Attendance, and the run of the Company's Paddocks for one Horse (if a Gelding).

One Free or Ticket of Leave Constable (for Stroud)	Salary £17 per Annum with Rations
Three Convict Constables One Police Clerk One Scourger	To receive such Gratuities not exceeding £10 per Annum as I may from time to time appoint in common with other assigned Servants of the Company subject to the Resident Magistrate's Recommendation.

4. I beg leave further to acquaint you that I must in future object to the Employment of the Company's Constables – Police Clerk – Police Office – Watch House – Irons – Handcuffs – Boats – Horses – Stationery, or any other Property whatsoever belonging to the Company except for purposes absolutely & exclusively connected with the Company's affairs or servants, without my permission as the Company's Agent, or the permission of the Person authorized to take charge of the Company's Business and Property during my occasional absence.

5. I request you will do me the favor to communicate this arrangement to the Free Constable now employed by the Company, and that you will also acquaint me as early as convenient, whether he wishes to continue to hold his present situation on the terms mentioned in this communication.

Letter No. 645

Port Stephens
12th June 1832

Honorable Colonial Secretary

Sir,

The Prisoner named in the margin now in the Service of Mr George Graham of Hunter's River having some time ago applied for a Ticket of Leave, for that District, but being now desirous of entering the Service of the A. A. Company.

I have the Honor to request that you will obtain the permission of His Excellency the Governor for Coombes' Ticket being made out – or if already made out, altered to the District of Port Stephens.

James Coombes, Hooghley, 7 years

Letter No. 646

Port Stephens
13th June 1832

Captain Moffatt J. P.
Resident Magistrate
Port Stephens

Sir,
   I have the Honor to acknowledge the Receipt of your letter of this day's date, and beg to state, in reply, that, in the Event of His Majesty's Government acceding to the arrangement you intend proposing by which the A. A. Company will be relieved from the payment of One Hundred Pounds per Annum now paid to the Resident Magistrate, there can be no objection whatever to my allowing you in that Capacity all the Advantages mentioned in my Communication of the 11th instant. The same Remark applies also to the use of one of the Company's Horses for all purposes connected with your Magisterial Duties.
   I can assure you that I feel scarcely less pleasure in the prospect of this arrangement, from the circumstance of its rendering the Resident Magistrate no longer dependent upon any payment from the Company – a situation in which, in my opinion, he ought never to have been placed - than from its offering a hope of some relief being at length afforded to the Company from the heavy Expense by which they have hitherto been so unjustly burthened in this Department of their Establishment.

Letter No. 647

Port Stephens
15th June 1832

Thomas Tulk
Walleroba

Thomas Tulk,
   Understanding that you have lately been on the Estate of the A. A. Company without my permission.
   I hereby refer you to my Public Advertizement on that subject, and give you notice that should you repeat your visit without such permission being first obtained, you will be proceeded against for a Trespass according to Law.

Letter No. 648

Port Stephens
15th June 1832

Mr B. Singleton
Williams River

Sir,
    I request you will have at Maitland by the 25th instant, without fail, One Thousand Pounds of Flour for the use of a Surveying Party under the direction of Mr Dangar Surveyor to the A. A. Company.

Letter No. 649

Port Stephens
15th June 1832

His Excellency
Major General Bourke
Governor in Chief

Sir,
    1. The Question relative to the Lands to be granted to the Australian Agricultural Company, which formed the principal subject of the conference with Your Excellency on the 4th of the present month, is of such vital importance to their interests, that it becomes my duty once more to draw Your Excellency's attention to some of the leading features of this case, and, at the same time, in order to obviate the possibility of future misapprehension, to place upon record my own views respecting it. This I shall endeavour to do in the Communication which I have now the Honor of making to Your Excellency.

    2. For this purpose, it will be necessary first to recapitulate briefly the circumstances which have led to my selection of those portions of Land, which, most unhappily for the Company's Interests, Your Excellency has declined granting to them.

    3. I need not inform Your Excellency that, in the original selection of the Company's Grant, so little pains were taken to survey the Land, that a very slight <u>actual</u> examination rendered it all but certain that it was unfit for the purposes of the Company.

    4. This fact having been represented to His Majesty's Home Government, the latter could not fail to perceive that the intentions and hopes of the Company must be altogether frustrated, unless some relief were afforded to them in their un-looked for dilemma. And accordingly, just before I left England to proceed to this Country, in July 1829, the Secretary of State consented to allow the Company to exchange a portion of their Original Selection, to a certain specified extent.

    5. In accordance with this permission, a demi-official Communication to that effect was then made to General Darling; and this was afterwards

followed up by Sir George Murray's Despatch (No. 23) dated the 21ˢᵗ of April 1830, conveying to the Governor the final Instructions of His Majesty's Government on this subject.

6. Some time before the receipt of this latter Communication, however, I had, in the beginning of June 1830, personally commenced an examination of the unexplored parts of the original Grant, accompanied by Mr Armstrong, one of the Company's Surveyors, and by the Superintendent of their Flocks.

7. In the same month, Mr Dangar, another Surveyor (who had lately arrived from England for the express purpose of assisting me in the new Selections) was despatched to survey the Lands to the North of the Manning River – a considerable tract of country which was, for a short time, expressly reserved by the Government for examination by the Company.

8. At the same time various minor excursions were made upon the Original Grant by other Officers of the Company's Establishment, to enable me to complete without delay its final examination.

9. The result of these journies accorded but too well with the previous accounts; and no doubt could any longer exist of the absolute necessity of relinquishing a very large portion of the first Selection.

10. Mr Dangar having continued his Survey till his Resources were expended, returned for a fresh supply; and, after (thus far) finishing his Maps, he again set out, in September 1830, to complete the examination of the whole Tract North of the Manning.

11. Having cherished a sanguine hope that this Tract, so advantageous in point of locality, would prove favourable to the Company's purposes, I was greatly disappointed in finding it quite the reverse, the proportion of available land being as small as in the Original Grant.

12. Mr Dangar was next employed from the month of November 1830 till April 1831 in surveying and completing his Maps of the 'Clergy and School Reserve', adjoining the Company's Estate, with reference to certain conditions relative to the leasing by the Company of a portion of that Reserve.

13. In March & April of 1831, I despatched Dr Nisbet, accompanied by the Superintendent of the Company's Flocks, to penetrate through the mountainous Country to the Westward of the same Reserve, which they did to a considerable distance, but without the smallest success in the discovery of available Land.

14. On the 21ˢᵗ of February 1831, after a personal Communication with the Governor on the subject of the Company's Lands, I drew up, by His Excellency's desire, and submitted to the Government a Memorandum, stating, among other things, the quantity and situation of the Original Grant, which I proposed to relinquish on the part of the Company – reporting that the land to the North of the Manning was unfit for the purposes of the Company – and requesting, with a view to my further Selection, "to be put in possession of all information of this nature in the Surveyor General's Office, as related to that portion of the Colony lying to the Westward and North Westward of the Company's present Estate, especially Liverpool & Goulburn* Plains, and the Country situated between these and the Company's Grant."

* This Error was not mine, but occurs in Cross's Map on the very spot I have since selected as the Peel's River Location

15. His Majesty's Government having immediately acceded to all these proposals, I applied without delay at the Surveyor General's Office, where, with no small difficulty, I procured, from some inferior person, a sight of the only Map (as he told me) which he was authorized to show. This Map was entirely devoid of information relative to the Country North Westward of the Company's Estate, nor did it even contain the paper on which Liverpool Plains ought to be.

16. Subsequent enquiries were attended with no better success, and this was the result of the "Instructions given to the Surveyor General" to put me in possession of all his information relative to the Lands in question.

17. Having thus failed to obtain information where it was usual for Grantees to seek it, I fitted out another exploring party with a view to the discovery of suitable Lands in the interior. Early in July 1831, I despatched Dr Nisbet and Mr Dangar to the North Westward of the Company's present Grant, with instructions to endeavour to penetrate in that direction, notwithstanding the discouraging prospect of Range after Range which there presented itself. With extreme labour, and a degree of enterprize which would have done credit to any object, these Gentlemen succeeded in travelling Westward up the Manning River, through as rugged a country as any in the known parts of this Colony, coming out over the Great Western Dividing Range, upon the heads of Peel's River.

18. Their Resources being almost exhausted by this effort, they could only make a partial discovery of land in the last mentioned locality; and then, travelling Southward, crossed the Liverpool Range to Segenhoe, whence, having obtained fresh supplies, they traversed with great difficulty the rough and useless country immediately Westward of the Company's Estate. Of this latter tract I laid before Your Excellency a Map by Mr Dangar, at the late conference.

19. The Maps of this laborious Journey being completed, I again, in November 1831, despatched Mr Dangar, to examine Liverpool Plains, the still more distant Country bordering upon Peel's River, and even beyond the River Mowherindi.

20. After an absence of ten weeks on this service, Mr Dangar returned in January of the present year, reporting to me that he had at length succeeded in discovering some portions of Land, which, tho' at a great and inconvenient distance, he considered more likely to suit the Company than any other that could be found.

21. On the 1st of March, a party under my own direction, accompanied by Mr Dangar and the Superintendent of the Company's Flocks, set out from Port Stephens, to make a further examination of the Country named by Mr Dangar, and to enable me to decide for myself without delay whether I should make application for it on account of the Company.

22. In the course of this journey, which occupied me six weeks, besides going over the former ground, our examination was carried a considerable distance higher up the Mowherindi till it was discovered to divide into two branches. Then following Peel's River to its sources, I crossed the Great Dividing Range; and, with the hope of discovering a route which might serve for conducting Stock from the Company's Estate, returned home by a new line across the Mountainous Country before mentioned.

23. Being now satisfied that the Colony did not contain a Tract of Country, so suitable as that which I had just visited, I completed the Map without delay, and, on the 5th of May, by my Letter to the Colonial Secretary, applied to Your Excellency for permission to select for the Company the two Portions delineated in the Map.

24. On the 4th of the present month, I had the honor of a conference with Your Excellency on this subject, in the course of which Your Excellency declined granting to the Company that Location which I was the most anxious to obtain, and proposed an enlargement of the other Location, which, so far as my present information goes, would entirely render null and void the Selections I have made.

25. It only remains for me to add at present, on this part of the subject, that these Selections were the result of an examination, during nearly two years unremittingly, of more than three millions and a half of Acres, and that the expence to the Company has exceeded Sixteen Hundred Pounds.

26. I have been obliged to trouble Your Excellency with all these details, in order to shew that, since the Consent of His Majesty's Government to an exchange of Lands was obtained, the Company has lost no time, and spared no expence, in endeavouring to make their Selections.

27. The necessity for my making this clear to Your Excellency arises principally from the Remark made to me by Your Excellency, that it was the fault of the Company's own Agents that the Original Selection was a bad one; and that the Company must abide by the consequences – or to that effect.

28. It is quite true that it was the Company's own Agents who committed this error; but I trust, Sir, you will excuse my remarking that I cannot perceive the justice of the inference which Your Excellency appeared to draw from this fact; namely, that the Company's Claims to a fresh selection of Land upon the same principles as at first, are on that account weakened.

29. If, indeed, this inference were admitted, what would become of the assurance of His Majesty's Secretary of State that he was "convinced that the Company's just interests required some relaxation of the first arrangement", and that, on this account, he had consented to the exchange of a large portion of the Original Grant?

30. For if these considerations, and the permission founded upon them, mean anything, I humbly conceive they imply that a just and liberal sense of the Company's Claims had induced His Majesty's Home Government to overlook with considerate indulgence the important error committed at the outset of this extensive undertaking; and that leave was therefore given to repair this error, by making a fresh Selection – to a certain limited extent indeed – but unshackled by any conditions except those <u>directly</u> specified.

31. I repeat, therefore, that I know not how to admit what I understood to be Your Excellency's inference, which would, in fact, amount to this; that His Majesty's Government is no longer disposed to view this matter in the same just and considerate light as when the permission to exchange was granted; that this indulgence is to be contracted within some narrower & undefined limits; and, in short, that this first error is still to be visited upon the Company by a refusal of what would originally have been considered their fair and reasonable Claims.

32. On the contrary, I think it is obvious that, if His Majesty's Government had determined on putting a nominal value of Five Pounds upon every acre of land in this Colony, instead of as many shillings, this circumstance could not, upon any principle of justice, affect the Company's previously admitted Claims; provided it could be shewn that no time had been lost, and no exertion or expence spared, by the Company's Agent, in making the allowed Selections.

33. On these grounds, then, I would now respectfully submit to Your Excellency's sense of justice whether I am not correct in considering that, in whatever degree the decision of this question is influenced by the <u>present</u> views of the Government as to the value and disposal of land in this Colony, instead of the views entertained when the exchange was consented to, precisely in that degree will His Majesty's Government commit a breach of faith in their dealings with the Australian Agricultural Company.

34. If, then, the Company have a just Claim to make their Selections on the same principle by which all other Grants were then regulated, I must contend that no just reason exists for the decided objection raised against the Company's possessing <u>any</u> portion of one of the Locations I had, with so much labour and expence, selected for their Grant.

35. That Your Excellency arrived at an opposite conclusion, in consequence of the representations of the Surveyor General that it would cut off all future Settlers from Liverpool Plains, and occupy almost the only desirable Tract of the Country in that neighbourhood, I am well aware. But the Surveyor General entirely failed to prove the correctness of this sweeping assertion, and I may safely defy him to do so. On the contrary, it is quite evident to every impartial person who knows the Country (which, to be sure, Major Mitchell does not) that there would still remain an immense tract of highly desirable Country; and that Liverpool Plains, to an extent so great that it has never yet been delineated, would be just as much open to future Settlers as it is this moment.

36. If I am not correct in this conclusion, why did not the Surveyor General propose some other Form & Situation for a Location for the Company in that neighbourhood, instead of urging Your Excellency to settle the matter by a simple refusal, and thus denying to the Company the right of every ordinary Settler to choose his Grant in a good location, rather than in a bad one?

37. With respect to the claims of those Individuals, or, as the Surveyor General feelingly called them, those "poor people", whose Cattle are now grazing on a portion of the lands which I selected for the Company, I trust I need scarcely submit to Your Excellency whether the just claims of a Chartered Company with a Capital of One Million Stirling are to be sacrificed to the pretensions (if any) of persons, whether poor or rich, who have no right whatever to the possession of a single acre of that Country.

38. The fact, however, is, that these persons are by no means disposed to set up any such claim, nor to complain of the Company's expected possession of that country as any hardship at all. On the contrary, when speaking of the alarm which the Surveyor General had sounded, they uniformly treated it as a matter of trifling inconvenience to remove their Herds to a somewhat

greater distance, only observing that they hoped a few months' notice would be given them.

39. The Surveyor General also urged, as an objection to my Selection, that the Colony was already too extended, and therefore that it was highly inexpedient that the Company's Grant should be made in the manner I proposed. With this objection, Sir, I have, of course, nothing to do as a question of expediency. It is for Your Excellency alone to determine this; and it did not form any objection on your part. But I cannot help reminding Your Excellency of the consistency with which this objection was urged by the Surveyor General, when, in the next breath, he used all his logic to drive the Company into one Location, <u>forty miles farther</u> from the present limits of the Colony than that which, on this very account, he objected to the Company's possessing!

40. In fact if the objections raised by the Surveyor General to the Company's possession of the Tract shaded green, were divested of the obscurity in which he involved it, they would, I am satisfied, amount simply to this; that the Tract in question is a desirable one, and that if the Company possesses it, nobody else can. These are truisms, which cannot be denied; and I declare, Sir, upon my honour, that I think <u>the fact</u> is precisely that and no more, and that if Your Excellency could personally have seen the Land, you would never have objected to my Selection of it for the Company.

41. The nearest and most desirable Location of the two being thus refused, on the grounds to which I have alluded, the next object of the Surveyor General, at the late conference, was to persuade me, as he had unhappily already persuaded Your Excellency, that the <u>Whole Quantity</u> of land required to complete the Company's Grant might, with advantage to the Company, be taken in <u>One Location</u> on the Peel's River, without interfering with Liverpool Plains at all!

42. This object the Surveyor General endeavoured to accomplish in two ways; 1st, by pushing the red shaded Location back to a Range, which, for this express purpose, as it appeared to me, he had opportunely transferred from Mr Dangar's Map to his own blank paper; and secondly, by making up any further deficiency by a few odds and ends of Land, if I may so express myself, on the opposite or right bank of Peel's River.

43. As to the first of these proposals, I must observe that the objection I made to this arrangement, being dependent on a physical fact, cannot be got rid of by any representations, however strenuously urged, on the part of the Surveyor General. Whatever arguments he may have adduced on this occasion, <u>Land without water is incapable of supporting man, sheep, or cattle.</u>

44. If, therefore, the intended Survey should shew (as we have much reason to suppose it will) <u>that a Tract of One Hundred and Sixty Thousand Acres without Water</u> is proposed to be added to this Location by making the Range the boundary, I am sure, Sir, that you would consider me wanting, either in common sense or common honesty, if I should accede to such a proposal.

45. I shall not add more on this point at present, since, in order to put beyond doubt the actual fact, I suggested, and Your Excellency has been

pleased to direct, that an actual Survey of the Range be made by the Surveyor of the Government and the Surveyor of the Company, conjointly.

46. I must however, say a few words as to the General Principle, upon which, <u>as relates to Water frontage</u>, it has hitherto been customary to regulate the Grants of Letters. And this I am especially anxious to do, because, in this respect also, Your Excellency appeared to me to apply to the Company a principle of Selection, which was never before applied to any other Grant in this Colony.

47. The Custom has hitherto been, to give about one mile of water frontage in a Grant of 2560 acres, or four square miles; so that no part of such a Grant is more than about four miles distant from the water.

48. The reasonableness and propriety of this arrangement are obvious, if we consider the principle upon which it was adopted, namely, that four miles is about the utmost limit of distance which Stock should have to go for water, in order to make the whole Grant available for their support. In this manner the interest of each individual Proprietor is best consulted on the one hand, and the Water-frontage of any Tract of Country properly economized on the other.

49. But, supposing the case of any larger Grant – say, for instance 7600 Acres, or twelve square miles – it never would have been dreamt of, as a reasonable arrangement, that the Grantee should still only have his one mile of water-frontage, and the rest of his Grant thrust back twelve miles from the water, so as to leave seven or eight square miles wholly destitute of this indispensible article. Otherwise, the possessor of the small Grant would be just as well off as the possessor of the large one; inasmuch as he would have just as much land capable of supporting animal life.

50. Will Your Excellency, then, deem me unreasonable if I claim for the Company that <u>their</u> Grant shall be made on the same principle? I do not say that, in so large a Grant, it is <u>possible</u> to carry it to the same extent as in a small one; but I must say that it is anything but just to disregard this principle altogether in the case of the Company; virtually to say to them "Whatever care we take to provide for the support of the Stock of all other Settlers, <u>yours</u> must do the best they can without water"; and to carve out for them, and for them only, a Grant of Land, which, however neat its boundaries may look upon the Map, contains an immense proportion utterly unavailable for any one useful purpose.

51. I have offered these remarks, Sir, because Your Excellency appeared to think that, according to the Regulations hitherto in force, the Government would be bestowing a great boon upon the Company in not pushing their Grant back from the water I know not how many more miles than I proposed. I maintain, on the contrary, that by so doing the Government would be infringing the very principle on which every other Grant in the Colony has been measured out.

52. Nor would there be any difficulty in shewing that, in thus undertaking to mark out a Grant for the Company, the Surveyor General has not, in other respects, any more than in the water-frontage, attended to the principles recognized in other Grants.

53. For instance, the stress which, on this particular occasion, he has laid on making Ranges the Boundaries, is entirely without precedent in this

Colony, even in the Company's Original Grant – the only one which could well furnish a precedent. And although I have no objection whatever to a Range as a Boundary, preferring, of course natural boundaries to any others, yet surely it is too much to expect that I should, on this account, consent to overlook the more important qualification of land capable of supporting animal life.

54. Nor can I omit to express the sense I entertain of this attempt, on the part of the Surveyor General, to drive the Company into One distant and inferior Location, and thus to blot out one of the most striking and important conditions contained in the permission of His Majesty's Home Government to exchange a portion of their Lands. If the Surveyor General could point out to me any One Location suited to the views of the Company, most gladly would I accept it; but I must claim Your Excellency's protection against this or any other endeavour to deprive the Company of the indulgence of selecting the Remainder of their Grant in Two Locations, except under circumstances which I, as their Agent, can approve.

55. In the course of this Communication, I have, without hesitation, assigned the representations of the Surveyor General as the cause of Your Excellency's decision on this Subject; because this was obviously the case in the course of the late conference. I should have esteemed it a fortunate circumstance for the Company, had it so happened that my application for these Lands had been made at a somewhat later period, when time had been afforded for Your Excellency to put into execution the wise and judicious plan which it is understood to be your intention to adopt, of seeing everything with your own eyes, and thus being enabled to form your own unbiased and impartial judgment. In this case, I am satisfied that I should not now have had to contend against the representations of a prejudiced Individual.

56. To prove that I am justified in using this last expression, I have only again to notice the circumstance which I before mentioned to Your Excellency in presence of the Surveyor General, that that Officer had, in a most unwarrantable manner, thought proper to excite an odium against the Company, and me as their Agent, throughout the line of the Hunter River Road, and even at the most distant Stock Station on Peel's River, by giving out that we were coming to turn everybody else out; and by asserting in one instance (as I am ready to prove by the most respectable testimony) that "what Sir Edward Parry was going to ask for, was quite inadmissible"!

57. I shall not here stop to remark upon the impossibility of the Surveyor General's knowing what I was about to ask for, since I did not at that time know myself. But it is of importance that Your Excellency should be clearly aware, as I have long been, that this conduct on the part of that Officer is the real key to the whole of his objections. Major Mitchell undertook to be the champion of those "poor people" whose case he seemed to regard with so much sympathy; and the consequence was, as I told him in Your Excellency's hearing, that he was content, in this affair, to do a popular thing, rather than a just one.

58. But I have still to place on record, in this Communication, one more circumstance, as regards the Surveyor General's objections. He told

some of the persons on Peel's River, that I was about to ask for the Land on <u>both sides</u> of that Stream, which was quite contrary to all Regulations in the granting of land. Whatever I might have done had I not heard this, I determined from that moment not to think of asking for both banks; and, as Your Excellency is aware, I made no such proposition. But what was the result? This objection, which the Surveyor General had magnified into importance so long as he had <u>one</u> object to effect, was carefully kept out of sight the moment he had <u>another</u> end in view. This latter end, as I have already explained, was to push the Company up into One Location. For this purpose, he wanted fifty or a hundred thousand Acres of land on the right bank, to throw into the scale as a convenient make-weight, and therefore not a syllable was said of the inadmissibility of the Company's occupying both sides of the River!

59. I cannot believe it possible, after this Statement of Facts, that upon the representations of a person so prejudiced; and so pre-determined to object to <u>anything</u> I should ask for, Your Excellency will be disposed to confirm a decision which strikes at the very root of the Company's prosperity.

60. Under all these circumstances, I feel, Sir, that I should be unworthy of the trust reposed in me, if I did not protest against that decision; and I do, therefore, most respectfully, but most earnestly, entreat Your Excellency to re-consider it. For I now unequivocally repeat the declaration I before made, that this decision, if carried into effect, must not merely cramp the Company's operations, and retard their final success, but in all probability put an end to their continued existence.

61. In conclusion, it becomes my duty, to request, as a matter of immediate and urgent necessity, that Your Excellency will be pleased to direct that a Licence of Occupation be granted to me, without delay, on account of the Company, for such a portion of the Green shaded Location near 'Warrah' – say Forty Thousand Acres – as may suffice to maintain Ten Thousand Lambs, which are expected to be added by birth to the Company's Flocks between this time and next October. As regards the immediate urgency of this measure, I beg leave, in addition to my own repeated representations on this head, to refer Your Excellency to the testimony contained in the Affidavit of the Superintendent of the Company's Flocks, appended to this Communication.

I have the Honor to be, Sir
Your Excellency's faithful & obedient Servant
W. E. Parry. Commissioner for managing the affairs of the A. A. Company in New South Wales.

Letter No. 650

Port Stephens
19th June 1832

Board for the Assignment of Servants

Gentlemen,
   In conformity with the Regulations I request that Fifty Convict Servants may be assigned to me of the following Description: vizt Shepherds or Agricultural Labourers.
   I reside at Port Stephens in the County of Gloucester. I am Commissioner to the A. A. Company and hold about 458,000 Acres of Land; of which 450 Acres are cleared, and 400 Acres are in tillage.
   I possess 306 Horses, 3000 Head of Cattle and 27,000 Sheep; I now employ 65 Free, and 401 Convict Servants; of whom 196 have been in my Service upwards of Three Years, and 116 upwards of one year; No assigned Servants have been returned by me to Government within the last Two Years, and none have absconded from my Service during that period, without having been since apprehended & returned, or under Colonial Sentence.
   My Agent, Mr Bunn residing at Sydney is fully empowered to receive such Servants as may be assigned to me & to defray all Expenses incurred on their account.

I am, Gentlemen &c &c &c

W. E. Parry. Commissioner for Managing the affairs of the A. A. Company in New South Wales.

I hereby certify upon Honor, the correctness of the above Statement.
W. E. Parry. J. P.

Letter No. 651

Port Stephens
19th June 1832

F. Mitchell Esq.
Sydney

Sir,
   With reference to the Arrangement made between us for Supplying Coals occasionally to you per the *Lambton* from Newcastle at 17/- per Ton, I request you will pay the several amounts to Captain Corlette on delivery of the Coals, as it will interfere very much with the existing Regulations for the Company's Accounts to have any Transactions of this nature upon credit.

Letter No. 652

Port Stephens
22nd June 1832

Mr B. Singleton
John's Mill
Williams River

Sir,
    Enclosed you have an Invoice of Four Hundred and One Bushels of Wheat shipped by the A. A. Company on board the sloop *Ellen*, Joshua Reeves Master, and consigned to you, which I request you will have ground into Flour according to the directions contained in the Memorandum at foot of the Invoice.

Letter No. 653

Port Stephens
27th June 1832

Adam Howitt
Carrington

Adam Howitt,
    In compliance with the request contained in your Letter addressed to me this day, you have my permission to quit the Service of the A. A. Company on the 1st of July next.
    You will, therefore, be ready to deliver up, on that day, or as soon as I may be able to procure you a conveyance from the Company's Estate, the Premises now occupied by you, together with all other Property belonging to the Company now in your possession.

Letter No. 654

Port Stephens
29th June 1832

Adam Howitt
Carrington

Adam Howitt,
    In reply to your letter of yesterday's date, I have to acquaint you that, in consideration of the unhappy situation in which you have placed your Wife and helpless family, I am induced to allow them to occupy the House in which you now live, for a reasonable time, until you can find the means of supporting them elsewhere. But I can only do this on condition that you leave with me sufficient funds for providing your Family with Rations, as I cannot burden the Company with that Expense after you have left their Service.

Letter No. 655

Port Stephens
29th June 1832

Robert Ball Esq
Sydney Gazette Office
Sydney

Sir,
In reply to your letter of the 21st instant, I regret that it is not in my power to give you any hopes of a situation in the Service of the A. A. Company. It being my intention to reduce rather than increase their Establishment.

Letter No. 656

Port Stephens
29th June 1832

H. C. Sempill Esq.
Sydney

Sir,
In reply to your letter of the 18th instant I beg to acquaint you that the A. A. Company will not require any Supply of Tobacco this year, being amply supplied from their own Estate.

Letter No. 657

Port Stephens
2nd July 1832

George Bunn Esq.
Sydney

Sir,
I beg leave to enclose to you a Draft on the Bank of Australia for (£45) Forty five Pounds to meet the Payments per Last Invoice.
The two 'Fox's Tooth Keys' are Instruments for extracting Teeth. Perhaps this Explanation may enable you to procure them.
Herewith you will receive Bills on the Governors & Directors of the A. A. Company for (£500) Five Hundred Pounds to your order, which I request you will endorse, & deposit in the Bank of Australia to the credit of the Company.

Letter No. 658

Port Stephens
5th July 1832

John Baker
Care of W. Croasdill Esq.
Newcastle

John Baker,
 In reply to your letter of the 25th ultimo, I am sorry to find that you have a difficulty in supporting your family, but it will not be in my power to allow you to reside on the Company's Estate, as you do not belong to their Establishment.

Letter No. 659

Port Stephens
9th July 1832

Board for the Assignment of Servants

Gentlemen,
 I request you will have the goodness to Sanction & cause to be arranged the Transfer of an Assigned Servant belonging to the A. A. Company whose name is Thomas Emmett Phillip per ship *Manlius* Sentence Life convicted at Lancaster 12th August 1826 to the Service of J. E. Stacy Esq., Surgeon to the Company's Establishment: also William Bannister assigned Servant to J. E. Stacy Esq., who arrived per Ship *Georgiana* Sentence 7 years Convicted at Oxford January 1831 to the Service of the A. A. Company, in exchange for the above, each party being agreed.

I have the honor to be
Gentlemen &c &c &c
W. E. Parry Commissioner to the A. A. Company

Approved
J. E. Stacy Surgeon to the A. A. Company

Letter No. 660

Port Stephens

12th July 1832
W. May
Carrington

William May
 In reply to your letter of this day requesting that your Agreement with the A. A. Company may be cancelled with as little delay as possible.

I have to inform you that I have no objection to your request, and for that purpose, have given directions that the usual form of Cancelment may be prepared immediately.

Letter No. 661

Port Stephens
12th July 1832

Colonial Secretary
Sydney

Sir,

I beg leave to enclose the Report of Mr Stacy, Surgeon to the Australian Agricultural Company, relative to the case of the Prisoner of the Crown named in the Margin; to which I may add that I have myself watched this poor Man's case with attention for a considerable time past, and I fear no hope can be entertained of his recovery.

I therefore, request you will do me the Honor to inform me whether he may be received into the Lunatic Asylum – a measure to which I am unwillingly obliged to resort in consequence of the disposition he now occasionally evinces to commit acts of violence.

Daniel Dimotte, Hercules, Life

Letter No. 662

Port Stephens
12th July 1832

Principal Superintendent of Convicts
Sydney

Sir,

I have the Honor to acquaint you that the Prisoner of the Crown named in the Margin has lately absconded from the Service of the Australian Agricultural Company, and has since been known to commit robberies in the neighbourhood of the Williams and Hunter's Rivers.

This man being free in a few days his conduct is the more unaccountable.

John Linsky, Mangles, 7 years

Letter No. 663

Port Stephens
12th July 1832

Board for Assignment of Servants

Gentlemen,
    Observing in the List of Assigned Servants published in the Government Gazette, that the two men named in the Margin are stated to have been assigned to the Australian Agricultural Company.

    I beg to acquaint you that I have never before heard of their Assignment to the Company, & to request that you will direct them to be forwarded to the Company's Agent Mr Bunn, as soon as convenient.

    I beg leave also to notice that Thomas Benton (*Surrey* 5) appears on the before mentioned List, as two separate men namely No's 113 and 151.

Margin:
William Goodwin, *Asia* 9, Brickmaker

George Hames, *Asia* 9, Brassfounder

Letter No. 664

John Mackie Esq., Sydney

and

Letter No. 665

Nicholas Aspinall Esq., Sydney

Port Stephens
12th July 1832

Sir,
    With reference to the Letter which I addressed to you on the 8th of February last on the subject of the Manufacture of Barilla, to which I had the pleasure of receiving your very obliging reply,

    I now forward to you per *Lambton*, to the care of Captain Corlette, a sack containing 3 bushels of Barilla, manufactured from Mangrove at Port Stephens, each bushel weighing 54 lbs.

    I request you will do me the kindness to inform me, by return of the *Lambton*, whether Barilla of this kind will answer your purpose, & what price (cash) per bushel you will be disposed to give for it, as a <u>constant</u> price throughout the year.

Letter No. 666

Port Stephens
12th July 1832

Board for Assignment of Servants

Richard Beecher, *Burrell*, 14 years

Gentlemen,
    William Ogilvie Esq. J. P. having applied to me to transfer to him from the Service of the A. A. Company the Prisoner named in the margin, whose wife is in Mr Ogilvie's service, in exchange for John Davis, *John*, 7 years whose assignment he has procured for this purpose.
    I request that this transfer may be permitted, for the reason above stated.

Letter No. 667

Port Stephens
13th July 1832

Captain Moffatt J.P.
Resident Magistrate
Port Stephens

Sir,
    1. I have the Honor to acknowledge the receipt of your letter of yesterday's date enclosing for my perusal a copy of the Honorable Colonial Secretary's Letter addressed to you on the 6th current and requesting I will inform you what my intentions are respecting the latter part of the 3rd Paragraph of that Communication.
    2. In reply I do myself the Honor to remark, in order to obviate future misconception, that in my letter addressed to you on the 11th ultimo (to which I presume Mr McLeay's Letter alludes) I did not intimate my intention to object to the occasional employment of the Court House, Constables, Clerk and other property belonging to the Company for purposes unconnected with their Affairs or Servants; because I was well aware that Cases of this nature must sometimes occur in which as a Magistrate and a Gentleman I should feel myself bound to lend all the means within my reach to preserve the Public Peace and to forward the ends of Public Justice. But what I did object to was, that anything of this sort should be done <u>without my permission</u>, as the Company's Agent, who am alone responsible for the due custody and Employment of their Property, whether Buildings, Servants or otherwise, committed to my charge.
    3. To this I may now add, by way of being more explicit, that whenever I may be disposed to grant such permission, I do it as a matter of mere Courtesy and from a sense of Public Duty, but by no means as a right which His Majesty's Government is authorised to demand at my hands. I do it on the part of the Company just as I should do it at my own Expense if I were resident in any other part of the Colony on my own private Estate, but on no other principle whatever.

4. I regret to find that His Excellency the Governor viewed this matter in a different light, conceiving that I am bound to place at the disposal of the Resident Magistrate, <u>for public purposes</u>, a portion of the property in my charge, belonging exclusively to the Company, to the Amount of about Three Hundred Pounds per Annum; since, in the letter before alluded to, His Excellency directs you to notify to me that if "I object to your using the Court House, Constables, Clerk or any other permanent part of the Police Establishment <u>for the purposes of the District generally</u>, His Excellency will feel himself obliged to withdraw the Magistrate".

5. Under these circumstances, I am compelled to say that, with whatever regret I may contemplate incurring the Penalty which His Excellency has been pleased to attach to a non-compliance on my part with this new Requisition, I cannot possibly consent to relinquish, in any shape or in any degree, my just right to be the sole judge in what cases the Company's Private Property is to be employed <u>for Public Purposes</u>, and in what cases it is not to be so employed.

Letter No. 668

Port Stephens
17th July 1832

Colonial Secretary
Sydney

Sir,

I have the Honor to enclose to you, for the use of H. M. Government, a copy of a new Survey of the Anchorages of Swan River lately received from the Admiralty.

Letter No. 669

Port Stephens
20th July 1832

Colonial Secretary
Sydney

Sir,

1. I have the Honor to enclose to you herewith an Account in Triplicate with the requisite Vouchers, for Coals supplied by the A. A. Company, to His Majesty's Colonial Government, during the Quarter ending the 30th ultimo, amounting to (£3.15.9) Three Pounds, Fifteen Shillings and nine pence.

2. I likewise enclose open for your perusal, a Letter to the Deputy Commissioner General, transmitting to him, similar accounts in Triplicate for Coals supplied, during the same period, to the Commissariat

Department, amounting to (£144.18.1) One Hundred & Forty four Pounds Eighteen Shillings and One Penny.

3. I have adopted this division of Accounts to the Colonial Department and the Commissariat Department respectively, in consequence of having understood from Messrs Laidley and Nicholson that they are in future to be furnished as separate accounts.

4. You will observe that all these Accounts are made out on the principle explained in my Letter addressed to you on the 15th of February last, and since sanctioned by H. E. The Governor for the two preceding quarters, namely that Six Shillings per Ton be paid, <u>on account</u>, for the one-fourth part of the whole quantity of Coals disposed of in each Quarter, and Eight Shillings per ton for all the Remainder of the Quantity Supplied to H. M. Government.

5. My reason for enclosing to you my Communication to the Deputy Commissary General, is, that an inspection of <u>all</u> the Accounts is requisite to shew the correctness of the Quantities charged at the respective prices.

6. I request that you will forward my letter to the Deputy Commissioner General as soon as possible, and that His Excellency may be pleased to direct that immediate payment be made of the whole Supply – amounting to (£148.13.10) One Hundred, & Forty-eight Pounds, Thirteen Shillings and Ten pence.

Letter No. 670

Port Stephens
20th July 1832

James Laidley Esq.
Deputy Commissary General
Sydney

Sir,

I have the Honor to enclose to you Accounts (No's. 1 and 2) in Triplicate, with the requisite Vouchers, for Coals supplied by the A. A. Company to the Commissariat Department during the Quarter ending the 30th ultimo and amounting to £116.7.5 and £28.10.8 respectively.

These Accounts are made out on the principle already sanctioned by H. E. The Governor for the two preceding Quarters; and I enclose them with this Letter, open, to the Honorable Colonial Secretary in order to shew the Correctness of the Quantities charged in these Accounts & in those Transmitted at the same time to the Colonial Department, the one depending upon the other.

I request you will cause the Amount (£144.18.1) One Hundred & Eighty [sic] four Pounds Eighteen Shillings & One Penny, to be paid into the Bank of Australia to the credit of the A. A. Company, with as little delay as possible.

Letter No. 671

Port Stephens
20th July 1832

James Laidley Esq.
Deputy Commissary General
Sydney

Sir,
   The Book Keeper at the Coal Works of the A. A. Company at Newcastle having represented to me that considerable inconvenience is experienced by the Quantities of Coals required in your Department at Newcastle being stated <u>to a Single Pound weight</u>, occasioning unnecessary minuteness both in measuring the Coals, and in keeping the Accounts.
   I beg leave to suggest to you whether some arrangement may not be made with the Deputy Assistant Commissary General at Newcastle, to avoid this Practice in future, which is not allowed with any other Purchaser.

Letter No. 672

Port Stephens
20th July 1832

The Honorable Colonial Secretary

Sir,
   1. I beg leave to submit to you, for the consideration and decision of His Excellency the Governor, the following Statement.
   2. The Australian Agricultural Company contract to furnish Rations of Meat and Flour to the Military Detachment stationed at Port Stephens.
   3. These Rations are furnished upon Requisitions made by the Commanding Officer, according to the enclosed Form [A]; each Requisition bearing the Receipt of the Serjeant of the Detachment.
   4. The Accounts are rendered by the Company to the Deputy Commissary General in the annexed Form [B], to which is appended a detailed Statement of each separate Requisition [C]; and the Originals of all the Requisitions accompany the Accounts.
   5. Notwithstanding this clear and simple arrangement, objections have been made to the full payment of the Accounts, in consequence, as the Deputy Commissary General informs me, of the Vouchers thus furnished <u>differing from those transmitted to him in the usual printed "Ration List" by the Commanding Officer.</u>
   6. I beg leave further to state, for His Excellency's information, that, in order to obviate such disagreements in future, it was lately suggested to me by the Deputy Commissary General, that my Accounts should be compared quarterly with those of the Commanding Officer at Port Stephens, previously to their being transmitted to the Commissariat Office.
   7. To this arrangement I willingly acceded; but, in endeavouring to carry

it into effect, as relates to the Accounts up to the 30th of June, I find that some difference again occurs between the two sets of Vouchers. Where the error lies, I cannot say; tho' it most probably arises from certain complicated fractional parts of a pound which frequently occur in the Commanding Officer's 'Ration List'. All that I can do is, to vouch for the Correctness of the Accounts rendered by the Company, as attested by the simple documents by which those Accounts are accompanied.

8. To make my explanation complete, I must add that, by a Memorandum relative to some of these Accounts for the last year, received from the Commissariat Office, it appears that the difference alluded to arose from some "Excess of Issues"; by which expression, I believe, is meant, that the Office had drawn more Rations than the Detachment was entitled to. His Excellency will, I am sure, perceive that I cannot presume to interfere in such matters, nor pretend to judge what quantities ought to be issued; my business only being to issue whatever quantities the Commanding Officer sets down in his Several Requisitions. It is, therefore, obviously unjust to refuse or even to delay payment to the Company in such cases.

9. Under these circumstances, I applied with confidence to His Excellency, requesting He will be pleased to direct that payment be in future made without delay for the Quantities of Rations <u>bona fide supplied by the Company</u>, as shewn beyond all possibility of doubt by the Officers Requisitions; instead of having any deductions made on account of Errors not committed on the part of the Company, and over which they can have no control.

Letter No. 673

Port Stephens
25th July 1832

James Laidley Esq.
Deputy Commissary General
Sydney

Sir,
I have the Honor to transmit to you herewith, Accounts (in Triplicate) for Supplies to the Military Detachment stationed at Port Stephens, between the 1st of January and 30th of June of the present year, together with the Vouchers complete for the same.

I also transmit herewith Accounts (in Triplicate) for Supplies to Sundry persons on account of H. M. Government to the 30th June of this year, with the Vouchers complete.

I request you will cause the several amounts to be paid into the Bank of Australia to the credit of the Company as early as possible; and I beg to remind you that an account rendered by the Company on the 14th February last, amounting to £20.5.7 for Supplies to Sundry Persons, yet remains unpaid.

Letter No. 674

Port Stephens
26th July 1832

George Bunn Esq.
Sydney

Sir,
    I herewith enclose to you a Draft on the Bank of Australia for (£200) Two Hundred Pounds, to meet the Current Expences on account of the Company.
    I also enclose a Memorandum from Mr Ebsworth, with reference to the Sketch of your a/c to the 30th April last; likewise a Requisition for Stores.
    I request you will take care that the Castings mentioned in your letter of the 18th instant, are sent by this trip of the *Lambton*.
    The Wheat now shipped on the *Lambton*, of which an Invoice is enclosed, is to be ground into Seconds Flour, and returned by the *Lambton* with as little delay as possible.

Letter No. 675

Port Stephens
26th July 1832

Dr Mitchell
General Hospital
Sydney

Sir,
    I have the Honor to enclose to you the Statements of the Cases of the Two Prisoners named in the Margin, assigned Servants of the Australian Agricultural Company and request you will receive them into the General Hospital, and cause them to be sentenced when cured thro' the Company's Agent – George Bunn Esq. George Street.

Peter Hely,
Boyne, 7 years

Florence
Macarthy or
Macarthur,
Eliza, 7 years

Letter No. 676

Port Stephens
9th August 1832

Mr B. Singleton
John's Mill
Williams River

Sir,
    I request you will forward to Port Stephens without delay the *Ellen*, with

a full cargo of Flour in the following proportions, vizt – ¼ of her Cargo in <u>Fine</u>, and ¾ of her Cargo in <u>Seconds</u> Flour.

P.S. An answer by the Bearer is requested.

Letter No. 677

Port Stephens
10th August 1832

Captain Moffatt J.P.
&c &c &c

Sir,

1. The Honorable Colonial Secretary having by letter of the 27th ultimo informed me that His Excellency the Governor, has been pleased to direct that Three Constables, upon your recommendation will be borne on the Establishment of the Colony from the 1st of that Month (July) at the rate of Two Shillings & Three pence per diem if free, and One Shilling & Nine Pence per diem if Prisoners.

2. I beg to acquaint you that, under this arrangement, I propose discharging from the Police Department the following Servants of the Company, so soon as you can make it convenient to supply their places by the recommendation of others to H. M. Government, namely: Mr John Field (Free), Charles Hancock (Holding a Ticket of Leave) and any one of the present Prisoners Constables.

3. If, however, you should be disposed to recommend to the Governor, Mr John Field as a fit person to receive the higher Salary allowed by the Government, I have no objection, in consideration of Mr Field's character as a steady & useful Constable, to make up to him, at the Expense of the Company, the other Three pence per day, & to continue to him all the other advantages named in my letter addressed to you on the 11th of June.

4. Should you also be disposed to recommend Charles Hancock (Ticket of Leave) as a fit person to receive one of the lower Salaries, I have no objection, if the Man himself is willing, to allow him to enter the Service of Government as a Constable, by cancelling his Agreement with the Company.

5. With respect to the Third Government Constable, I request you will make choice of any Prisoner now belonging to the Police Department whom you may consider most proper to discharge therefrom

Letter No. 678

Port Stephens
10th August 1832

Captain Moffatt J.P.

Sir,
   In reply to the latter part of your Letter of this day's date, I beg to acquaint you that I propose retaining in the Company's Police Department the same number of Persons named in my Letter addressed to you on the 11th of June, with the exception of the three now intended to be borne on the Colonial Establishment by H. M. Government.

Letter No. 679

Port Stephens
14th August 1832

Dr Bowman
Inspector Of Hospitals
Sydney

Sir,
   His Excellency the Governor having directed that the Prisoner of the Crown named in the Margin be received into the Lunatic Asylum, I have forwarded him herewith, together with the enclosed Statement of his case, & request you will do me the Honor to acquaint the Bearer in what way he is to be disposed of on his arrival at Sydney.

Daniel Dimotte,
Hercules

[Letter No. 679a]

The following <u>Advertizement</u> was this day transmitted to the
Sydney Gazette
Sydney Herald
Sydney Monitor
The Australian

YOUNG CLEVELAND

In consequence of the Increase of the Australian Agricultural Company's Cleveland Stock, I intend offering for sale at the ensuing Parramatta Fair the Entire Horse,

YOUNG CLEVELAND

This superior Horse was bred by Roger Calvert Esq. in 1824. Got by Old Cleveland out of a Mare by Dale's Coaching Stallion and imported on the *Australia* in 1827 under the name of the 'Brewer'.

He is a bright bay with Black Legs, stands 16 hands high, is sound – a sure foal Getter and quiet either for the saddle or Harness.

The Horse and his Stock may be seen and any further particulars obtained on application to Mr Henry Hall at Port Stephens, until the middle of September – when he will be removed to Sydney for Inspection.

W. E. Parry. Commissioner to the A. A. Company
Port Stephens 13th August 1832
Three Insertions

[Letter No 679b]

The following <u>Advertizement</u> was this day transmitted to the
Sydney Gazette
Sydney Herald
Sydney Monitor
The Australian

For Sale at Port Stephens

A Vessel of about 18 Tons burthen, built in a superior manner of the best seasoned Timber, she is just launched, and is fitted with a windlass and spars complete.

This Vessel is well adapted for the Hawkesbury, Illawarra, or Newcastle Trade, and will carry an excellent Cargo for her tonnage with a light draught of water.

Terms – Moderate

Apply to Mr Corlette commander of the *Lambton*.

W. E. Parry. Commissioner to the A. A. Company
Port Stephens 13th August 1832

Letter No. 680

Port Stephens
13th August 1832

Mr James Cox
Maitland

Sir,

William Berry, Minerva not *Mariner*

In reply to your Letter of the 27th ultimo respecting the Prisoner named in the Margin, I beg to acquaint you that I have in my possession Mr Hely's Official Printed Communication, dated the 25th of February last intimating the Sanction of His Excellency the Governor to your transfer of Berry to me, under the established Regulations.

Letter No. 681

Port Stephens
13th August 1832

Board for the Assignment of Servants

Gentlemen,
    In conformity with the Regulations I request that six carpenters may be assigned to me of the following Description; vizt Shepherds or Agricultural Labourers.
    I reside at Port Stephens in the County of Gloucester. I am Commissioner to the A. A. Company and hold about 458,000 Acres of Land; of which 450 Acres are cleared, and 400 Acres are in tillage.
    I possess 306 Horses, 3000 Head of Cattle and 27,000 Sheep; I now employ 65 Free, and 395 Convict Servants; of whom 196 have been in my Service upwards of Three Years, and 116 upwards of one year; No assigned Servants have been returned by me to Government within the last Two Years, and none have absconded from my Service during that period, without having been since apprehended & returned, or under Colonial Sentence.
    My Agent, Mr Bunn residing at Sydney is fully empowered to receive such Servants as may be assigned to me & to defray all Expenses incurred on their account.

Letter No. 682

Port Stephens
14th August 1832

Cornelius Smith
Care of Mr S. Lord
Sydney

Cornelius Smith,
    I acknowledge the receipt of your Letter of the 1st instant in which you express a wish to engage yourself in the Service of the Australian Agricultural Company.
    In reply I have to acquaint you that I have no occasion for your Services, there being no situation vacant in the Company's Service.

[Letter No. 682a]

The following Advertizement was this day transmitted to the
Sydney Gazette
Sydney Herald
Sydney Monitor
The Australian

Pure Merino Rams to be Sold at Maitland

The Australian Agricultural Company will have for Sale by Private Contract at Wallis's Plains on Wednesday the 26th of September next – Fifty Pure Merino Rams of Superior quality. Price from Three Pounds to Five Pounds,

Terms. Cash.

Apply to Mr Charles Hall at Hewitt's Inn Maitland on the Monday and Tuesday preceding.

W. E. Parry
Commissioner to the A. A. Company
Port Stephens 14th August 1832.

Three Insertions each

Letter No. 683

Port Stephens
14th August 1832

Alexander McLeay Esq.

Sir,
With reference to that part of your Letter of the 27th ultimo which intimates to me that H. E. the Governor has been pleased to accede to my request to have temporary occupation of (40,000) Forty Thousand Acres of Land near 'Warrah', on Liverpool Plains, on account of the A. A. Company.

I request you will do me the Honor to acquaint me whether I am at liberty to take possession of the same, & in what manner the limits are to be defined, in order to enable me to proceed with the requisite Buildings.

Letter No. 684

Mr Thomas Parnell, Richmond

Letter No. 685

Mr Philip Thorley, Richmond

and

Letter No. 686

Mr William Nowlan, Patrick's Plains

Port Stephens
14th August 1832

Sir,
    His Excellency the Governor having been pleased to grant me, on account of the A. A. Company, temporary occupation of 40,000 Acres of Land at 'Warrah', on Liverpool Plains, where I understand you have Stock grazing at present.
    I take the earliest opportunity of acquainting you with the same, to enable you to remove your Stock, it being my intention to occupy the Land with Sheep as soon as possible.
    I beg to assure you that, in making this arrangement, I shall be happy to meet your convenience in any way in my power.

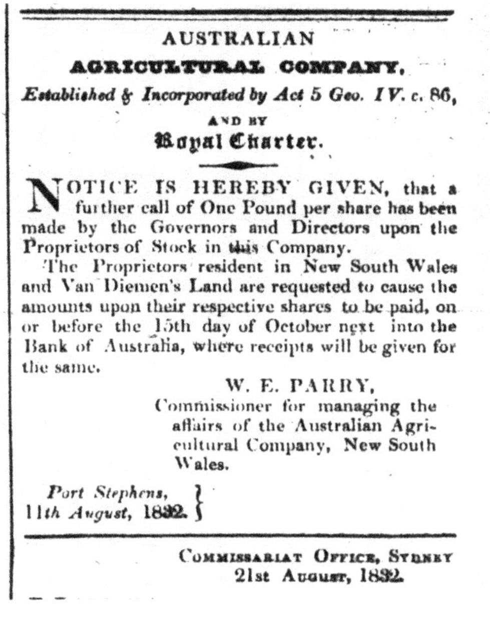

Illustration 1:
Sydney Herald,
23 August 1832
(Letter No. 687a)

Letter No. 687

Port Stephens
14th August 1832

George Bunn Esq.

Sir,

1. I herewith enclose to you Bills on the Governors and Directors of the A. A. Company for (£1000) One Thousand Pounds, which I request you will endorse, and lodge in the Bank of Australia, to the credit of the Company.

2. I request you will comply with the accompanying Requisition as soon as convenient; and I beg to advise you that I did not receive, per last voyage of the *Lambton*, any Invoice of her Cargo.

3. I beg to call your attention to the accompanying Letter from the Assignment Board relative to two men named therein, who appear in the Advertized List as Assigned to the Company, but have never been heard of here or at Newcastle. I request you will give me any information in your power respecting them by return of the *Lambton*, and should they not be forthcoming, that you will endeavour to leave them out and send them down to Port Stephens, as I am in great want of men.

[Letter No. 687a]

Australian Agricultural Company Established & Incorporated by Act 5 Geo IV Cap. 86 and by <u>Royal Charter</u>.

Notice is hereby given that a further Call of One Pound per Share has been made by the Governors & Directors upon the Proprietors of Stock in this Company.

The Proprietors resident in New South Wales and Van Diemen's Land are requested to cause the Amounts upon their respective Shares to be paid, on or before the 15th day of October next into the Bank of Australia, where Receipts will be given for the same.

W. E. Parry Commissioner for managing the affairs of the Australian Agricultural Company in New South Wales.

Port Stephens.
11th August 1832

Sydney Gazette	
Sydney Herald	Three Insertions each
Sydney Monitor	
Australian	

Forwarded to Graham's – 15th August 1832

Letter No. 688

Port Stephens
15th August 1832

George Bunn Esq.
Sydney

Sir,
    Enclosed you will receive <u>22</u> Letters addressed to some of the Colonial Proprietors of Stock in the A. A. Company respectively, which I request you will cause to be forwarded to them without delay.
    With reference to any further Proceedings which the Governors & Directors may institute on this head, I request you will insert opposite each name in the accompanying List the manner in which you have disposed of the respective Letters, and that you will return the List to me, Signed by yourself for transmission to the Court of Directors.

Forwarded to Graham's – 15th August 1832

-oOo-

    List of 22 (Twenty two) Proprietors of Stock in the A. A. Company to whom Circulars are addressed announcing the Twelfth Call – One Pound per Share – transmitted to George Bunn Esq. to be forwarded by him

Name	Address	How disposed of
The Honorable A Berry Esq. M. C.	Sydney	
George Bunn Esq.	do	
The Executors of the late J. T. Campbell Esq.	do	
The Honorable Robert Campbell Esq. M. C.	do	
Mr D. G. Forbes	do	
Mr F. N. Forbes	do	
F. A. Hely Esq.	do	
Patrick Hill Esq.	Liverpool	
The Rev. Richard Hill	Sydney	
James Macarthur Esq.	Parramatta	
Thomas Macvitie Esq.	Sydney	
The Rev. Samuel Marsden	Parramatta	
James Murdoch Esq.	V. D. Land	
Peter Murdoch Esq.	do	
James Norton Esq.	Sydney	
The Executors of the late John Ovens Esq.	do	
The Executors of the late John Oxley Esq.	do	

G. T. Palmer Esq.	Parramatta
A. B. Spark Esq.	Sydney
His Honor Mr Justice Stephen	do
The Executors of the late Charles Throsby Esq.	Glenfield
Edward Wollstonecraft Esq.	Sydney

Port Stephens 15th August 1832

Letter No. 689

Port Stephens
15th August 1832

John Henderson Esq.
Newcastle

Sir,

Enclosed you will receive 3 Letters addressed to some of the Colonial Proprietors of Stock in the A. A. Company respectively, which I request you will cause to be forwarded to them without delay.

Forwarded to Graham's 15 August 1832

-oOo-

List of 3 (Three) Proprietors of Stock in the A. A. Company to whom Circulars are addressed announcing the Twelfth Call – One Pound per Share – transmitted to John Henderson Esq. to be forwarded by him

Name	Address	How disposed of
The Honorable E. C. Close Esq. M. C.	Hunters River	
John Henderson Esq.	Newcastle	
Robert Scott & Helenus Scott Esq.	Glendon, Hunter's River	

Port Stephens 15th August 1832

[Letter No. 689a]

20th August 1832
His Excellency Major General Bourke

    Petition of Michael Devitt – *Mariner* – Life to be reunited to the Family from which he was separated at the Time of his Transportation.
    Recommendations of this Petition to the favorable consideration of H. E. The Governor,

Signed by
W. E. Parry Petitioner's Employer, for the A. A. Company
R. G. Moffatt J. P. & Captain 17th Regiment – First Magistrate
J. Edward Ebsworth J. P. – Second Magistrate

Letter No. 690

                                                                       Port Stephens
                                                                    25th August 1832

Captain Moffatt J. P.

Sir,
    With reference to the Information which I transmitted to you yesterday relative to the claim of William Barnes, an Indented Servant of the A. A. Company, to a reward paid to John Field, Constable, for the apprehension of Two Men illegally at large at Tellighary in the Month of April last.

    I have the Honor to acquaint you that, as it appeared to me, on the face of that information, that the reward (tho' justly paid to John Field <u>from the Evidence originally brought before you</u>) ought, in all probability, to have been awarded to William Barnes, I laid the case before our Brother Magistrate, Mr Ebsworth, at whose request, & in whose name as well as my own, I now beg to acquaint you with our joint opinion thereupon.

    It appears to us,

    1st That William Barnes was, as stated in his Letter, the first to apprehend the Two Men in question, at Telligherry, a Station distant from Stroud between two & three Miles.

    2d That he sent the Men, this distance of 2 to 3 Miles to Stroud, in charge of Richard Merchant. another Indented Servant of the A. A. Company.

    3d That Richard Merchant brought the Men to his Superintendent, Mr Swayne, at Stroud, by whose direction he delivered them to Thomas Beckett a Constable.

    4th That the circumstance of Barnes' not appearing before you, ought not by any means to invalidate his claim to the Reward if it be his due in other respects; since he could not, by any possibility, living as he does in the Bush, be aware when the case was to be tried, unless informed by the proper authorities.

Letter to A. McLeay

5th That neither could his Claim be considered less because he applied to you only "a Month ago" – that is, about 3 Months after the apprehension of the Prisoners.

6th That your remark (in which we quite agree) that the Persons who run a risk of an Action for false imprisonment ought to have the emolument, is another strong reason why Barnes is entitled to the Reward if our present information be correct; since he was the first to run that risk by apprehending the Men.

7th That the fact of Field's having brought the Prisoners from Stroud to Carrington, (to which he seems to attach some merit) does not constitute in the slightest degree, a claim to the Reward, which we consider intended by H. M. Government to encourage the Apprehension of Prisoners illegally at large, and not as a Fee for the performance of a Constable's ordinary duty in conveying such persons from one place to another after they have been apprehended and delivered to the police.

8th That, therefore if this new information be correct, there can be no doubt of the Reward being due to William Barnes – since if the two Prisoners were at large after this, i.e. at the time Field states that he took them into Custody, the fault lies with the Constable Beckett and not with Barnes.

Under these circumstances, we beg leave to suggest to you whether, upon the additional information now before us, it will not be proper to institute before the Bench an investigation (in which we shall be happy to assist) into the real facts of the case, to give Barnes an opportunity of proving his Claim, if correct, & thus, in a manner which will give no room for future question, to render justice to all parties.

Letter No. 691

Port Stephens
27th August 1832

Captain Moffatt J. P.

Sir,
Referring to your Letter of the 25th instant relative to a Claim made by William Barnes for certain Rewards therein alluded to.

We observe, with regret, that in that communication you impute to us, an intention of throwing a doubt on your former decision in this Case, and a desire to institute an enquiry for the purpose of altering that decision without a reference to His Majesty's Government.

Upon this imputation, we beg to remark, that we never entertained any such intention or desire – on the contrary you cannot fail to perceive, on a re-perusal of the Documents before you, that we directly expressed our conviction of the justice of your decision "from the evidence originally brought before you" – and that we merely suggested to you "whether upon the additional information now before us, it would not be proper to institute before the Bench" a fresh investigation, in which we should be happy to assist – it being our intention, of course, that should the additional information appear to the Bench to give William Barnes a just Claim to the Reward, the proper reference might be made to His Majesty's Government thereupon – if not, to let the matter stand as it now does.

We, therefore, request that, in any future correspondence with us, as Magistrates of the Territory, you will be good enough to avoid any imputations such as these, which are not borne out by the facts of the case.

We have moreover – to remark upon your observation that you are "the only acting Magistrate in the District" that we cannot admit the accuracy of that observation; since we are, and always have been, ready and willing to act as Magistrates in all Cases in which, it would be legal for us to do so. In fact, we have, as you are aware always done so, when called upon, and should have been ready to act if required in the very case, which is now the subject of our correspondence.

It is satisfactory to us, however, to find that you are willing to adopt our suggestion, by "recommending, as the best way of settling the claim, that Statements be taken from the different Parties on Oath" and that the case be then, if necessary, referred for final decision to H. M. Government.

We, therefore, request you will name to us, any day and hour next Week, either here or at Stroud, when it will be most convenient to you, for taking the Statements of the Parties, when we shall be ready to attend, in our places, on the Bench. We name next Week, in consequence of Beckett's absence, and the probability also, of the unavoidable absence of Sir E. Parry.

With reference to your letter of the 25th instant, suggesting for our consideration, the propriety of applying for the opinion of H. M. Attorney General, in the case of Mr Stubbs therein alluded to, we beg to acquaint you, that, in compliance with your wishes, we propose making the application.

We have the Honor to be
W. E. Parry J. P.
J. E. Ebsworth J. P.

Letter No. 692

Port Stephens
27th August 1832

The Honorable Colonial Secretary

Sir,

We have the honor to acquaint you that Captain Moffatt the Resident Magistrate at Port Stephens has applied to us, to sit on the Bench, in the case of a Summons against Mr Richard Stubbs, free Store Keeper, at this place, for allowing certain Servants of the A. A. Company to get drinks in a House, for which Mr Stubbs holds a license to sell Spirits &c.

The House is situated at Stroud, on the Estate of the A. A. Company and is rented by Mr Stubbs from the Company whose property it is.

Sir Edward Parry, is the Sole Attorney & Agent for the Company in New South Wales, and Mr Ebsworth's appointment from the Directors, is that of Assistant to Sir E. Parry. Mr Ebsworth has the sole charge and control of all the Company's Servants and Property in Sir E. Parry's occasional absence, and in case of his death, would immediately become the sole Agent and Attorney of the Company.

The Rent to be paid by Mr Stubbs, is fixed by Sir E. Parry on the recommendation of a Board of the Company's Officers, of whom Mr Ebsworth is one.

Under these circumstances, we declined acting, a few days ago, in this case, conceiving that it would be illegal for us to do so, under the 12th Section of the Act of the Government and Council No. 11 dated 12th May 1830 – but as it is a matter of great inconvenience to the Public Service, that such alleged offences should remain untried, we are induced on Captain Moffatt's suggestion to request that you will move His Excellency the Governor to be pleased to direct that a legal opinion be obtained, whether, under all the circumstances, it would be legal for us to act magisterially in such a case.

We should also esteem it a favor, if, as a separate question, we may be informed, whether the circumstance of our holding Shares in the Company's Stock, would affect the legality of our sitting in the above case.

We have the Honor to be
W. E. Parry J. P.
J. E. Ebsworth J. P.

Letter No. 693

Port Stephens
28th August 1832

Richard Julian Hamlyn Esq.
Cumming's Hotel
Sydney

Sir,

In reply to your Letter of the 16th instant, I regret to say that there is no situation vacant in the Service of the Australian Agricultural Company which is in my power to offer to your acceptance, the Medical Department of the Company's Estate being quite complete.

Letter No. 694

Port Stephens
28th August 1832

George Bunn Esq.
Sydney

Sir,
    In reply to your Letter of the 24th instant, on the subject of men returned to the A. A. Company from the General Hospital at Sydney, I request you will pay the account herewith returned, which, however, appears to require the Signature of the "Surgeon in charge".
    I also request you will take charge of any of the Company's men who may hereafter be discharged from the Sydney Hospital, until the arrival of the *Lambton*, providing for them as economically as circumstances will permit; as it appears that the Regulations laid down by His Majesty's Government on this head require that the Agent should take such men immediately into his charge.

Letter No. 695

Port Stephens
29th August 1832

Board for Assignment of Servants
Sydney

Gentlemen,
    With reference to my Letter addressed to you on the 12th July last relative to the Two Prisoners named in the Margin, and to your reply thereto.
    I have the Honor to acquaint you that I have now received these Two Men from Mr Bunn.

Margin: William Goodwin, *Asia*, 14 yrs

George Hames, *Asia*, Life

Letter No. 696

Port Stephens
29th August 1832

George Bunn Esq.
Sydney

Sir,
    Herewith you will receive a Draft on the Bank of Australia for (£60) Sixty Pounds on account of your current disbursements for the A. A. Company.
    I beg to advise you that the Invoice of a former Shipment, alluded to in the 3d Paragraph of your letter of the 23rd current was not enclosed, as

intended by you.

I may also mention that the <u>Official</u> Communication, alluded to in the same Letter, on the subject of the 2 missing Men, does not appear to have been forwarded by the Lambton; but the information on this subject conveyed to me in your Private Communication of the 23^d current is sufficient, & the Men have now been received.

I request you will return to me the Letter of the Board of Assignment, on this subject enclosed to you in mine of the 14th current (No 687)

I request you will comply, as soon as possible, with the enclosed Requisition attending particularly to the Red Ink Memorandum at foot thereof.

Letter No. 697

Port Stephens
29th August 1832

James Becket (Ticket of Leave)
Care of Alexander Macauley
Accountant
Parramatta

James Beckett [sic],

I have to acknowledge the receipt of your Letter of the 13th instant & acquaint you that the A. A. Company have no occasion for your Services.

Letter No. 698

Port Stephens
29th August 1832

His Honor, the Chief Justice
Sydney

Sir,

I have the honor to forward inclosed an account for Sums due by you to the A. A. Company amounting to Twenty Nine Pounds five Shillings and four pence (£29.5.4) and request the favor of you to pay the amount into the Bank of Australia at your early convenience, to be placed at my Credit as Commissioner to the Company.

Letter No. 699

Port Stephens
8th September 1832

Mr Yeoman
Maitland

Sir,
I request you will inform me, <u>per bearer,</u> whether the *Ellen* has been despatched with Flour for the A. A. Company agreeably to the request contained in my Letter to Mr Singleton of the 9th ultimo.

If she has not been dispatched, and you cannot ensure her being here by the 15th instant, I request you will make <u>immediate</u> arrangements for sending Four Tons of fine Flour, & Eleven Tons of Seconds Flour overland to Sawyers Point, acquainting by the bearer what day it will be there, that the Company's boats may be ready to receive it.

[Letter No. 699a]

Memo
12th September 1832
His Excellency General Bourke

Petition of Lukin Foreman to be re-united to his Family from which he was separated at the time of his Transportation.

Recommendations of his Petition to the favorable consideration of His Excellency the Governor was signed by

W. E. Parry Petitioner's Employer for the A. A. Company
R. G. Moffatt – J. P. Captain 17th Regiment 1st Magistrate
and J. E. Ebsworth J.P. Second Magistrate

[Letter No. 699b]

The following (3) Advertizements were this day transmitted to the
Sydney Gazette
Sydney Monitor
Sydney Herald, and
The Australian

FOR SALE
At the ensuing Parramatta Fair the Entire Horse

YOUNG CLEVELAND

This Superior Horse was bred by Roger Calvert Esq. in 1824 got by 'Old Cleveland' out of a Mare by Dale's Coaching Stallion, and imported on the *Australia* in 1827 under the name of the 'Brewer'.

He is a Bright Bay, with Black legs, stands 16 Hands high, is sound, a sure Foal getter, quiet either for Saddle or Harness.

Also,

A Handsome Entire Sorrel Pony with silver Mane and Tail foaled in March 1830, got by the imported Welch Pony 'Spangle' out of a Hector Mare and now stands 14 Hands high.

These Horses may be seen at Jones' Livery Stables – York Street Sydney from the 20th instant until they are removed to Parramatta. The Terms and any other particulars may be obtained on application to Mr Henry Hall at Cummings Hotel, Sydney, after the 26th instant.

W. E. Parry, Commissioner to the Australian Agricultural Company
Port Stephens 13th September 1832

-oOo-

WANTED

By the Australian Agricultural Company an Active Single Man who has been accustomed to the Management of Cattle – as Head Stock Keeper at Port Stephens.

Application to be made by letter to Mr Henry Hall at Port Stephens or personally in Sydney or Parramatta from the 26th instant to the 16th of October.

Testimonials as to Character and Ability will be required.

W. E. Parry, Commissioner to the Australian Agricultural Company
Port Stephens 13th September 1832

-oOo-

SHEARERS WANTED

Wanted by the A. A. Company at Port Stephens Eight good Shearers to commence Shearing on the 25th October.

Applications to be made to Mr James Corlette on board the *Lambton* cutter or to me at Port Stephens.

W. E. Parry, Commissioner to the A. A. Company
Port Stephens 13th August 1832

Letter No. 700

Port Stephens
13th September 1832

George Bunn Esq.
Sydney

Sir,
1. I herewith enclose to you a Draft on the Bank of Australia for (£70) Seventy Pounds to meet the current expenses on account of the A. A. Company.
2. Mr Ebsworth requests me to mention to you that he cannot understand how it is that there is a difference of 7/6 between the Balance of the Amount Current rendered by you to the 30th April 1832 and your rough sketch returned to you with the alterations in red ink as you requested.
3. As a trifling difference of this kind requires as much time & labour in going thro' the Company's Books as if it were ever so large an amount, I request you will be good enough to state by return of the *Lambton* wherein the difference consists, that is, why the Balance of your amount is not £13.17.3 instead of £13.9.9.
4. The Invoice to the Documents alluded to in the 4th Paragraph of your Letter of the 6th instant have not yet reached me, as we have had no communication with the Hunter lately, but I expect to receive them in the course of the next week.
5. I beg to call your attention to the enclosed Requisition, but I wish the *Lambton* to be dispatched to Newcastle for a Cargo of Coals for Sydney the moment Captain Corlette can dispose of a number of Hides & a few other articles for England respecting which he has received my Instructions & after that to return to Port Stephens without delay.

Letter No. 701

Port Stephens
13th September 1832

James Laidley Esq.
Deputy Commissary General
Sydney

Sir,
I have the Honor to enclose to you herewith the two undermentioned Drafts on the Bank of Australia, to your Order in payment of the Two Accounts against the A. A. Company by H. M. Government namely.

No. 1401 – £70.12.1
No. 1402 – £37.2.10

Amounting in the whole to (£107.14.11) One Hundred & Seven Pounds, Fourteen Shillings and Eleven Pence, the Receipt of which I request you will acknowledge by your signature on the Forms herewith enclosed.

[Letter No. 701a]

The following Advertizement was transmitted to the
Sydney Gazette and
Sydney Monitor

TO COVER THIS SEASON
At Mr Thomas Jones' Vineyard Cottage Patterson's River
PRINCE
A Cleveland Colt Bred by the Australian Agricultural Company in January 1830 Got by their Cleveland Stallion BARNABY Imported per Frederick in 1827.

PRINCE is a Beautiful Dark Bay without any white – stands 15 Hands high and is free from vice.

Terms Two Pounds each Mare – Groomage half a Crown. A Liberal Allowance to Persons sending more than one Mare

(Patterson's River) 1st September 1832.

Letter No. 702

Port Stephens
17th September 1832

Mr George Yeoman
John's Hill
Williams River

Sir,

In reply to your Letter of the 10th instant, I beg to acquaint you that the First Flour received from you is of so dark & musty a quality that I cannot receive any more of that kind on account of the A. A. Company, as it is very little inconvenience to obtain it from Sydney by the *Lambton*.

I request, therefore, that, unless you can furnish good first flour, you will send the whole quantity proposed to be sent on Saturday to Sawyers Point, of the Seconds kind – also from 80 to 100 Bushels of Bran, if there is any room in the dray.

As a Party of the Company's Servants are going out to Liverpool Plains on the 1st of October, I request you will have ready by that day, 500 lbs of First Flour and 500 lbs of Seconds Flour, at your Store at Maitland, for which Mr Charles Hall will give the necessary receipt.

Letter No. 703

Port Stephens
18th September 1832

George Bunn Esq.
Sydney

Sir,

 I now beg leave to acknowledge the receipt of your Letter of the 23rd ultimo, sent by the way of the Hunter containing an explanation, which is quite satisfactory, relative to the two Men therein alluded to.

 Observing, however by a Printed Memorandum dated from the Office of the Principal Superintendent of Convicts on the 8th of March 1832, which you enclosed to me (and which I now return) that a Man named Edmund Allen – *Asia* 8, No 51 – was assigned to the Australian Agricultural Company on that day; which Man I have never before heard of, I request you will, on the part of the Company, make the necessary enquiry, and cause him to be sent down to Port Stephens as soon as possible, as we are much in want of Men.

Letter No 704

Port Stephens
21st September 1832

The Honorable The Colonial Secretary
Sydney

Sir,

 I request you will do me the honor to call the attention of H. E. the Governor to the ninth Condition of the Charter of Incorporation of the Australian Agricultural Company which stipulates that the Quit Rents to accrue due upon the Company's Lands during the Second Term of Five Years after the date of their Grant "shall be remitted if Six hundred Convicts shall have been regularly employed and maintained by the Company for and during the greater part of such Second Term of Five Years".

 I beg leave to acquaint you, for His Excellency's information that in accordance with the Terms of the above mentioned Condition, I am desirous on the part of the A. A. Company of redeeming the Quit Rent thus to become due in the manner therein specified, namely by employing and maintaining Six hundred Convicts from and after the thirty first day of March of the ensuing Year (1833) that is about two hundred Convicts, more or less, in addition to those now employed and maintained on the Company's Estate at Port Stephens.

 I request you will further convey to His Excellency my assurance that this communication is not intended to refer in any way to the Company's extreme want of Men, but Solely to express my readiness and wish on the part of the Company to fulfil <u>their</u> part of the Ninth Condition of their charter for the purpose of redeeming the Quit Rent.

W Hewitson, *John*, 7 Years. Tried at Maitland, 14 August 1831. Sentence 12 Months to an Iron Gang.

Anthony Murphy, *Agamemnon*, Life. Tried at Port Stephens, 22 September 1831. Sentence 12 Months to an Iron Gang.

John Water, *Florentia*, 14 Yrs. Tried at Sydney, January 1832. Sentence 6 Months to an Iron Gang.

John Bryant, *Clyde*; William Wilson, *Clyde*.

William Edwards, *Surry*, Life; William Brown, *Waterloo*, Life.

Letter No. 705

Port Stephens
22nd September 1832

Principal Superintendent of Convicts
Sydney

Sir,
    The Sentences of the Three Prisoners of the Crown named in the Margin lately in the Service of the A. A. Company having expired, two of them for a considerable time past, & the Company being in extreme need of Men,
    I have earnestly to request that you will be good enough to cause these Men to be returned, without delay, to the Service of the Company – or, should this application not be regular, that you will inform me to whom I ought to apply.

Letter No. 706

Port Stephens
24th September 1832

Board for Assignment of Servants
Sydney

Gentlemen,
    Being desirous of exchanging with the Australian Agricultural Company, the two Men first named in the Margin (lately assigned to my private Service) for the two Men last named in the Margin (now in the Company's Service).
    I request you will be pleased to obtain for me the sanction of His Excellency the Governor to this exchange.

[Letter No. 706a]

    The following Advertisement was this day (26th September 1832) transmitted to the

Sydney Gazette	
Sydney Herald	Three Insertions each
Sydney Monitor	
Australian	

To cover this Season
at the Australian Agricultural Company's Stud
Establishment, Alderley – Port Stephens

The Imported Blood Horse
GRAMPUS

Bred by the Earl of Egremont in 1824 – Stands 16 hands high, and was got by 'Whalebone', out of 'Rectory', by 'Octavius' – vide *Stud Book* Vol. 3, p. 151

His Performances may be found in the Racing Calendar – Vols 55 & 56

The Cleveland Stallion
NOBLE

Bred by the Company in 1827. A Bright Bay. Stands 16 hands high got by 'Old Cleveland' out of an Imported Mare by 'Sorcerer'

The Cleveland Stallion
GRANBY

Bred by the Company in 1828 – A Dark Bay – Stands 15 ¼ hands high, got by 'Barnaby' out of an Imported Mare.

'Barnaby' was a well known Yorkshire Horse, sent out for the purpose of crossing 'Old Cleveland's Stock.

Illustration 2:
Sydney Herald, 4 October 1832
(Letter No. 706a)

The Imported Welch Pony
SPANGLE
A Beautiful Dapple Grey with Silver Mane & Tail. Stands 13 ½ hands high.

Terms
'Grampus'   £6.-.-
'Clevelands'   £3.-.-
'Welch Pony' £1.10.-
Groomage   £5.-.-

A liberal allowance will be made to Persons sending more than One Mare according to the numbers sent.

No charge will be made for Grass if the Mares are taken away after due notice. All Expenses to be paid before the Mares are taken away.

Letter No. 707

Port Stephens
26th September 1832

George Bunn Esq.
Sydney

Sir,
   I herewith enclose to you a Draft on the Bank of Australia for (£100) One Hundred Pounds, to meet the Current Expenses on Account of the Australian Agricultural Company.
   The *Lambton* is to return as soon as possible to Port Stephens, with the Remainder of the Goods per *Governor Halkett* and also the remainder of the Flour charged in your last Invoice.
   I also request that a Crown or Mortice Wheel (the model of which was forwarded to Sydney on the 28th of May last) may be sent, without fail by the *Lambton*.

Letter No. 708

Port Stephens
1st October 1832

To Captain Moffatt J.P.

Sir,
   With reference to our former Correspondence with you, on the subject of the claim of William Barnes, we beg to acquaint you that, as you expressed your unwillingness to assist in any further investigation of the case, we

considered it proper to recommend William Barnes, in answer to his application, to make Affidavit to the Facts, and to submit his Affidavit to the Bench of Magistrates of this District. But as Barnes is a Servant of the A. A. Company, we thought it might be better, under all the circumstances, not to administer the Affidavit ourselves; more especially as, in your Letter of the 27th of August, you expressed your readiness, as a point of duty, to swear the Aggrieved Party if required.

As, however, it would appear, by a Communication received from William Barnes last night, that you have declined doing so upon his application to you on your first visit to Stroud, we request you will inform us whether this Statement is correct. If so, we shall no longer feel any hesitation in administering the required oath; after which we purpose referring the whole of the Documents on this subject to His Excellency the Governor for his decision.

We have the honor to be
Sir
Your obedient humble Servant
W. E. Parry J. P.
J. E. Ebsworth J. P.
subject to His Excellency the Gove

Letter No. 709

Port Stephens
3rd October 1832

Captain Moffatt J. P.

Sir,
   Mr Ebsworth and myself having occasion today to consult and copy for transmission to H. M. Government, certain of the Records of the Police Office, & understanding that you are likely to be absent most of the day, I request you will leave the keys of the Records with the Constable for that purpose.

Letter No. 710

Port Stephens
5th October 1832

To Captain Moffatt J. P.

Sir,
   In your Letter of the 2d instant, addressed to Mr Ebsworth and myself, you have incidentally introduced some Remarks upon my holding a Court

lately at Stroud; which my duty as a Magistrate will not allow me to pass unnoticed.

Those Remarks being calculated to produce an incorrect and unfavourable impression upon the mind of His Excellency the Governor, to whom you was aware that we were about to refer your Letter, I shall take care that the real facts of the case are made known in the proper quarter. But, in the mean time, I feel myself called upon to protest most decidedly against the Principle which you seem disposed to set up; as regards the Magisterial Duties of this District.

The manner in which you mention the circumstance of my having held a Court at Stroud, plainly implies that you imagine, in some way or other, that I ought not to have done so. It clearly betrays a jealousy of my having acted magisterially at all in this instance. I am bound, therefore, distinctly to inform you that I consider myself as competent, and as much required, by my duty as a Magistrate, to hold Courts in this District, as you are, in all cases in which I can legally do so; and that, whatever may be your objection to my thus acting, I shall always continue to do so, when called upon in any similar instances for the future. If you think I am wrong in this view of the matter, it may save much trouble if you will say so, in order that His Majesty's Government may determine whether my competency is thus to be questioned – and not only this, but my authority weakened, since your written sentiments on this subject are sure to be publickly made known through the medium of the Chief Constable and the Clerk.

I must further remark, however, that, when you mention the fact of my holding a Court at Stroud "for the first time since your arrival at Port Stephens", to try & decide on Charges brought against a Constable, you have omitted to mention some <u>other</u> facts of some importance in this case; namely, that there are only <u>two persons</u> (besides the Constables), resident at Stroud, who are <u>not Servants of the A. A. Company</u>; and that it was not quite four weeks previous to my holding the Court, that I became legally competent to try a Charge against one of the Constables; since it was only on the 10th of the preceding month that any of the Constables <u>ceased</u> to be Servants of the Company, in consequence of His Excellency's Commands that three of them should be maintained by His Majesty's Government.

I am unwilling to believe that you intentionally omitted these important facts, which, to any candid mind, will, I apprehend, afford a sufficient explanation of the circumstance to which you so pointedly allude in your Letter.

But the same Paragraph of your Letter contains a much more serious assertion – namely, that I "tried and decided on charges brought against a Constable, <u>after you had refused to enquire into the affair further</u>".

I really believe, Sir, that you will, on a re-perusal of this sentence of your Letter, be as much astonished at it as I have been. I feel quite convinced, indeed, that it is either an inadvertency, or a mere obscurity of expression. But as, according to my ideas of language, it can convey to the Governor only one meaning, and that meaning (as I am sure you will be ready to admit) directly opposed to the truth, I request you will oblige me by a written assurance that you had never tried those charges against the Constable, nor had even heard of them, until I placed the Depositions in your hands; in one of the two instances, for the express purpose of receiving your assistance and advice.

In conclusion, I shall only add that as, on several occasions of late, you seem to have imagined that the Police of this District is <u>exclusively</u> under your Control, thus intimating that you consider as a right, what your brother Magistrates have only conceded to you as a matter of mere courtesy, I, as one of those Magistrates, have felt it the more incumbent upon me to make this Communication, lest you should suppose that I admit any such right on your part. And I now take the opportunity of stating that, since you are not disposed rightly to appreciate the intention of my non-interference with the Police, I shall no longer feel any delicacy in exercising my full Magisterial Authority, whenever I may see occasion to do so, and that I shall strenuously resist every act which may tend to call in question or to weaken that Authority.

Letter No. 711

Port Stephens
5th October 1832

James Macarthur Esq.
Parramatta

Sir,
On the 21st of November of last year, I had the Honor of addressing to you a Letter on the subject of a certain Claim made by Mr Wetherman, Storekeeper to the Australian Agricultural Company. Having received no reply to this Communication, I fear it may have miscarried. I, therefore, now transmit to you a Copy of it, to which I beg the favor of an answer at your earliest convenience.

Letter No. 712

Port Stephens
5th October 1832

James Laidley Esq.
Deputy Commissary General
Sydney

Sir,
I have the Honor to transmit to you herewith an account (in Triplicate) amounting to Thirty three pounds sixteen shillings and nine pence (£33.16.9) for Supplies to the Military Detachment stationed at Port Stephens – between the 1st of July and 30th of September of the present Year, together with the Vouchers complete, for the same.

I also transmit herewith an account (in Triplicate) amounting to Five Pounds four shillings and eight pence (£5.4.8) for Supplies to sundry Persons on account of H. M. Government to the 30th of September of this year, with the Vouchers complete.

I request you will cause the several amounts to be paid into the Bank of Australia, to the Credit of the Company as early as possible; and I beg to remind you that the whole of the accounts referred to in my Communication to you of the 25th July, still remain unpaid.

Letter No. 713

Port Stephens
5th October 1832

James Laidley Esq.
Deputy Commissary General
Sydney

Sir,

I have the Honor to transmit to you herewith a memorandum of Account Current, between H. M. Government and the Australian Agricultural Company to the 30th of June 1832, for Supplies furnished to the Military Detachments and other Persons at Port Stephens, on account of H. M. Government.

The intention of this Memorandum, is to facilitate the settlement of Various Accounts which have been long outstanding, and respecting which I had the Honor, to communicate with you personally at Sydney, in the early part of June last.

I beg leave again to draw your attention to the absolute necessity of my being acquainted with the reasons for the several deductions which appear to have been made from the Accounts rendered by the Company; more specially as the several sums paid do not agree, in any one instance, with the Items charged in the Company's Books.

You will also observe that independently of any Items which have been or may be disputed, no payment has been made by His Majesty's Government for the Supplies furnished to the Military, nearly four years ago, namely between 24th May and 24th December 1828, amounting to One Hundred and Sixty one Pounds – Seventeen Shillings and five pence (£161.17.5), for which the accounts were duly rendered to Mr Scott at Newcastle, by your desire, before the close of that year.

I also beg leave to remind you that, independently of the Balance of Two Hundred and Eighty four pounds – ten shillings and four pence three farthings (£284.10.4¾) appearing in the accompanying Memorandum, there is also due for Coals to the 30th of June, the Sum of One Hundred and forty four Pounds – Eighteen Shillings and a penny, as per Account transmitted to you on the 20th of July last, and Thirty nine pounds – one & five Pence (£39.1.5) being the Amount of two Accounts transmitted to you in a separate

Letter this day – making a Total of £468.9.10¾ due from H. M. Government to the A. A. Company of which I earnestly request a speedy settlement.

Letter No. 714

Police Office Carrington
Port Stephens

10th October 1832
To The Honorable The Colonial Secretary

Sir,

We request you will do us the honor to lay before His Excellency the Governor the following Statement.

On the 24th of August last, Sir Edward Parry received a Letter (of which Enclose A is a Copy) from William Barnes, a free Servant of the Australian Agricultural Company, stating his Claim to a Reward for apprehending two Prisoners illegally at large. Sir Edward Parry never having heard of this business before, in consequence of his absence in the interior, immediately referred the Letter to Captain Moffatt, the Resident Magistrate at this place, together with the Note, forming the present Inclosure B, to which Inclosure C, with the Copy of the Police Records D, is Captain Moffatt's reply, and E the rejoinder of Sir Edward Parry.

Having on the same day obtained additional information on the subject from Mr Swayne, one of the Parties referred to by Captain Moffatt, Sir Edward Parry inclosed it to Captain Moffatt (F and G), to which H, with it's Inclosure I is the reply.

Sir Edward Parry being unable to agree with Captain Moffatt, in opinion that a Claim of this nature respectfully made by a free and respectable Individual could thus be, with propriety, dismissed without a hearing, referred the foregoing Correspondence to Mr Ebsworth, one of the Bench of Magistrates of this District, for his opinion and advice: and the Letter (Inclosure K) was in consequence addressed to Captain Moffatt, stating our joint Opinion, this was replied to by Inclosure L.

Captain Moffatt having thus acquiesced in our suggestion as to the propriety of further inquiry, by recommending as his own opinion, that the Statements of the different parties should be taken on Oath, with a View to our obtaining the opinion of His Majesty's Government, we requested Captain Moffatt (Inclosure M) to name the time and place most convenient to him, for this purpose, when we should be ready to attend in our places on the Bench. To this Communication we received the reply N in which Captain Moffatt declines assisting in the inquiry, which we understood him to have recommended in his preceding Communication.

As we conceived it would have been highly improper to enter upon this inquiry ourselves without Captain Moffatt's assistance, it was suggested to us, by the last Paragraph of that Gentleman's Letter (N) that the only remaining mode, in which William Barnes could be allowed an opportunity of substantiating his Claim, if a just one, was for himself and Richard Merchant to make Affidavits to the facts and submit them to the Bench of Magistrates. In reply, therefore, to Barnes's original application Sir Edward Parry addressed to him on the 28th of August, the Communication marked O.

Considering that it might be more proper for Captain Moffatt than for either of us to swear the Aggrieved Party to any Statement he wished to make, more especially as Captain Moffatt had expressed his readiness to do so, if required, we intimated to Barnes our wish that he would wait until the next visit of Captain Moffatt to Stroud. He accordingly did so, and on the 30th of September Sir Edward Parry received from him a Letter (P), stating that Captain Moffatt had declined swearing him. He then addressed to Captain Moffatt the communication marked Q, to which R is Captain Moffatt's reply. The Affidavits twice made by William Barnes and Richard Merchant respectively, are transmitted herewith.

Having now no other course left, we beg leave, respectfully to submit the whole Case, so far as we are acquainted with it, to His Excellency the Governor. This we do, with much reluctance in the present imperfect state of the Evidence; and we feel that some apology may be necessary for transmitting several Documents which are not strictly in Official Form. But being strongly impressed with the importance of holding out every encouragement to persons living in Solitary Situations "in the Bush" to apprehend Prisoners illegally at large, in order to give full effect to the beneficial intentions of His Majesty's Government, in offering liberal Rewards for this Service, we cannot, consistently with our Sense of Duty, permit a case of this kind to pass unnoticed. The grounds on which we consider that some further inquiry is called for, having been already detailed in our Communication (Inclosure K) we only consider it necessary to add, for His Excellency's information that Stroud, where the Constable appears to have taken charge of the two men, is a Village with a population of 140 persons, and that Barnes's Residence is above Twenty three miles from the Police Office at this place, where the two Prisoners in question were brought up for examination.

We have the Honor, to be
Sir, &c &c &c
W. E. Parry J. P.
J. E. Ebsworth J. P.

P. S. With reference to any enquiry which His Excellency may be pleased to order in this business, it may be necessary to add that Thomas Beckitt, the Constable to whom Merchant swears that he delivered the two Prisoners, is expected to leave the Company's Estate with a Ticket of Leave about the 1st of December next.

Letter No. 715

Port Stephens
12th October 1832

To The Honorable The Colonial Secretary

Sir,

Understanding that it is the wish of His Excellency the Governor to obtain a Return of the number &c of the Aborigines residing in each district of the Colony.

We have the Honor to enclose herewith a List containing as many of the Names as could be collected in this District amounting, with their Wives and families to 512 Souls, known to reside on the Estate of the Australian Agricultural Company.

It is supposed, by those who have the best opportunity of judging, that these do not constitute more than one-third of the whole number resident within the Limits of the Company's Original Grant. The neighbourhood of the Myall River and Lakes is especially populous, but as they are very shy in that quarter, in consequence, as we imagine, of several murders known to have been committed by them upon Runaways from Port Macquarie, we have not much intercourse with them.

We request you will communicate to His Excellency the Governor the respectful expression of our hope, that he will be pleased at the next annual Issue of Blankets to the Aborigines, to extend this Indulgence to the Natives of this District.

We have the Honor
W. E. Parry J. P.
J. E. Ebsworth J. P.

Letter No. 716

Port Stephens
12th October 1832

To Dr Mitchell
General Hospital
Sydney

Sir,

I have the Honor to enclose to you the Case of the Prisoner of the Crown named in the Margin, an Assigned Servant of the Australian Agricultural Company, whom I request you will receive into the General Hospital. Mr George Bunn, George St, Sydney, will receive him, when cured, on the part of the Company.

Patrick Thompson,
Mangles 4, Life

Letter No. 717

Port Stephens
12th October 1832

George Bunn Esq.
Sydney

Sir,
With reference to your Letter of the 3rd instant relative to Edmund Allen a prisoner said to have been Assigned to the A. A. Company on the 8th March and forwarded from the Barracks to Port Stephens I beg to acquaint you that I have again made strict enquiry & that no man of that name has ever been forwarded to the Company's Estate. I therefore request that you will make further enquiry on this subject as the Company is in great want of Men.

Letter No. 718

Port Stephens
14th October 1832

Captain Moffatt J. P.

John Mills,
Surry, 14 yrs

Sir,
With reference to my Remark upon the Letter of the Prisoner named in the Margin, which you referred for my explanation on the 8th instant, it may perhaps save trouble to inform you that, as Mills was sent to Port Macquarie by the Sydney Bench in February 1824, he has no claim to a Ticket of Leave, according to the Government Regulations till February 1833, his term of probation commencing in February 1827.

Letter No. 719

Port Stephens
16th October 1832

Captain Moffatt J. P.

Sir,
In reply to your Letter of this day's date, I beg to acquaint you that I am quite aware of the Regulation to which you allude in the last Paragraph, but you will observe that by this Regulation the time has not yet arrived for Mills's application.
I am however much obliged by your reminding me of the Regulation in question, & have the Honor to remain, &c

Letter No. 720

Port Stephens
18th October 1832

To William Sharpe Esq.
North Shore, Sydney.

Sir,

I have the Honor to acknowledge the receipt of your Letter of the 10th current, and in reply have very much to regret my inability to comply with your wishes, there being no situation vacant or likely to be vacant in the Service of the Australian Agricultural Company.

Had it been in my power, I should have had much pleasure in attending to the recommendations of the highly respectable Individuals, to whom you refer me.

Letter No. 721

Port Stephens
18th October 1832

To The Honorable Colonial Secretary

Sir,

1. Mr Dangar having completed his Map of that part of the country adjacent to Newcastle, which he lately surveyed in conjunction with Mr White, for the purpose of ascertaining the limits of the Fifteen hundred (1500) acres of Coal Grant for which I applied, on behalf of the Australian Agricultural Company, in my Letter addressed to you on the 30th of January last.

2. I have now the Honor to forward to you, for the information of H. E. the Governor, a Sketch of Mr Dangar's Map; and I beg leave to acquaint you that the following limits comprehend the portion of Land, which I wish to be granted to the Company

3. The figure A B C D on the Map includes the Fifteen Hundred (1500) Acres applied for by my Letter of the 30th of January; but as we are now sufficiently acquainted with the Strata, to enable me to determine on the locality of the whole Grant of Two Thousand (2000) Acres, I wish to take the remaining Five hundred (500) Acres by drawing a North Line from C, in the direction of E, and thence Eastward, so far as may be found necessary to include the 500 Acres between those lines & the River. Should the North line meet the River <u>before</u> it includes 500 Acres, I wish to add the remaining portion Westward of, and parallel to, the line C D.

4. As the small figure A B F G in the Map, consisting of Sixty seven (67) Acres and upwards includes the Western part of the Town and two Government Windmills, I wish to obtain only the <u>Mining</u> right to this portion, which is indispensable to the Company's operations; and I would propose that the <u>surface</u> right of that portion be relinquished by the

Company in consideration of their obtaining a Grant of the Two small Town Allotments applied for by my Letter addressed to you, on the 4th of October 1831.

5. With respect to the Water Frontage, I wish to obtain for the Company the whole quantity allowed by H. M. Government (of <u>not less</u> than five hundred (500) yards), by measuring the requisite distance from F, which is the North Western extremity of the Intended Town, Westward towards H.

6. I beg leave again to express a hope that a <u>Breadth</u> of One hundred (100) Yards will not be considered as exceeding the intention of H. M. Government in agreeing to a "liberal allowance" of Water Frontage to each of the Company's Locations.

7. From the point at which the allowed Water frontage terminates between F and H a line may be drawn due South, till it meets the Public Maitland Road, which Road will advantageously form the Boundary as far as may be found practicable.

8. The Strip of Water Frontage from which the Company will thus be excluded, though it has been comprehended in the present Survey, may be made up to the Company by a corresponding quantity in either of the Localities alluded to, in the 3d Paragraph of this communication.

9. I request you will do me the honor to submit these proposals to H. E. the Governor as soon as convenient. Mr Dangar will be ready to accompany a Government Surveyor in any final measurement and marking out of the Company's Boundaries, which H. E. may be pleased to direct.

Map 2:

The proposed Newcastle Coal Grant as discussed in Letter 721 – based on AO Map 6268, State Records of NSW

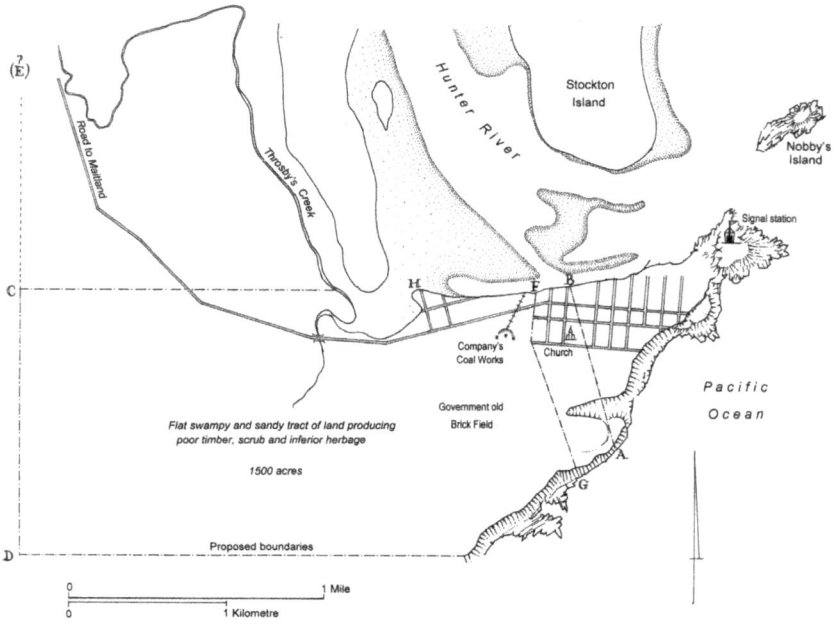

Letter No. 722

Port Stephens
19th October 1832

To Captain Moffatt J. P.

Sir,

Having on the 13th of August furnished Ryan, the Government Constable with the Sum of One Pound on account of the A. A. Company to enable him to procure Rations, till he receives his Pay, I shall feel much obliged by your obtaining for me, payment of the same, when the next Quarterly Payment of the Government Constables takes place.

Letter No. 723

Port Stephens
26th October 1832

To James Mudie Esq.
11 George Street
Sydney

Sir,

I beg leave to acknowledge the Receipt of your Letter of the 15th current, and in reply to inform you that, whenever the A. A. Company has an Establishment at Liverpool Plains, it is my intention to advertize for Tenders to supply it with Flour, when I shall be happy to receive your proposals on this subject.

Letter No. 724

Port Stephens
26th October 1832

To James Laidley Esq.
Deputy Commissary General
&c &c &c

Sir,

I have the honor to acknowledge the Receipt of your Letter of the 22d current, and beg leave to return herewith the three cash accounts therein alluded to with my Signature attached to the several Receipts – namely

Duplicate Cash Accounts for Coals supplied to the Commissariat Department for the quarter ended 30th June and amounting to	£143.17.10½
likewise Cash Accounts for Provisions supplied to the Detachment up to 30th June last also in Duplicate and amounting to	£66.12.5
and similar Accounts for Provisions supplied up to 30th September last and amounting to	£33.16.9¼
Making a total of	£244.7.0¾

Two Hundred and forty four Pounds – seven shillings and three farthings.

You will observe that I have filled up the Receipt for the last Amount, which was inadvertently left blank in your Office.

I will do myself the honor of replying to the several points contained in your letter by an early opportunity; and in the mean time I request you will do me the favor to pay the above amounts into the Bank of Australia to my Credit as Commissioner to the A. A. Company.

P. S. Observing in your Account for Supplies to the Military to the 30th of June 1832, that a deduction of 4/9 has been made from my Account rendered, I beg to draw your attention to my Memorandum thereupon, and I earnestly request an explanation of this deduction. W.P.

Memo: In the Accompanying Account for Coals 6/- per Ton having been mentioned as prime Cost, Sir Edward Parry annexed the following Note:

Memo: The above 6/- per ton not the Prime Cost, but paid on account, till the Prime Cost is determined on.

Letter No. 725

Port Stephens
26th October 1832

To The Honorable Colonial Secretary

Sir,

1. I have the honor to enclose to you herewith an Account in triplicate with the requisite Vouchers for Coals supplied by the Australian Agricultural Company to H. M. Colonial Governor during the quarter ending the 30th ultimo amounting to (£44.17.6) Forty four pounds – seventeen shillings and six pence.

2. I likewise enclose open for your perusal (for the reasons given in my Letter addressed to you on the 20th of July last) – a Communication to the Deputy Commissary General transmitting to him similar Accounts in triplicate for Coals supplied during the same period to the Commissariat

Department amounting to (£126.2.5). One hundred and twenty six pounds – two shillings and five pence.

   3. I request that you will forward my Letter to the Deputy Commissary as soon as convenient after ascertaining the accuracy of the Account against His Majesty's Colonial Government and that His Excellency may be pleased to direct immediate payment to be made of the whole Account, amounting to (£170.19.11.) One Hundred and Seventy pounds, nineteen shillings and eleven pence.

   4. I beg leave to remind you that the Account against His Majesty's Colonial Government transmitted to you in my Letter of the 20th of July last still remains unpaid.

   5. I likewise beg leave to inform you, that the Deputy Commissary General has declined paying the Company the sum of (£1.0.2½) One Pound and two pence halfpenny, being a part of the Account transmitted to him, through you, on the 20th of July last, in consequence as he informs me of that Sum being due for Coals supplied to the Beacon at Newcastle and which should therefore be paid by the Colonial Treasury.

   6. I am aware that this confusion arose from the change made in Supplying H. M. Government with Coals under the name of Two Different Departments, and before any systematic arrangement had been made for furnishing the Company with regular Vouchers for the supplies to the Colonial Department. As however Mr Nicholson will be ready on application to explain the circumstances, I request you will be pleased to take the necessary steps for ascertaining the correctness of this additional claim against H. M. Colonial Government. and cause the Amount (£1.0.2½) to be paid with the other accounts.

Letter No. 726

Port Stephens
26th October 1832

To James Laidley Esq.
Deputy Commissary General

Sir,

   1. I have the honor to enclose to you herewith Accounts (No. 1 and 2) in triplicate with the requisite Vouchers, for Coals supplied by the A. A. Company to the Commissariat Department; during the quarter ending the 30th ultimo, and amounting to (£90.9) Ninety pounds Nine Shillings and (£35.13.5.) Thirty five pounds, thirteen shillings and five pence respectively.

   2. I request you will cause the amount (£126.2.5.) One hundred and twenty six pounds two shillings and five pence, to be paid into the Bank of Australia to the credit of the A. A. Company with as little delay as possible.

   3. With reference to a part of your Letter addressed to me on the 22d current I beg to acquaint you that I have applied to the Honorable Colonial Secretary for payment of the Sum of (£1.0.2½) One pound and two pence

half penny for Coals supplied to the Beacon, and included in my Account transmitted to you up to the 30th of June last; and I request you will be good enough to give the necessary explanation, should application be made to you for that purpose.

Letter No. 727

Port Stephens
26th October 1832

To John Nicholson Esq.
Master Attendant

Sir,
    I have the honor to acquaint you that the Deputy Commissary General has declined paying the A. A. Company the Sum of (£1.0.2½) One pound and two pence halfpenny for Coals supplied to the Beacon Light at Newcastle and included in my Account against the Commissariat Department for the quarter ending the 30th of June last.

    As you are aware that this confusion arose from the change made about that time in the mode of supplying <u>Two</u> Departments of H. M. Government instead of One as formerly, I request you will communicate with the Honorable Colonial Secretary and the Deputy Commissary General on this subject, so as to ascertain the correctness of this claim, and to obtain immediate payment of the same by the Colonial Department.

Letter No. 728

Port Stephens
27th October 1832

To the Principal Superintendent of Convicts
Thomas Peck, Native of V. D^s Land, 14 years

Thomas Peck, Native of V. D. Land, 14 years

Sir,
    The Prisoner of the Crown named in the Margin now in the Service of the Australian Agricultural Company whose Ticket of Leave is advertized in the Government Gazette of the 1st Current being desirous of remaining in the Service of the Company – I request that his Ticket of Leave may be changed from Newcastle to Port Stephens for that purpose.

Letter No. 729

Port Stephens
27th October 1832

To George Bunn Esq.
Sydney

Sir,
   In reply to your Letter of the 22nd Current on the subject of the Company's Wool, I beg leave to acquaint you that, if you can positively guarantee the Craigievar being at Port Stephens by the last day in January, and her leaving the Colony for London by the middle of February, I should have no objection to making this arrangement for the Company's Wool upon the terms you propose – namely (7) seven farthings per pound. I would undertake to say that the *Craigievar* should not be detained more than five days from her anchoring at this Settlement, till all the Wool is put on board. As however, I intend sending One of the Company's officers to Sydney in a very few days, I will give him Instructions to determine finally on this subject.
   I enclose herewith a draft on the Bank of Australia to meet the Payment of the last Invoice; and a Requisition for 12 Kennels, with which I request you will comply.
   As I am anxious to get the *Lambton* back to Port Stephens not later than the 6th proximo in order to take advantage of the next Spring tide to examine her bottom, I request you will despatch her from Sydney in time for that purpose.

   P. S. Herewith you will receive Bills on the Governors & Directors of the A. A. Company for (£1000) One thousand Pounds Nos 247 to 252 which I request you will endorse, and place to my Credit in the Bank of Australia, as Commissioner to the Company. W. E. P.

Letter No. 730

Port Stephens
7th November 1832

Honorable Colonial Secretary
&c &c &c
Sydney

Sir,
   It has very recently come to my knowledge that the Ticket of Leave of the Prisoner of the Crown named in the Margin has for several years past been deposited among the Papers of the A. A. Company, in whose Service he has been, without its being endorsed by a Magistrate at the intervals directed by the Government Order of the 28th of May 1830.

Robert Field, Ocean, Life

Robert Field's Ticket of Leave enclosed

This irregularity appears to have been occasioned by the Ticket of Leave having been originally lodged with the Company's Principal Agent, and as the man has ever since been residing at the distance of 55 miles from the residence of any Magistrate, and has been receiving a Salary quarterly like the Free Servants of the Company, it seems to have escaped notice that he was a Prisoner at all.

As, however, the circumstances have now come to my Knowledge, I consider it my duty to make you acquainted with the case, for the information of H. E. The Governor, and I request, on the part of Field that, as he has bona fide been in the Service and on the Estate of the Company during the whole period exceeding 6 years with an excellent character, this non-compliance with the Regulations, proceeded entirely from ignorance of them, His Excellency may be pleased to view with Indulgence this deviation from the Established Rule.

As I have lately engaged in the Service of the A. A. Company some other men holding Tickets of Leave, whose duties may, and in some instances already do, render it necessary for them to be stationed at the distance of about 60 miles from the residence of any Magistrate & nearly 40 from any place occasionally visited by a Magistrate except by Mr Ebsworth and myself, I request to be informed whether our Initials (as Magistrates) upon the Certificates of any such men will be considered as a sufficient compliance with the Government Regulations. It is scarcely necessary to point out to His Excellency that, unless this be allowed, the loss to the Company arising from the necessity of their Ticket of Leave Servants travelling always 80, and sometimes nearly 120 miles every Month, would render it scarcely possible for me to employ in their Service any persons of that description which I am otherwise very desirous of doing – especially such Men of good characters as receive their Tickets while in the Service of the Company.

Letter No. 731

Port Stephens
7th November 1832

A. W. Scott Esq.

Sir,

Observing by the Books of the A. A. Company that the sum of £5 was advanced to you on loan on the 20th February 1827 by Mr Dawson late Agent to the Company, I have to request that you will pay the Amount to the Bearer Mr J. C. White or lodge the same at the Bank of Australia to my Credit as Commissioner to the Company together with Interest at the rate of 8 percent per annum for 5½ years being £2.4.

Letter No. 732

Port Stephens
7th November 1832

Mr Jeremiah Warlters
21 King Street
Sydney

Sir,

In reply to your Letter, of the 20th ultimo I beg to acquaint you that the Cattle to which I suppose you allude, and which you consider to have been yours, were impounded, advertized, and sold according to Law, and the Account transmitted to the Resident Magistrate as the Act directs. I find on reference to the Accounts that, the Cattle were sold for less than the Expenses incurred. I need not inform you that it was not in my power consistently with the Law, to have acted otherwise than I did.

On a Petition from Alexander Macdonald to His Excellency the Governor for a Ticket of Leave.

At the request of the Petitioner Alexander Macdonald, we hereby certify that he has been in the Service of the Australian Agricultural Company for six years and a quarter, during which time, tho' he has occasionally indulged in drinking, his conduct has been generally good. He has had charge of a small vessel belonging to the Company, for the greater part of the time, and has constantly been employed in the conveyance of Stores, without any impeachment of his character for honesty; we, therefore, recommend his case to the favorable consideration of His Excellency

Port Stephens 7th November 1832
W. E. Parry J. P.
J. E. Ebsworth J. P.

Letter No. 732 [sic]

Stroud
12th November 1832

To Captain Moffatt J. P.

Sir Edward Parry presents his Compliments to Captain Moffatt, and forwards to him, for his information, the accompanying Minutes of an Enquiry made this day, which he requests Captain Moffatt will cause to be lodged among the Police Records.

Australian Agricultural Company

Established & Incorporated by Act 5th Geo: IV Cap: 86 & by Royal Charter

Notice is hereby given that a further Call of One Pound per Share has been made by the Governors & Directors upon the Proprietors of Stock in this Company.

The Proprietors resident in New South Wales and Van Diemen's Land, are requested to cause the Amounts upon their respective Shares to be paid on or before the fifteenth day of January next, into the Bank of Australia, where Receipts will be given for the same.

W. E. Parry Commissioner for managing the Affairs of the A. A. Company in New South Wales.

Port Stephens 15th November 1832

Sydney Gazette	Three Insertions each.
Sydney Herald	Forwarded per *Lambton* 16th
The Monitor	November 1832
The Australian	

Letter No. 733

Port Stephens
15th November 1832

To George Bunn Esq.

Sir,

Enclosed you will receive 21 Letters addressed to some of the Colonial Proprietors of Stock in the A. A. Company respectively, which I request you will cause to be forwarded to them without delay.

With reference to any further Proceedings which the Governors and Directors may institute on this head, I request you will insert opposite each name in the accompanying List, the manner in which you have disposed of the respective Letters, and that you will return this List to me, signed by yourself for transmission to the Court of Directors.

-oOo-

List of 21 (twenty one) Proprietors of Stock in the Australian Agricultural Company to whom Circulars are addressed announcing the Thirteenth Call – One Pound per Share – transmitted to George Bunn Esq. to be forwarded by him:

Names	Address	How disposed of
The Honorable A. Berry Esq. M. C.	Sydney	
George Bunn Esq.	do	
The Executors of the late J. T. Campbell Esq.	do	
The Honorable R. Campbell Esq. M. C.	do	
Mr D. G. Forbes	do	
Mr F. W. Forbes	do	
Fred A. Hely Esq.	do	
Patrick Hill Esq.	Liverpool	
The Rev. Richard Hill	Sydney	
Thomas Macvitie Esq.	do	
The Rev. Samuel Marsden	Parramatta	
James Murdoch Esq.	V. D. Land	
Peter Murdoch Esq.	do	
James Norton Esq.	Sydney	
The Executors of the late J. Oxley Esq.	do	
The Executors of the late J. Ovens Esq.	do	
G. T. Palmer Esq.	Parramatta	
A. B. Sparke Esq.	Sydney	
His Honor Mr Justice Stephen	do	
The Executors of the late C. Throsby Esq.	Glenfield	
Edward Wollstonecraft Esq.	Sydney	

Port Stephens
15th November 1832

Letter No. 734

Port Stephens
15th November 1832

John Henderson Esq.
Newcastle

Sir,
    Enclosed you will receive (3) three Letters addressed to some of the Colonial Proprietors of Stock in the A. A. Company respectively, which I request you will cause to be forwarded to them without delay.
    With reference to any further Proceedings which the Governors and Directors may institute on this head, I request you will insert opposite each

name in the accompanying List, the manner in which you have disposed of the respective Letters, and that you will return this List to me, signed by yourself for transmission to the Court of Directors.

-oOo-

List of 3 (three) Proprietors of Stock in the Australian Agricultural Company to whom Circulars are addressed announcing the Thirteenth Call – One Pound per Share – transmitted to John Henderson Esq. to be forwarded by him.

Name	Address	How disposed of
The Honorable E. C. Close Esq. M. C	Hunter's River	
John Henderson Esq.	Newcastle	
Robert Scott and Helenus Scott Esqres	Glendon, Hunter's River	

Port Stephens November 15th 1832

Letter No. 735

Port Stephens
16th November 1832

A. B. Spark Esq.
Sydney

Sir,

Mr White having communicated to me that the *Arundel* is ready to receive Wool for the Port of London, and that she is likely to sail in all December, I request you will inform me, by the return of the *Lambton* whether you can receive on board that Vessel at Sydney, and stow in such a manner as to avoid any risk of damage from the Oil, from Eighty to One hundred and twenty bales of the Australian Agricultural Company's Wool; and if so, at what rate per pound?

Should the terms be satisfactory, I can undertake to say that about that number of Bales can be shipped by the last week in December.

It would be a Convenience to me to be informed when the *Arundel* can positively receive the first Forty Bales, in order to avoid the necessity of re-landing them from the *Lambton* at Sydney.

Letter No. 736

Port Stephens
16th November 1832

Thomas Macvitie Esq.
Managing Director
Bank of Australia

Sir,
My Draft upon the Bank of Australia No 1456 for £8.2.6 (Eight pounds, Two Shillings & Sixpence) in favor of William Newman, <u>without his Endorsement</u> having been stolen I request you will stop the payment of the same, should it be presented at the Bank.

Letter No. 737

Port Stephens
16th November 1832

To Deputy Assistant Commissary General Paty
Newcastle

Sir,
In reply to your Letter of the 23rd ultimo I have the honor to enclose to you herewith Certified Copies of the <u>only two Accounts</u> in my possession furnished by the Commissariat at Newcastle against the A. A. Company. Amounting to £70.12.1¼ or Rations, and £37.2.10¼ for Stores; both which Accounts have been paid by the Company.

I beg leave to add that, in your Letter of the 16th July last (of which you have now sent me a Copy,) it would appear that the three Accounts first named therein are merely a repetition, in a different form of the Account for £70.12.1¼ above mentioned.

Letter No. 738

Port Stephens
16th November 1832

Dr Mitchell
Sydney Hospital

Sir,
I request you will have the goodness to receive into the General Hospital the Prisoner of the Crown named in the margin an assigned Servant of the Australian Agricultural Company whose case is herewith enclosed. Mr George Bunn, George Street, Agent for the Company, will receive him from the Hospital when cured.

John Matthewson.
Albion, Life

[Letter No. 738a]

CONTRACT FOR FLOUR

Persons desirous of supplying the Servants of the Australian Agricultural Company at 'Warrah', Liverpool Plains with <u>Flour</u> for One Year - from the 1st of February 1833 are requested to address Tenders to me under cover to Mr Henderson Newcastle, on or before the 1st of January next.

The following quantities of Flour to be delivered quarterly at the Company's Station at Warrah – vizt

350 lbs good First's Flour and 3,500 lbs good Second's Flour
on the   1st February 1833
              1st May 1833
              1st August 1833
              1st November 1833 respectively

In the event of any slight variation in the quantity required fourteen days notice of the same will be given to the Contractor, prior to the intended delivery.

Tenders to specify in words the price per 100 lbs at which the Flour will be delivered at the Company's Station.

No Tender will be accepted for less than the whole quantity required, nor unless it be delivered at Warrah.

Payment to be made in Cash or by Drafts of the Company upon the Bank of Australia, as soon as an Account made out and Certified in such form as the Company may prescribe shall be presented to me.

The Contractor will be required to give Security for the due performance of his Contract.

**Signed W. E. Parry. Commissioner to the A. A. Company
November 16th 1832**

Sydney Gazette *Sydney Herald* *Sydney Monitor* *Australian*	One Insertion each

---

Letter No. 739

Port Stephens
17th November 1832

Thomas Macvitie Esq.

Sir,

Mr White having informed me that you have not received any Authority for paying the Outstanding Drafts upon the late Committee of Management of the A. A. Company, I beg to hand you a Copy of the Letter which I addressed to you on the 25th April 1832 and which I then enclosed to the Gentlemen of the Committee to be forwarded by them to you if they approved the transfer of the Balance of their Account to mine. I conclude that they inadvertently omitted to do so, when they made the transfer.

I also beg to acquaint you that the Draft (No. 433) for £10 in favor of G. Hadell having been paid prior to the transfer the Sum Total of the remaining outstanding Drafts will be £24.18.7.

Letter No. 740

21st November 1832

To G. Bunn Esq.

Sir,
I beg leave to inclose 2 Packets for Captain Corlette, a Letter for Thomas Macvitie Esq. Managing Director of the Bank of Australia, and a Packet for Richard Stubbs Esq. which I request you will have the goodness to cause to be delivered as early as possible.

I have the honor &c
J. Edward Ebsworth

Letter No. 741

Port Stephens
21st November 1832

To G. A. Oliver Esq.
In the absence of Sir Edward Parry, Mr Ebsworth requests the favor of Mr Oliver causing the accompanying Parcels for Mr Henderson Newcastle and Mr Bunn Sydney, to be placed on board the *William IV* on her Voyage down the Hunter tomorrow morning.

Letter No. 742

Port Stephens
21st November 1832

James Laidley Esq.
Deputy Commissary General

Sir,
With reference to an advertizement dated "Commissariat Office, Sydney 25th September 1832", and which I presume to be published by your

Authority, calling for tenders for Supplies for His Majesty's Service for 12 Months commencing January the 1st 1833.

I do myself the Honor to acquaint you that I have deferred making any regular tender for these supplies on the part of the A. A. Company because I am unable to furnish several of the Articles such as Rum Bread and Mutton & the advertizement states that "Offers for supplying any of the articles separately will not be admitted".

But in the event of no other tender being made for supplying the Military Detachment at Port Stephens, I beg further to acquaint you that I am willing on the part of the A. A. Company and on the condition hereinafter mentioned to furnish Meat and Flour, at the following Prices; being the same as for the current year

          Flour, per lb   2$^{3/4}$d   (two pence three farthings)
          Beef, per lb   2$^{1/4}$d   (two pence farthing)

But, it will not be in my power to undertake this Contract, unless I receive some assurance that the Company shall be actually paid for the whole of the Supplies bona fide delivered to the Military, on the Requisition of any person you may name, and for which regular vouchers are transmitted with the Accounts.

I request, therefore, that it may be understood that I offer this Tender, only on the condition just mentioned, or some other which you may perhaps be able to suggest, for ensuring to the Company full payment for all the provisions supplied, as attested by complete and unexceptionable vouchers in any form you may wish.

Letter No. 743

Port Stephens
26th November 1832

James Laidley Esq.
Deputy Commissary General
Sydney

Sir,

With reference to your Letter of the 22^d ultimo, in which you state that the Memorandum which I had the Honor to enclose to you on the 5th of the same Month, "has reference to transactions which took place prior to your assuming the charge of the Commissariat of this Colony".

I request you will have the goodness to inform me, to <u>which</u> of the transactions named in the Memorandum that remark is intended to apply; in order to enable me to refer to the Assistant Commissary of Accounts, as suggested in your Letter. Referring to your observation that "all transactions with the Commissariat Department are final, with which there cannot exist any running or open Account", I beg leave to remark that, so far as those transactions relate to the Australian Agricultural Company, I cannot admit that they are "final" until they are paid, which is not yet the case in the instances to which I have alluded. In all cases where the Accounts transmitted to you by the Company are supported by proper vouchers, it is evident that the necessity for "a running or open Account" is occasioned by your non-payment of the amounts claimed, & not by any error or neglect of the Company, much less by any wish on the part of their Agents to have any such recurring or open Accounts with His Majesty's Government. But as often as His Majesty's Government are charged in the Company's Books with one Amount, and a different and smaller amount is paid there <u>must</u> exist a balance against the Government, such as those pointed out in the Memorandum which you decline recognizing.

The Memorandum, as you are aware, was not intended as a formal Account *Current* but that mode of shewing the Company's Claims against His Majesty's Government was adopted as the plainest and most simple for facilitating a settlement of the claims. I need scarcely say that I am ready to render the several accounts afresh in any form you may be pleased to point out; but I am sure you will admit that no just debt can be cancelled, nor any claim invalidated, because the Regulations of Your Department oblige you to deviate from the usual method of carrying on Money transactions.

With reference to the unsettled Accounts transmitted by your desire to your Officer at Newcastle Mr Scott, I trust you may be enabled to make a speedy settlement of this part of the sum owing to the Company, in which I believe there can be no doubt or disagreement.

Letter No. 744

Port Stephens
26th November 1832

Mr Simeon Lord
Macquarie Place
Sydney

Sir,

In reply to your Letter of the 29th of October I beg leave to acquaint you that it is not in my power to accept the price you propose therein for the Sheep Skins belonging to the Australian Agricultural Company.

Letter No. 745

Port Stephens
26th November 1832

W. Scott Esq.
Ash Island

Sir,

I have the Honor to acknowledge the receipt of your Letter of the 12th current and reply to mine of the 7th; and I beg to express my regret that any application should have been made to you on account of a Sum of Money which you state to have been paid – the more so, as you appear to have taken offence at my having made the application.

But I feel confident that on further consideration, you will perceive that I could not consistently with my duty to the Company, have failed to apply to you for the Settlement of a debt which appears against you on the Company's Books.

I can only say that in making this application, as a matter of ordinary business, I meant no offence whatever; and I shall now be obliged by your informing me <u>to whom</u> the payment was made, to enable me to close this transaction in the Company's Books.

Letter No. 746

Port Stephens
26th November 1832

A. B. Spark Esq.
Sydney

Sir,

In reply to your Letter of the 23rd current, on the subject of shipping the Australian Agricultural Company's Wool in the Arundel, at the rate of three halfpence per lb gross weight with primage.

I beg to acquaint you that, having received tenders for the conveyance of the Company's Wool to London at five farthings per pound, it will not be in my power to ship it on the *Arundel* at any higher rate of freight.

I have, therefore, instructed Captain Corlette to ascertain from you whether you may be willing to receive on board the *Arundel* from Eighty to One Hundred and Twenty Bales on those terms; in which case he will tranship into that vessel from the *Lambton* Forty Bales forwarded to Sydney herewith; and the remainder will follow as soon as possible.

Letter No. 747

Port Stephens
26th November 1832

George Bunn Esq.
Sydney

Sir,

With reference to the last Paragraph of your Letter of the 23rd current, I beg to acquaint you that having previously received an offer to take the Company's Wool on board the *Arundel*, I have consented to Ship on that vessel from Eighty to One Hundred & Twenty Bales provided the Agent will receive them at the rate of Five farthings per pound, with Primage accustomed.

But in the event of his not agreeing to these Terms, Captain Corlette is instructed to tranship the 40 Bales now forwarded per Lambton, into the *City of Edinboro'* upon the above mentioned Terms, as offered by you; and on the understanding that the remainder of the Company's Wool will be forwarded to Sydney as fast as possible, to be shipped on the same vessel, provided it can be stowed in a proper manner as each successive Cargo of Forty Bales arrives at Sydney in the *Lambton*.

Should the Agent of the *Arundel* consent to receive the number of Bales mentioned in the first paragraph of this letter, I shall be willing to ship the remainder – say from seventy to one hundred and ten bales on the City of Edinburgh on the terms you propose, by the 31st of January. I request you will inform me, by return of the *Lambton*, whether this proposal will meet your views.

Letter No. 748

Port Stephens
26th November 1832

James Norton Esq.
Sydney

Sir,

I beg leave to submit to you the following circumstances, upon which I request you will favor me with your legal opinion.

The following clause occurs in the Agreement of Mr William Burnett lately discharged from the Service of the A. A. Company.

"In case for any reason the Court of Directors or the said Commissioner or other Principal Agent of the said Company shall think fit to put an end to this Agreement they shall be at liberty to do so upon giving Six Months Notice to the said William Burnett or paying him Six Months Salary in advance and providing him at the expence of the Company a passage to England if he should require the same".

When Mr Burnett and his family removed from Port Stephens to Sydney, I proceeded by his own request to engage a passage for them to England. While the negociation was going on at Sydney Mr Burnett informed me by Letter that it was not his wish to embark immediately, but requested that he might be allowed to receive £300 as his passage money, leaving him at liberty to take his passage when convenient.

To this I replied by agreeing to allow him £250 which Sum was by his Consent paid to him for that purpose. About the same time I likewise agreed to allow Mr Burnett at the rate of Twenty Shillings per day for his expenses in Sydney until the Sailing of the Ship in which I had nearly engaged to take his passage. This amounted to £15.

Soon after this arrangement had been completed Mr Burnett took his own passage in another Ship, but not a passage for his wife and family, who have remained in the Colony ever since.

Since his departure more than one application has been made to me by Mrs Burnett and one of her sons for the payment of the £15. This I have declined paying (tho' without assigning any reason) because I conceive that Mr Burnett has practised upon the Company a deceit, almost amounting to a fraud in the other transaction above mentioned.

I request you will favor me with your opinion whether, in case of Mrs Burnett's personal application to me for the £15, I should be justified in refusing to pay it.

Letter No. 749

Port Stephens
27th November 1832

George Bunn Esq.
Sydney

Sir,

I beg to acquaint you that in the Invoice of Goods per last voyage of the *Lambton* dated 23rd instant there appears deficiencies as follows.

148 lbs of Harness Leather instead of 152 lbs charged
21 lbs of Bees wax " 3 lbs do

I agree with you in thinking that what the Consignees of the *Governor Halket* have sent to you as a Report of Survey on the three cans of oil (not turpentine) said to have leaked out on board that ship, is not at all satisfactory. I know nothing of either of the parties whose Signatures appear at foot of the paper, one of which should have been nominated on the part of the Company.

I therefore return the document in question, and request that you will take such further steps as you think necessary for recovering the Value of the same, or for delivering to the Company an equal quantity – 18 gallons of oil and three cans: should it appear that the ship is chargeable with the damage.

In reply to your communication of the 24th current I beg to acquaint you that an arrangement has already been made at the Bank of Australia for the payment of the Draft (No. 623) on the late Committee of Management for £16.10.8 – the second and third of Rantzsch's Bill on the Governors & Directors (No. 246) for £270 – are forwarded herewith according to his desire – I request you will obtain from Rantzsch for me a Receipt for the same.

I enclose herewith a Draft on the Bank of Australia for (£75) Seventy five pounds to meet the *current* payments on account of the Company.

Letter No. 750

Port Stephens
24th November 1832

Board for the Assignment of Servants

Gentlemen,

In conformity with the Regulations I request that Two Blacksmiths, One Horse-shoer, One Bricklayer may be assigned to me of the following Description;

I reside at Port Stephens in the County of Gloucester. I am Commissioner to the A. A. Company and hold about 500,000 Acres of Land; of which 460 Acres are cleared, and 450 Acres are in tillage.

I possess 330 Horses, 3,000 Head of Cattle and 32,000 Sheep; I now employ 60 Free, and 414 Convict Servants; of whom 196 have been in my Service upwards of Three Years, and 116 upwards of one year; No assigned Servants have been returned by me to Government within the last Two Years, and none have absconded from my Service during that period, without having been since apprehended & returned, or under Colonial Sentence.

My Agent, Mr Bunn residing at Sydney is fully empowered to receive such Servants as may be assigned to me & to defray all Expenses incurred on their account.

Letter No. 751

Port Stephens
28th November 1832

To The Honorable Colonial Secretary

Sir,

We have the Honor to acknowledge the receipt of your Letter of the 17th instant enclosing for our information a Copy of the Attorney General's opinion on the subject which we referred to you, in our Letter of the 10th ultimo.

Having communicated with Captain Moffatt thereupon, we proposed to him, in accordance with the Attorney General's opinion, that the Bench of Magistrates should again examine Thomas Beckett, into whose charge, as Constable, the two runaways were said to have been delivered.

Captain Moffatt having declined assisting in this examination, we have this day taken Beckett's deposition, together with those of Mr John Swayne and Mr Henry Hall, of which three Depositions we have now the Honor to transmit to you Copies, for the further information of His Excellency the Governor.

W. E. Parry J.P.
J. E. Ebsworth J.P.

Letter No. 752

Port Stephens
29th November 1832

To George Bunn Esq.

Sir,
    1. In the absence of Sir E. Parry, I beg leave to acquaint you that the description of the Steel & Iron belonging to the A. A. Company not yet delivered from the *Renown* is as follows

				cwt	qr	lb
Three	3	Bars German Steel	weighing	1	0	2
One	1	Bar Low Moor Iron ½ by 2½ in	do		1	24
Two	2	Bundles 1 in. Hoop iron	do	1		
Two	2	Bundles 1¼ in. do	do	1		
One	1	Bundle 1½ in. do	do		2	

    2. In the event of any of the above Goods not being found and delivered to the Company on the clearing out of the *Renown's* Cargo I request you will take such steps as may be necessary for recovering from the Owners or Agents of that Vessel, the Value of them in the Sydney Market – or for causing Articles of like description and quality to be delivered by them – which latter mode of arranging the business would be preferred by the Company.

    3. With reference to your Account current to 31st October last I have to remark that you have omitted to charge the Company with one Pound and Three Shillings £1.3.0. Hospital Fees paid by you 21st August last on account of the Company – which makes the Balance of your transactions, with Sir Edward Parry, as Commissioner to the Company £33.17.2. in your favor, instead of as in your a/c £32.14.2.

    4. It appears upon inspection of the 12 Kangaroo Skins included in your Invoice of the 23d instant, that they are not the Articles applied for – being blacked, instead of plain, brown Tanned Skins – they are therefore returned by the *Lambton* to be exchanged.

    5. I enclose a Requisition for some Drugs Spirits & Castings, to which I request your attention.

Letter No. 753

Port Stephens
1st December 1832

George Yeoman Esq.
John Mill
Williams River

Sir,

I request you will send by the *Ellen* to Port Stephens the Ten Tons of Flour mentioned in the enclosed Requisition, so as to be here <u>not later</u> than the 14th instant & to take back a Cargo of the Company's Wheat to be ground.

If you cannot make certain of this, I request that you will send as much of the above quantity as possible to Sawyers Point by Drays, by that day, in which case the wheat can partly be sent by the same drays.

An answer is requested by the Bearer.

Letter No. 754

Port Stephens
6th December 1832

Captain Moffatt J. P.
&c &c &c

Sir,

H. M. Government having intimated to me, by Letter from the Honorable The Colonial Secretary dated the 10 September last that you would be called upon to pay to the A. A. Company the Sum of Four Shillings & nine pence (4/9) for Supplies to the Military Detachment at Port Stephens between 1st January & 30th June 1832, over & above the quantities which it appears are allowed by H. M. Government to be drawn for that purpose.

I request you will be good enough to pay the same as soon as convenient.

Required by the A. A. Company at Port Stephens Fifteen Tons of Sugar for Prisoners Rations, to be delivered on board the *Lambton* in Sydney Harbour on or about the 31st day of January next.

Persons desirous of supplying the same are requested to address Tenders (accompanied by Samples) to me to the care of George Bunn Esq. Sydney on or before the 15th January.

Payment to be made in cash or by Drafts on the Bank of Australia, within One Month after delivery of the Sugar.

W. E. Parry Commissioner to the A. A. Company

Port Stephens – 7 December 1832

Sydney Gazette	
Sydney Herald	One Insertion each
Sydney Monitor	
Australian	

Letter No. 755

Port Stephens
7th December 1832

Charles H. Chambers Esq.
Sydney

Sir,
In reply to your Letter of the 3rd current addressed to me I now beg leave to enclose to you Copies of certain Documents transmitted to me by Mr Dutton in answer to my Communication of the 29th August 1831, relative to the Claim advanced by Carl Rantzsch & others against that Gentleman

I believe that these must be the Documents to which Carl Rantzsch refers; but I shall be ready to afford to him any further information in my possession, on this subject.

Letter No. 756

Port Stephens
8th December 1832

George Bunn Esq.
Sydney

Sir,
Herewith you will receive a Draft on the Bank of Australia for (£35) Thirty five Pounds to meet the payment of the last Invoice.

I also enclose to you Bills on the Governors & Directors of the A. A. Company for (£500) Five Hundred Pounds drawn to your order, which I request you will endorse, & lodge in the Bank of Australia to the credit of the Company – Nos 254 to 257.

With reference to your remark respecting the Company's Iron, I beg to acquaint you that the number of Bars received at Port Stephens is as follows:

	Iron	Steel
On the 5th November		10
do 26th November	135	2
do 6th December	1	

being three bars of Steel deficient, as before stated by Mr Ebsworth.

Letter No. 757

Port Stephens
4th December 1832

Principal Supervisor of Convicts
Sydney

Sir,
    On a Memorandum attached to a Warrant for sending back to the A. A. Company the Prisoner of the Crown named in the Margin, it was intimated that no Report had been made of his being a Runaway from the Company's Employment.
    On enquiry at Newcastle I find that no such Report was required on the part of the Company, the Man having applied to the Bench at that Place as being Free by Servitude, and <u>received from one of the Magistrates a Pass until his Certificate of Freedom arrived.</u> In consequence of this permission he left the Company's Employment; and it was therefore the business of the Bench to make the necessary Report.

Patrick McGarvie, Phoenix

Letter No. 758

Port Stephens
14th December 1832

James Laidley Esq.
Deputy Commissary General – Sydney

Sir,
    In reply to your Letter of the 1st instant I do myself the Honor to acquaint you that I will give immediate directions to Mr Henderson to cause the Public Carts at Newcastle, to be repaired by the Company's Workmen, on the Requisition of the Deputy Assistant Commissary General, so far as the business of the Company will permit.

Letter No. 759

Port Stephens
14th December 1832

William Smyth
Wheelwright
Maitland

William Smyth,
    In reply to your Letter of the 5th instant I have to acquaint you that I have requested the Governors and Directors of the A. A. Company to receive from your Agent in London the sum of £50 on your account, to be repaid to you by me as soon as I receive their Instructions to that effect.
    You should, therefore, write to your Agent in London to desire him to pay the Money in Kings Arms Yard as soon as possible.

Letter No. 760

Port Stephens
15th December 1832

Messrs Hughes & Hosking
Sydney

Gentlemen,
    Finding that you have lately become purchasers of Coals at Newcastle to a considerable Amount I am desirous of dealing with you in return on account of the A. A. Company whenever they may require a Supply of Flour, should you be sellers of that Article.
    I have, therefore, to request that you will deliver to Captain Corlette, by return of the *Lambton* to Port Stephens
    Fine Flour   Five Tons.
    Seconds do   Five Tons.
on the understanding that the Sydney Price is to be paid for it, and that the Account be settled by Drafts on the Bank of Australia within One Month after delivery.

Letter No. 761

Port Stephens
15th December 1832

Colonial Secretary
Sydney

Sir,
    With reference to the first Paragraph of the Government Notice of the 3d instant:, it may be proper for me to acquaint you that I have some time since

transmitted to the Deputy Commissary General certain outstanding Claims of the A. A. Company upon the Colonial Treasury, to a considerable amount; and also to remind you that other Accounts transmitted to you still remain unpaid.

Concluding that the expression "as soon as possible before the end of the year" cannot be intended to apply to such Accounts as become due, for the Quarter ending the 31 December, I beg leave to acquaint you that no time will be lost, after the end of the year, in transmitting, thro' the proper channel any such Accounts which the Company may have against H. M. Government.

Letter No. 762

Port Stephens
19th December 1832

Colonial Secretary
Sydney

Sir,

I have the Honor to acknowledge the receipt of your Letter addressed to me on the 14th ultimo on the subject of the Ticket of Leave men employed by the A. A. Company on their Estate at Port Stephens and, I now, in compliance with the Governor's directions, enclose to you a List of the Persons of this description at present in the Company's Service.

I beg you will convey to His Excellency my best acknowledgments for the arrangement He has been pleased to allow, together with my assurance that every care shall be taken that the Ticket of Leave men in the Company's Service be not allowed to deviate in other respects, from the Government Regulation, on that head.

Individuals employed on the Estate of the A. A. Company Holding Tickets of Leave.

James Berry	*Champion*	Seven Years
Nathan Burrows	*Florentia*	Seven Years
James Coombes	*Hoogley* 2	
Robert Field		Life
James Gilchrist	*Countess of Harcourt*	Seven Years
Joseph Habberfield	*Florentia*	Seven Years
William Hart	*Cambridge*	Seven Years
Bartholomew McCarthy	*Eliza* 3	Seven Years
Thomas Peck	A native of Van Diemen's Land	Fourteen Years
James Goodwin	*Guilford* 7	Fourteen Years

Letter No. 763

Port Stephens
24th December 1832

Captain Moffatt J. P.

Sir,

His Excellency The Governor having been pleased to dispense with the Regular Muster of those Ticket of Leave men employed by the A. A. Company whose distance from a Magistrate would render such Muster inconvenient, I have the Honor to transmit to you herewith, for your information, a copy of the List of all the Ticket of Leave Men in the Company's Service, which, by direction of His Excellency, has been forwarded to the Colonial Secretary.

Letter No. 764

Port Stephens
22nd December 1832

The Honorable Colonial Secretary

Sir,

1. Mr Dangar having completed the Map of his recent Survey, made in conjunction with Mr White, Government Surveyor, of that portion of land which is included between Peel's River and the Dividing Range to the South Westward of it, for the purpose of ascertaining, the precise position of the Range and of the River respectively, and the real quality of the land enclosed by those boundaries,

2. I have now the Honor to transmit to you herewith, for the information of His Excellency the Governor, a Sketch of Mr Dangar's Map; and, with reference to my former Communications on this subject, I beg leave to submit, for His Excellency's consideration, the following Observations & Proposals.

3. The whole Area proposed by His Excellency as one Location of the two intended to be granted to the Australian Agricultural Company, as shewn by the <u>Red</u> boundary line ABCD, has been ascertained to consist of (481,456) Four hundred and eighty-one thousand, four hundred and fifty six Acres, reckoning to the Summit of the Range.

4. Of this Tract – The Portion bounded by a <u>yellow</u> line, consisting of about (100,000) One Hundred Thousand Acres, is wholly without a stream of water, and, on that account, a mere waste. The yellow line is drawn at the distance of four miles from the permanent streams.

5. The Tract bounded by a <u>Blue</u> line, amounting to (40,960) Forty thousand, Nine Hundred and Sixty Acres, is in some parts mountainous, in others rocky, with very small intervals of tolerable land.

6. The Portion CDGH, amounting to (29,747) Twenty-nine thousand, Seven hundred and forty seven Acres, contains two thirds, or 19,831 Acres of Land, which, from its rough character, is of no value for any purpose.

7. In addition to the above, there are (10,240) Ten thousand two hundred and forty Acres of precipitous, and therefore useless land, immediately

Map 3A:
The Company Locations

The original location.
(1) The Port Stephens Estate after reduction.

The new locations as requested by the Company.
(2) The Liverpool Plains Estate (Warrah).
(3) The Peel River Estate (Goonoo Goonoo).

Map 3B and 3C:
Locations discussed in Letter No. 764, 22 December 1832 – based on AO Map 3362, State Records NSW.

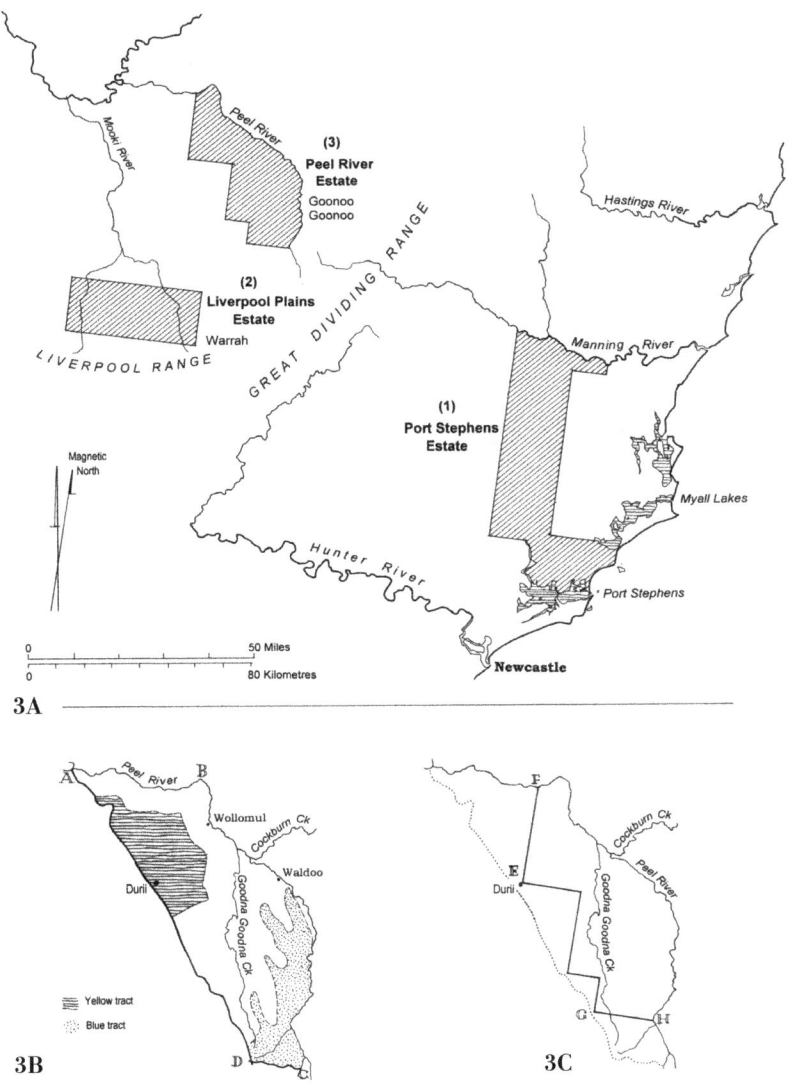

bordering on the Range.

8. Thus it appears that, from the various causes above-mentioned, (171,031) One Hundred & Seventy one thousand and thirty one Acres, being considerably more than One Third of the whole proposed Tract ABCD, is of little or no value.

9. This proportion of unavailable Land being much greater than I should be justified in consenting to receive as one of the two Locations intended to be granted to the Company, I beg leave to propose as follows:

10. That a Magnetic North Line, EF, be drawn as the Western Boundary of the proposed Location, from a Remarkable Pointed Hill in the Dividing Range (about a mile to the Eastward of 'Durii', which is not in the Range); and that the rough Tract CDGH be altogether excluded; thus making the Proposed Location EFHG to include (348,345) Three Hundred & Forty eight Thousand, Three hundred & forty five Acres; of which (89,280) Eighty nine thousand, two hundred & eighty Acres, or more than one fourth of the whole, will still consist of unavailable land, as above described; namely, of the yellow portion 40,960 Acres, the blue Tract, also 40,960 Acres; and 7,360 Acres of the precipitous sides of the Range.

11. The Land on the opposite or right bank of Peel's River, having been ascertained to be a still narrower strip than was before supposed, and nothing having been discovered worthy of notice to the North Eastward, though the Surveyors pursued their way up the Valley of Cockburn's River (the only opening in that direction) for about thirty miles, it is not in my power to propose any addition to this Location on that Bank of Peel's River

12. Should the Governor accede to the above Proposal, in which it has been my anxious endeavour to conform, as far as possible, to His Excellency's wish of making the Range a Boundary, there will remain to be selected for the Company a Second Location consisting of (193,735) One Hundred & Ninety three thousand, Seven hundred and thirty five Acres.

13. This Second Location it is still my wish to take for the Company, as shewn by the Green Shading in Mr Dangar's former Map accompanying my Letter addressed to you on the 5th of May last. And, as by your Letter of the 27th of July, His Excellency intimated his readiness to grant the required quantity of land, or more, on or near Liverpool Plains, if selected in a particular manner, I have only respectfully to request that His Excellency will be pleased to propose to me some other situation and shape, if He still objects to the selection I made.

14. As Mr Dangar is now unoccupied, and is retained in the Company's Service at a heavy expence, solely for the purpose of assisting in the Settlement of their Grants, I take the liberty of requesting as early an answer as the Public Service will allow, as well to this Communication, as to my application of the 18th of October last for the decision of the Company's Coal Grant at Newcastle.

[Letter 764a]

Application to the Board for the Assignment of Servants.

Port Stephens
28th December 1832

Usual printed form [as Letter No. 750]

For Two Wheelwrights

Land held	500,000 Acres
Land cleared	460 Acres
Land in tillage	450 Acres
Horses	330
Cattle	3,000
Sheep	32,000
Convict Servants	410 (of whom) about 200 – 3 years about 120 – 1 year returned none absconded none, except such as delivered to Police
Free Servants	60

In the Margin as follows:
Gentlemen

    I beg leave very earnestly to request attention to this application, the Company's Free Wheelwright having just fractured his Skull, and a Convict Wheelwright having been seriously burned; by which accidents the Company's Estate is left without either Wheelwright, or a person who can repair a Plough.

Illustration 3:
Australian Agricultural Company Annual and Half Yearly Reports 1824-1849 [Bound set, NBAC Reference Z713/11]

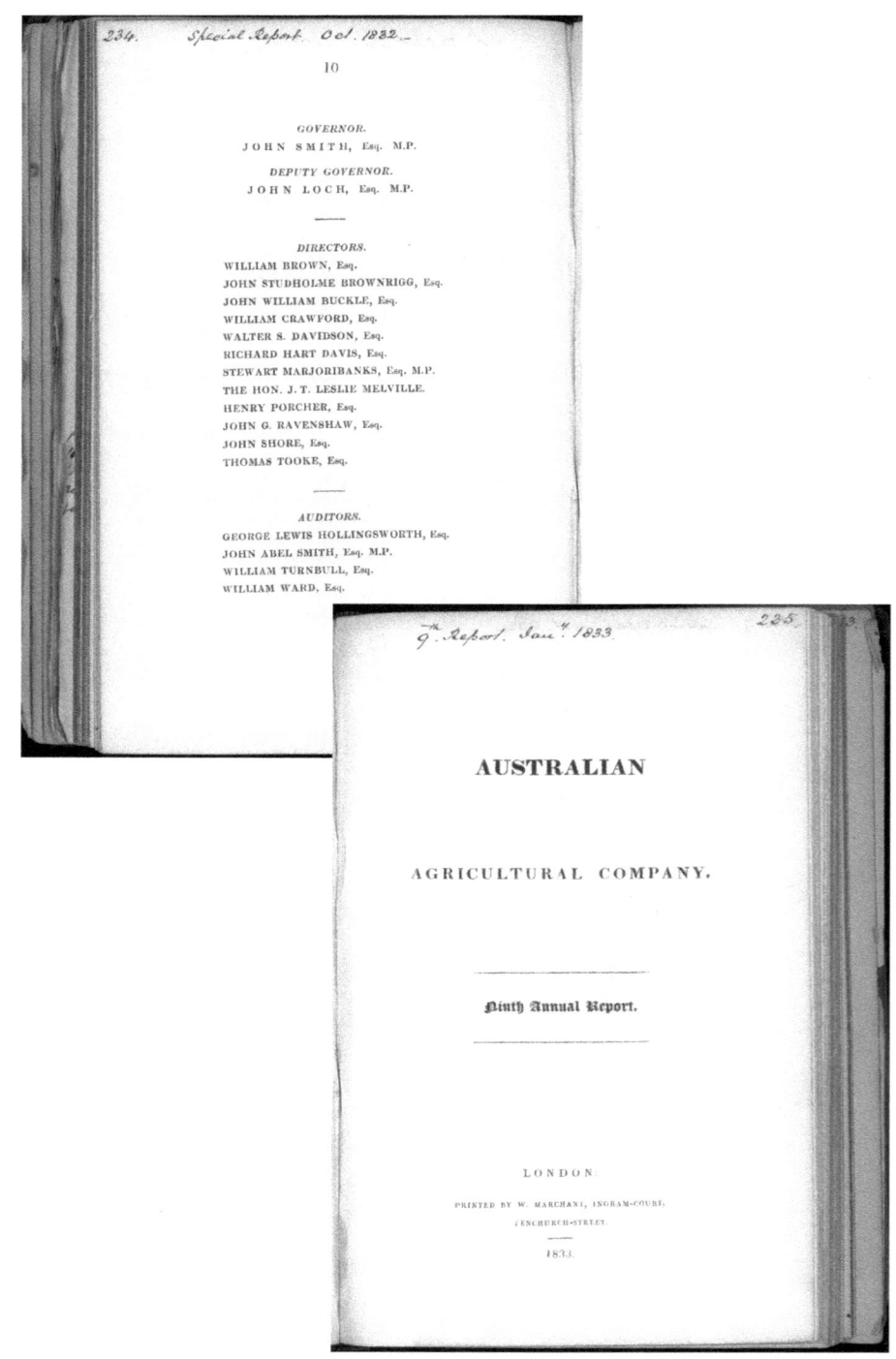

letters 1833

Letter No 765
H. C. Sempill Esq. J. P.
Segenhoe

Letter No 766
John Larnack Esq.
Castle Forbes

and

Letter No 767
Mr John Smith
Newcastle

Port Stephens
4th January 1833

Sir,

I have the Honor to acknowledge the receipt of your *Letter of (Mr Sempill's the 1st December last, Mr Larnack's - 29th do) offering, in pursuance of my Advertizement to that effect to Supply the Establishment of the A. A. Company at 'Warrah' Liverpool Plains with Flour.

And I take the earliest opportunity of acquainting you that, as a Tender has been made at a lower Rate, it will not be in my power to accept your offer.

* Mr Smith's – "Your Tender of the 31st December last"

Letter No. 768

Port Stephens
4th January 1833

Colonial Dumaresq Esq.
St Helier's

Sir,

I have the Honor to acknowledge the receipt of your Letter of the 7th ultimo offering to Supply the Establishment of the A. A. Company at 'Warrah' Liverpool Plains with Flour, in the Quantities & at the Periods Specified in my Advertizement to that effect, namely:

350 pounds of 1st Flour at 16/- per 100 lbs	to be delivered at the Company's Station at Warrah Liverpool Plains 1st February – 1st May – 1st August – 1 November 1833 respectively.
3,500 pounds of 2^{ds} Flour at 14/- per 100 lbs)	

And I beg leave to acquaint you that I accept your Tender for the Same upon these Terms.

Letter No. 769

Port Stephens
8th January 1833

Dr Mitchell
General Hospital
Sydney

Sir,
    I have the Honor to enclose to you the case of the Prisoner of the Crown named in the Margin, an Assigned Servant of the A. A. Company whom I request you will receive into the General Hospital.
    Mr George Bunn, George St. Sydney, will receive him, when cured, on the part of the Company.

Margin: James Davidson, *Minstrel*, Life

Letter No. 770

Port Stephens
8th January 1833

A. C. Innes Esq. J. P.

Sir,
    I have the Honor to enclose to you an Account for Supplies furnished to you and your Servants at Sundry times, by the A. A. Company amounting to (£7.14.8) Seven Pounds, fourteen Shillings & Eight pence.
    I request you will pay the Same into the Bank of Australia to my Credit as Commissioner to the Company.

Margin: Account & 4 Vouchers enclosed

Letter No. 771

Port Stephens
8th January 1833

To His Honor Chief Justice Forbes

Sir,
    I have the Honor to enclose to you your Account with the Australian Agricultural Company, amounting to (£29.15.11) Twenty Nine Pounds, Fifteen Shillings, and eleven pence.
    I request you will pay the same into the Bank of Australia, to my Credit as Commissioner to the Company.

Letter No. 772

Port Stephens
8th January 1833

To Peter McIntyre Esq.
Sydney

[Letter has been water damaged and is unreadable – would appear to be the same as the letter to Chief Justice Forbes No. 771, for a different sum of money]

Letter No. 773

Port Stephens
9th January 1833

James Laidley Esq.
Deputy Commissary General
Sydney

Sir,
 I have the Honor to transmit to you herewith an Account (in Triplicate) amounting to Thirty four Pounds Two Shillings & Three pence (£34.2.3) for Supplies to the Military Detachment stationed at Port Stephens, between the 1st of October & 31 December 1832 together with the Vouchers complete for the same.
 I also transmit herewith an Account (in Triplicate) amounting to Three Pounds, Eighteen Shillings & Eight pence (£3.18.8) for Supplies to Sundry persons on account of H. M. Government to the 31st of December last with the Vouchers complete.

Letter No. 774

Port Stephens
17th January 1833

Messrs Hughes & Hosking
Sydney

Gentlemen,
 As the *Lambton* occasionally takes a Cargo of Coals from Newcastle to Sydney, I request you will have the goodness to inform me, by return of that Vessel, whether you would be willing to take the Coals <u>for Cash,</u> and if so, upon what terms.

Letter No. 775

Port Stephens
17th January 1833

William Cowell
Sydney

William Cowell,

In reply to your Letter of the 14th instant, received yesterday, I am sorry that it will not be in my power, in justice to the Company, to make the exchange of Men which you desire, as Saunders is a quiet well-behaved man, and McQuaid of doubtful character.

Letter No. 776

Port Stephens
18th January 1833

Henry Hall Esq.
Stroud

Sir,

Observing that your present Agreement with the A. A. Company will expire on the 17th April next, I request you will inform me whether it is your wish to remain in the Company's Service beyond that time to enable me, in either case, to make the requisite arrangements.

Letter No. 777

Port Stephens
18th January 1833

James Steel
Newcastle

James Steel,

Observing that your present Agreement with the A. A. Company will expire on the 3rd April next, I request you will inform me whether it is your wish to remain in the Company's Service beyond that time to enable me, in either case, to make the requisite arrangements.

Letter No. 778

Port Stephens
18th January 1833

John Swayne Esq.
Tellighary

Sir,

Observing that your present Agreement with the A. A. Company will expire on the 8th of April next, I request you will inform me whether it is your wish to remain in the Company's Service beyond that time; to enable me, in either case, to make the requisite Arrangements.

Letters Nos 779-782

Port Stephens
22nd January 1833

Sir,

I beg leave to hand you annexed particulars of Stores supplied on your Account by the A. A. Company amounting to £ * * * * and I request you will have the goodness to pay the same into the Bank of Australia to my Credit as Commissioner to the Company as early as possible.

I also request you will favor me with an early reply to this Communication, as I shall now be compelled under my Instructions from the Court of Directors of the Company, to resort to Legal Measures for recovering all outstanding Debts due to the Company if not immediately paid.

The above Letter was addressed to the Following Individuals.

			Amount.
Hugh Noble Esq.	Sydney	No. 779	£ -.14.1
Samuel Terry Esq.	do	No. 780	£7.6.5
Thomas Hyndes	Sussex St Sydney	No. 781	£ -.19.8
A. P. Onslow Esq. care of Alexander McLeay Esq.	Sydney	No. 782	£10.1.7

Letters Nos 783-803

Port Stephens
22nd January 1833

Sir,

I beg leave to hand you annexed an Account for the Services of the A. A. Company's Stallion amounting to £ * * * * and I request you will have the goodness to pay the same into the Bank of Australia to my Credit, as Commissioner to the Company as early as possible.

I also request you will favor me with an early reply to this Communication, as I shall now be compelled under my Instructions from the Court of Directors of the Company to resort to Legal Measures for recovering all outstanding Debts due to the Company, if not immediately paid.

The above Letter was addressed to each of the Following Individuals.

Name	Address	No.	Amount
Mr J. Brown		No. 783	£5.15.-
Thomas Walker Esq.	Sydney	No. 784	£17.5.-
Edward Cox Esq.	Fern Hills, Mulgoa Penrith	No. 785	£23.0.-
W. H. Moore Esq.	Sydney	No. 786	£17.5.-
Sir John Wylde care of J. J. Moore Esq.	Cumberland Cottage, Liverpool	No. 787	£16.10.-
J. J. Moore Esq.	do	No. 788	£14.8.-
George T. Palmer Esq.	Parramatta	No. 789	£37.14.-
Thomas Cowper Esq.	Clifton, Campbell Town	No. 790	£17.5.-
Andrew Allan Esq.	Bailey Park, Penrith	No. 791	£17.5.-
Mr Henry Howey	Goulburn	No. 792	£5.15.-
Rev. S. Marsden	Parramatta	No. 793	£39.10.-
John Mackaness Esq.	Hyde Park. Sydney	No. 794	£23.11.-
T. B. Wilson Esq.		No. 795	£5.10.-
Executors of the late John Thomas Campbell Esq.	Sydney	No. 796	£5.15.-
James Murdoch Esq.	58 Kent Street Sydney	No. 797	£5.15.-
Jonathon Hassall Esq.	Matavia, Campbell Town	No. 798	£15.14.-
John Piper Senior Esq.	Alloway Bank, Bathurst	No. 799	£8.18.-
W. John Gaggin	Sydenham, Alcorn's Inn	No. 800	£8.18.-
Executors of the late John Oxley Esq.	Sydney	No. 801	£23.-.-
William Howe Esq.	Glenlee, Campbell Town	No. 802	£5.5.-
George Cox Esq.	Wimbourne, Penrith	No. 803	£23.-.-

Letter No. 804

Port Stephens
22nd January 1833

R. Campbell Junior & Co
Sydney

Gentlemen

I have the Honor to acknowledge the receipt of your Letter of the 15th Current tendering to supply the A. A. Company with Fifteen Tons of Sugar (according to Sample) at (£15) Fifteen Pounds Sterling per Ton.

And I beg leave to acquaint you that I accept this Tender on the part of the A. A. Company.

Letter No. 805

Port Stephens
23rd January 1833

George Bunn Esq.
Sydney

Sir,

With reference to the Paper purporting to be an Affidavit, enclosed in your Letter of the 20th ultimo relative to the Three Tin Cans of Oil belonging to the Company which baked [sic] out on board the *Governor Halkett*, I beg to acquaint you that unless a Survey was held upon the same, I do not consider an Affidavit on the part of the Chief Mate sufficient. The paper in question was not sworn at all.

I also beg to remind you that five bundles of Hoop-Iron & Three Bars of German Steel ex *Renown* alluded to in Mr Ebsworth's Letter addressed to you on the 29th November are still missing.

And I request you will endeavour to obtain from the respective Parties a final answer, acquainting them that I must otherwise be under the necessity of referring the questions to the Company's Solicitors.

Letter No. 806

Port Stephens
31st January 1833

H. Hall Esq.
Stroud

Sir,

With reference to your Letter addressed to me on the 26th current, I request you will inform me on what terms you are disposed to retain your present Situation in the Service of the A. A. Company say, for a term of three Years from the expiration of your present Agreement.

[Letter No. 806a]

Form of a Letter to be addressed to Individuals near the Company's Stations at Warrah Liverpool Plains, as circumstances may require.

Warrah – Liverpool Plains

Sir,
 Having observed some of the Cattle/Sheep in your charge upon the Land in possession of the A. A. Company I hereby give you notice that unless they are immediately removed, and kept off the Company's Land, the Proprietor of the Cattle/Sheep will be prosecuted according to Law.

Letter No. 807

Port Stephens
1st February 1833

To John Swayne Esq.

Sir,
 With reference to your Letter addressed to me yesterday, I beg to acquaint you that I can consent to the large increase of your Salary alluded to therein, only on the understanding (to be expressed in the Agreement) that, besides Wool Sorting, which occupies but a small portion of each year, your duties shall extend to those of an Assistant Superintendent, whenever required, & that you continue to assist in the writing which may be necessary in the Sheep Department.
 I also beg to acquaint you that I am not disposed to make any future Agreement, on the part of the Company, for a less period than three years. I request your early answer, and remain…

Letter No. 808

Port Stephens
1st February 1833

William Cowell, Builder
Sydney

William Cowell
    A bed of very superior Limestone having been discovered near Stroud, on the Estate of the A. A. Company, I am desirous of knowing whether you think that, if sent to Sydney in some considerable quantities, it might be sold at a remunerating price. One bushel of the lime procured from this stone is said to be as good as two bushels and a half of that obtained from Shells.
    If you can give me any information on this subject, I shall be much obliged to you, as you are probably in the way of knowing what demand there would be for limestone.

Letter No. 809

Port Stephens
1st February 1833

To Charles Beal
Carpenter & Builder
Sydney

Charles Beal,
    As there is a considerable quantity of good timber, of various kinds, on the Estate of the Australian Agricultural Company, which I am willing to dispose of, I request you will be good enough to inform me whether you think it might be worth while to send up occasionally, by the *Lambton*; for Sale in Sydney, a quantity of sawn timber; and, if so, of what kinds and dimensions.

Letter No. 810

Port Stephens
1st February 1833

The Honorable The Colonial Secretary

Sir,
    Having lately signed Receipts, forwarded to me by the Colonial Treasurer, for the Sum of (£48.13.3) Forty Eight Pounds thirteen Shillings and three pence, being for Coals supplied to the Master Attendants Department from 4th June to 30th September 1832.
    I beg leave to acquaint you that the above amount does not include the

Sum of (£1.0.2½) One Pound and two pence halfpenny – due by H. M. Government to the A. A. Company for Coals during that period, as reported to you in the 5th & 6th Paragraphs of my Letter (No. 725) dated the 26th October last.

    I have therefore again to request that you will be pleased to take the necessary steps for procuring the payment to be made to the Company.

Letter No. 811

22nd January 1833

Thomas Walker Esq.
Concord
    (a copy of Letter No 784. – addressed to the care of John Blaxland Esq., Newington)

[Letter No. 811a]

Copy
Voucher No [xx]   of Abstract D
1832.
£48.13.3 sterling

Colonial Treasury, Sydney,
    Received from Campbell Drummond Riddell, Treasurer, pursuant to Warrant of Government, No 172. Dated 26th December 1832 – the Sum of Forty Eight Pounds. thirteen Shillings and three Pence Sterling, being for Coal supplied the Master Attendants' Department from 4th June to 30 Sept 1832 – as by accompanying account of Particulars, and for which I have signed Duplicate Receipts of the same Tenor and Date.

Signed W. E. Parry – Commissioner to the A. A. Company
Witnesses to the Payment
Port Stephens 1st February 1833

Letter No. 812

Port Stephens
2nd February 1833

George Bunn Esq.
Sydney

Sir,
1. I herewith enclose a Set of Bills on the Governors and Directors of the Australian Agricultural Company, for (£1,000) One Thousand Pounds, drawn to your Order, which I request you will endorse, and lodge to my Credit, in the Bank of Australia, as Commissioner to the Company.

2. With reference to the 2d Paragraph of your Letter of the 29th January, I will forward to you, by an early opportunity, a Memorandum of the Cost & Charges of the Articles deficient ex *Renown*.

3. Referring to the 1st Paragraph of the same Communication, I request you will oblige me with your opinion whether a Survey said to have been held upon the Tin Cans, in which Survey <u>nobody acted on the part of the Company</u>, and a subsequent paper called an affidavit, <u>but not sworn to at all</u>, constitute, according to the ordinary usage in such cases, a satisfactory explanation of the damage.

4. With reference to the payment advised by you in your letter of the 14th ultimo, I beg to acquaint you that Thomas Emmett, one of the Convicts for whom £1.10.0 of the whole amount (£4.10.0) was paid; was not a Servant of the Company, but of Mr Stacy, who informs me that he has transmitted to Mr Puddefoot funds for the payment of this demand. I request, therefore, you will credit the Company with £1.10.0 accordingly.

Letter No. 813

Port Stephens
2nd February 1833

To Messrs R. Campbell Junior & Company
Sydney

Gentlemen
On weighing the Sugar forwarded by you per the *Lambton*, there appears to be a deficiency of £1.3.11, which, at 15/- per cwt, amounts to £1.7.9. For the difference between that and the Amount (£124.4.8) charged in your Invoice, I now transmit a Draft on the Bank of Australia, vizt No 1612, for (£122.16.11) One Hundred and Twenty – Two Pounds, Sixteen Shillings, and eleven pence.

Letter No. 814

Port Stephens
7th February 1833

Richard Stubbs Esq.
Carrington

Sir,

The numerous instances of drunkenness disorderly conduct & neglect of duty which continually occur on the Company's Estate, in consequence of the ready access to Spirituous Liquors at the Public Houses, have forced upon me the conclusion (after a fair trial of nearly three years) that I cannot consistently with my duty to the Company & to the Individuals under my control, Sanction a longer continuance of this evil.

If, therefore, it should not be worth your while to continue the Free Store without a license (for the renewal of which, I understand Captain Moffatt will not give his sanction) I request you will inform me what is <u>the earliest period</u> at which you can make it convenient to wind up your business at Carrington so as to incur no serious loss by your removal.

In giving you this notice, I trust you will believe that I am actuated by no other motive but that of a most imperative duty, & without any intention of casting blame on yourself. On the contrary, I believe that you have done all in your power to lessen the evils which the unlimited sale of Spirituous Liquors must, I fear, ever bring with it; but the disorders which have lately occurred, producing a constant stagnation of the Company's business, & the entire breaking up of the Stroud School, convince me that no Public House ought ever again to be allowed on the Company's Estate.

Letter No. 815

Port Stephens
7th February 1833

Captain Moffatt J. P.
Resident Magistrate

Sir,

I have the Honor to acknowledge the receipt of your Letter of yesterday's date on the subject of the irregularities which are going on at the Public House at Stroud, & which, without the assistance of a Second Magistrate, who may legally sit with you in such cases, it is not in your power to check by any Magisterial Proceedings.

I request you will accept my best thanks for your communication, & at the same time I beg to acquaint you that in consequence of the numerous irregularities occasioned by excessive drinking at both the Public Houses, I have this day given Mr Stubbs notice that it is my intention to discontinue this serious evil upon the Company's Estate at the earliest possible period.

Letter No. 816

Port Stephens
7th February 1833

Richard Stubbs Esq.
Carrington

Sir,
    In reply to your Letter of this day's date I beg to assure you that I regret extremely that the determination which I intimated to you in my Communication of this morning should be viewed by you as likely seriously to affect your future prospects.
    You must, however, be aware that it could only be in the anticipation of the probable necessity of the change now determined on, that I stipulated, in my Letter addressed to you on the 6th of March 1830, that I should be at liberty to discontinue your situation as Free Storekeeper at my own option by giving <u>One Quarter's</u> Notice – a stipulation with which in your reply dated the 11th of the Same Month you fully & unequivocally expressed yourself satisfied. In fact, I considered the whole as a matter of experiment – which experiment, you must admit, has now been fairly tried.
    But it is by no means my intention, as you seem to apprehend, to hasten your removal, nor indeed have I any wish that you should remove at all provided there be no Public Houses. I would, therefore, propose that this alteration should take place this day Six Months, being a Notice of <u>Two</u> Quarters instead of <u>One</u>.
    You cannot however fail to observe that, independently of any wish of <u>mine</u>, Captain Moffatt's determination not to sanction a renewal of your Licenses would alone prevent your retailing Spirits on the Company's Estate after the next Licensing day.
    I can only, therefore, repeat that it is impossible for me to tolerate, any longer than may be absolutely necessary, the frightful & growing evils to which the Public Houses on the Company's Estate give rise.

Letter No. 817

Port Stephens
8th February 1833

James Steel,
Newcastle

James Steel,
    In reply to your Letter of the 1st instant suggesting some alteration in any future agreement with the Company at the expiration of your present one, I have to observe that your present annual cost to the Company in Salary, Rations, and Flannels (independent of House-Rent and Coals) is about £160, which is a larger Amount than I could consent to pay to any other person in your situation.

But as your conduct has hitherto been satisfactory to your Employers, I am willing to make a fresh Agreement with you, for not less than three years, on the following terms: namely,
For the 1st year   £165 } to include all allowances, except
For the 2nd year   £170 } Lodging and Coals.
For the 3rd year   £180 }
But I can only consent to make the above Agreement on condition that a Written Agreement be also made with your Son Michael, for the same period, on the same terms as at present.

No Letter No. 818

Letter No. 819

Port Stephens
8th February 1833

John Swayne Esq.
Tellighary

Sir,
In reply to your Letter of the 4th instant I beg leave to acquaint you that I am willing to make a fresh Agreement with you, on the part of the A. A. Company for three years, on a Salary of £150 for each of the two first years, and £165 for the last year; but I should not feel justified in exceeding those Amounts. I request an early answer & remain…

Letter No. 820

Port Stephens
9th February 1833

Colonial Secretary
Sydney

Daniel Dimotte, Hercules, Life

Sir,
On the 12th July last I had the Honor to represent to you the case of the Prisoner of the Crown named in the margin, an Assigned Servant of the Australian Agricultural Company; in consequence of which His Excellency the Governor was pleased to consent to his being received into the Lunatic Asylum, as intimated to me by Mr Harrington's Letter of the 21st July last.
Dimotte was accordingly forwarded to Sydney on the 14th of August, but after remaining for some time in the General Hospital, he was returned to the Company on the 26th November without having been sent to the Lunatic Asylum.

I have therefore once more to entreat His Excellency's benevolent interposition, on behalf of this afflicted man whose state of insanity continues the same as before.

Letter No. 821

Port Stephens
9th February 1833

H. Hall Esq.
Stroud

Sir,
　I have to acknowledge the receipt of your Letter of the 6th instant proposing certain Terms on which you are willing to renew your Agreement in the Service of the A. A. Company.
　In reply I beg to acquaint you, that with every possible disposition to appreciate the value of your Services in the responsible Office which you fill, I should not feel justified in acceding to the full extent of your proposal; but that I am willing to renew your Agreement on the following Terms namely:

Salary for	First Year	£215.
	Second	£230.
	Third	£250.

　As I am about to order you a considerable Money Allowance for Visitors at Stroud House, together with additional Rations & Three Servants to be supported by the Company, I should hope that the foregoing Terms will be satisfactory to you.
　Requesting an early answer, I remain…

Letter No. 822

Port Stephens
9th February 1833

Mr G. A. Oliver
Kinross, Hunter's River

Sir,
　I beg leave to acknowledge the receipt of your Account against the A. A. Company for services rendered from 1st July 1831 to the 31st December 1832, amounting to £30, and I now hand you the Company's Account against you for Articles furnished from their Stores leaving a Balance in your favor of £26.10.-.
　I beg leave to suggest that in future a Regular Account be kept by you of the Services done for the Company, & that the same be rendered to me every Quarter, to avoid any arrears. It must, however, be understood that

the Company is not to be charged with any Services rendered to private Individuals, except on the Company's business, for which, in the case of persons going <u>from</u> the Company's Estate, Mr Ebsworth or myself will always send you a Requisition, which Requisitions will form the proper vouchers to accompany your Accounts.

All Persons coming <u>to</u> the Company's Estate, by way of Kinross, must themselves pay you any expenses which they incur. Should such expenses be on the business of the Company, the parties will apply to me for reimbursement.

The Company's Servants are not, on any occasion, to be furnished with Rations, nor their Horses with Corn, except by a Special Requisition to that effect.

P. S. Should a Messenger be required to bring over Letters from the Company's Establishment at Newcastle, I shall be obliged by your sending one, on the written Requisition of Mr Henderson or Mr Croasdill to that effect, but not otherwise.

Letter No. 823

Port Stephens
9th February 1833

Richard Stubbs Esq.
Carrington

Sir,

In acknowledging the receipt of your Communication of yesterday's date, it is only necessary for me to refer to the two Alternatives, to one or the other of which I understand you to request my assent.

To the first of these – namely your continuing a public house at Stroud for one year longer – I cannot consent, under the conviction of the effects of this evil which I have already expressed; which conviction, I may add, has been rather strengthened than otherwise by your Communication to which I am now replying.

To the second of your proposals, in so far as relates to the Stores being carried on after the expiration of the six months, I see no objection whatever; much less do I object to the residence of Mr Stubbs and family on the estate, so long as may be convenient to you, on the payment of a moderate rent to the Company. Indeed, in both my former Letters to you, I have already intimated that I am far from wishing you to remove at all, provided there be no public-houses.

With respect to any other person taking the Free Store, I do not at present see any objection to this; but I should reserve to myself the power of adopting very rigid Regulations in any future Establishment of this kind.

As relates to the payment of any debts due to you by the Company's Servants, you will, I am sure, perceive the impossibility of my pledging myself, in any particular manner, to exert my influence in the recovery of them. As I understood that it was your rule to give no trust, I cannot but express my surprize at the amount of the debts detailed in your letter. You must be aware that I have no power to retain or appropriate a single farthing which may at any time become due by the Company to their Free Servants; and as to the Prisoners, I candidly confess that my <u>first</u> impulse would be to stop altogether the Gratuities of any Prisoner who should have the impudence to mortgage to you the amount of those small sums which I have been in the habit of giving them when their conduct appeared to deserve it.

I can only, therefore, promise, in general terms, to render you every assistance in my power, in recovering your debts, consistently with what I consider to be my duty, in each specific case which you may wish to refer to me.

Letter No. 824

Port Stephens
14th February 1833

Dr Mitchell
General Hospital
Sydney

Sir,
I have the Honor to enclose to you the case of the Prisoner of the Crown named in the Margin, an Assigned Servant of the A. A. Company whom I request you will receive into the General Hospital.

Mr George Bunn, George Street – Sydney, will receive him, when cured, on the part of the Company.

(Signed) In the absence of Sir Edward Parry Commissioner to the Company
J. E. Ebsworth

William Coombs, Sesostris. Life

Letter No. 825

Port Stephens
14th February 1833

John Paul, Senior Esq.
Sydney

Sir,
In the absence of Sir Edward Parry, I beg leave to enclose particulars of the Contents of 22 Packages of Goods forwarded to you by the Cutter *Lambton* – being Surplus Stores belonging to the A. A. Company which I request you will have the goodness to offer for Sale by Auction without

reserve on account of the Company as early as may be convenient to you.

I further request that you will forward with as little delay as possible after the Sale an Account Sales of the same, and pay the Net Proceeds into the Bank of Australia to the Credit of Sir Edward Parry Commissioner to the Company.

(Signed) J. E. Ebsworth

Letter No. 826

Sydney
21st February 1833

Honorable Colonial Secretary
Sydney

Sir,

The two Prisoners of the Crown named in the Margin, lately Assigned Servants of the A. A. Company & now holding Ticket of Leave, having requested me to apply to His Excellency the Governor to be allowed to receive some small Sums of Money as specified against each name deposited in the former Savings Bank on their arrival in the Colony, I do myself the Honor to acquaint you that the conduct of both these Men is highly deserving of H. Excellency's indulgent consideration & to request that their wishes may be complied with should H. E. see no objection.

Margin notes:
James Goodwin. *Guilford*, 14 yrs. Ticket of Leave Port Stephens. About £2.17.- in 1827

Thomas Broadhurst. *Marquis of Huntly*, 14 yrs. Ticket of Leave Windsor. £2.4.- in 1827

Letter No. 827

Cummings Hotel
Sydney
22nd February 1833

John Blaxland Esq. M. C.

Sir,

I do myself the Honor to acknowledge the receipt of your Letter dated Newington the 12th instant but bearing the Sydney Post Mark of yesterday.

I very much regret having fallen into error, as to your being Agent to Mr Walker of Concord; but I beg to assure you that I did not incur that error without making the enquiry which you hastily remark, it would have been "wise in me to make", before addressing to you my Letter of the 22d ultimo – Until I have access to my Papers at Port Stephens, I can only speak from memory, but I believe I am correct in stating that I addressed that letter to you in consequence of an intimation from Mr Walker of Sydney, that you were Agent to Mr Walker of Concord.

I beg to add that, had you done me the kindness, to offer or to require one word of explanation on this subject, when I had the pleasure of meeting

& speaking to you yesterday in George Street, it would have prevented the necessity of a reply, apparently forwarded after you saw me, & written in a tone, which, I am quite sure, your better judgment will disapprove, as equally "uncourteous", and unmerited by me.

Letter No. 828.

Port Stephens
26th February 1833

George Bunn Esq.
Sydney

Sir,
    I beg leave to enclose herewith my Draft on the Bank of Australia No 1615 to your Order for Twenty Pounds (£20) to meet the payments for Articles included in your last Invoice.
    I request you will have the goodness to cause the accompanying Dispatch addressed to The Governors & Directors of the A. A. Company to be deposited in the Post Office at Sydney – and the other Letters to be delivered with as little delay as possible according to their respective addresses.

Letter No. 829

Port Stephens
27th February 1833

J. E. Stacy Esq.

Sir,
    With reference to your Letter addressed to me on the 28th February 1832, enclosing one of the same date for the Governors & Directors of the Company (which latter I forwarded to the Court of Directors, with a strong recommendation that your request should be complied with) I herewith enclose for your information a Copy of the Reply of the Court of Directors to those Communications.

Letter No. 830

Port Stephens
27th February 1833

Henry Dangar, Esq.

Sir,
With reference to your Letter addressed to me on the 25 February 1832, a Copy of which I immediately transmitted to the Court of Directors of the Company, requesting their Instructions thereupon, I now beg leave to hand you an Extract from a Letter just received from the Court of Directors on the subject of your Communication.

Letter No. 831

Port Stephens
27th February 1832

Thomas Cowper. Esq.
Clifton, Cowpastures

Sir,
In reply to your Letter of the 4th current I beg to assure you that the Claim of the A. A. Company therein referred to, for £17.5.- will not be urged till the beginning of July next, at which period I request you will pay it into the Bank of Australia to the Company's Credit.

Letter No. 832

Port Stephens
27th February 1833

James Macarthur Esq.
James Bowman Esq.
H. H. McArthur Esq.

Gentlemen,
I beg leave to enclose to you a Copy of a Letter I have received from Mr Henry Howey in reply to an Application from me for payment for the Services of one of the Company's Horses, and I request you will do me the favor to state, for the information of the Directors of the Company, whether you consider Mr Howey's Claims upon the Company such as he could substantiate by an Action at Law.
An early Answer will oblige…

Letter No. 833

Port Stephens
1st March 1833

A. B. Spark Esq.,
A. W. Scott Esq., Treasurers for the Hunter's River Sweepstakes

Gentlemen
    As one of the Committee of the Hunter's River Sweepstakes, I request you will favor me with a List of any nominations there may be in addition to those advertized in the *Sydney Gazette* of 22nd February 1831, and also that you will inform me whether it has been determined when they are to be run for.
    I beg leave to suggest that some Gentleman be appointed to the Committee in the room of Dr Nisbet, who, I believe, was appointed one of the Stewards, but who is not about to return to the Colony.

Letter No. 834

Port Stephens
1st March 1833

Henry Dangar Esq.

Sir,
    H. M. Local Government having again declined granting to the Company the Locations which I selected for them near Liverpool Plains & the Peel's River,
    I request you will favor me with your Opinion whether, under all the circumstances of the case (with which you are acquainted, equally with myself) it can be of any Service to the Company to prolong the dissension with the Local Government respecting the Lands already surveyed on the part of the Company; or, whether a fresh selection can be made in any other part of the Colony, within your knowledge, at a reasonable distance from their present Establishment.

Letter No. 835

Port Stephens
4th March 1833

Henry Dangar Esq.

Sir,
    H. M. Local Government having again declined granting to the Company the Portions of Land near Peel's River & Liverpool Plains, which, by your recommendation & with your assistance, I have selected for completing

their Original Grant; and the reasons urged by H. M. Government for thus refusing to accede to my Selections rendering it useless either to prolong the late discussions, or to attempt to make a fresh Selection in some still more distant part of the Colony.

It becomes my duty, under my Instructions from the Court of Directors, to give you Notice that your Services will not be required by the Company after the Fourth day of September of the present year, being Six Calendar Months from the present date.

In making this announcement, I am desirous of assuring you how highly I appreciate the zeal & ability with which you have performed the arduous duties with which you have been entrusted; & that nothing but the very distant prospect which there now appears to be of deciding the Question of the Company's Grant would have induced me to discontinue the Services of a permanent Surveyor, in whose skill and exertions I have so much confidence.

I beg further to assure you that I shall feel great pleasure in Communicating to the Court of Directors the high opinion I entertain of your Services & Conduct, & in furthering your future views by all the means in my power.

Letter No. 836

Port Stephens
5th March 1833

Honorable Colonial Secretary
Sydney

Sir

I have the Honor to enclose to you herewith, an account, in Triplicate, for Coals supplied by the A. A. Company to the Colonial Department of H. M. Government, during the Quarter ending 31st December 1832. Amounting to (£19.4.-) Nineteen Pounds & Four Shillings.

The Master Attendant's Certificate is wanting to complete the Vouchers for this Account which Certificate appears to have been lost between Sydney & Newcastle. I have now enclosed to Mr Nicholson a fresh Certificate for his signature, requesting him to forward it to you. The want of this Certificate has delayed my forwarding this Account for six weeks past.

I likewise enclose open for your perusal a communication to the Deputy Commissary General transmitting to him a Similar Account, in Triplicate, for Coals supplied during the same period to the Commissariat Department, amounting to (£92.14.-) Ninety-two.

I request that you will forward my Letter to the Deputy Commissary General as soon as convenient, & that His Excellency will be pleased to direct immediate payment to be made for the whole Sum, amounting to (£111.18.-) One Hundred & Eleven Pounds & Eighteen Shillings.

You will observe that, on this occasion the Quantity of Coals supplied to H. M. Government not having exceeded one-fourth part of the whole quantity disposed of, it is charged only at 6ˢ/- per Ton on account, pending the settlement of the Question respecting Prime Cost. The Manager's usual Affidavit is, therefore, unnecessary.

Letter No. 837

Port Stephens
5th March 1833

James Laidley Esq.
Deputy Commissary General

Sir,
　I have the Honor to enclose to you herewith, an Account in Triplicate (with the requisite Vouchers) for Coals supplied by the A. A. Company to the Commissariat Department of H. M. Local Government during the Quarter ending 31st December 1832 & amounting to (£92.14.-) Ninety-two Pounds Fourteen Shillings.
　You will observe – that, on this occasion – the quantity of coals supplied to H. M. Government no have exceeded one fourth part of the whole quantity disposed of, it is charged only at 6/- per ton on account, pending the Settlement of the Question respecting Prime Cost. The Manager's usual Affidavit is, therefore unnecessary.
　I request you will cause the Amount to be paid into the Bank of Australia to the Credit of the A. A. Company with as little delay as possible.

Letter No. 838

Port Stephens
5th March 1833

Messrs R. Campbell Jr & Co
Sydney

　I beg to acknowledge the receipt of your Letter of the 7th ultimo & in reply to acquaint you that as the Waste of Sugar alluded to in my letter of the 2nd ultimo appears to have been occasioned by the bad packages in which it was contained, & that circumstance was not objected to at the time of Shipment by the Master of the *Lambton*, I herewith enclose to you a Draft for (£1.7.9) One Pound-Seven shillings & nine pence, being the price of the deficient quantity
　I request you will inform the Master of the *Lambton* whether you wish to deliver to the Company the remaining Quantity to complete the Fifteen Tons – In that case, it should be understood that no unsound packages can be received.

Letter No. 839

Port Stephens
7th March 1833

George Bunn Esq.
Sydney

Sir,
   I enclose to you herewith a Draft on the Bank of Australia for (£30.) Thirty Pounds on account of your disbursements for the Company.
   I also enclose to you Bills on the Governors & Directors of the Australian Agricultural Company for (£800) Eight Hundred Pounds, drawn to your Order; which I request you will endorse, and, lodge in the Bank of Australia to my Credit as Commissioner to the Company.
   Herewith you will receive a Memorandum of your A/C with the late Committee of Management to which I request your earliest attention and reply: I request you will comply with the enclosed Requisition by the return of the *Lambton*

Letter No. 840

Port Stephens
11th March 1833

Henry Dangar. Esq.

Sir,
   Having maturely considered the various points alluded to in your Letter addressed to me on the 6th *Current* relative to the terms of your Agreement with the A. A. Company, I beg leave to acquaint you in reply, that, being very desirous of complying with your wishes to the full extent of my power, I am willing, on the part of the Company, to afford you the Following Accommodation.
   I should have no objection to your leaving Port Stephens immediately, if there were not a few duties to be completed, which cannot be performed without the assistance of a Surveyor, and I am sure you would not consider it reasonable or proper that I should have to engage another Surveyor for this purpose, perhaps immediately after your departure.
   These duties consist in the final measurement & marking of the Company's Coal-Grant at Newcastle, the same of their Estate (late Thew's) on the Williams River, the completing of the Maps of the Farms, now in progress, the visit to inspect the Road thro' Mr Myles' Property on Williams River, and perhaps one or two other trifling matters.
   With the exception of the Coal Grant at Newcastle, the duties just enumerated need not, I should think, detain you above 3 or 4 weeks from this time; but the Coal Grant depending entirely on the Government from whom I have not yet received any reply to my Application of the 18th October last, I beg to propose that in order to allow me to meet your wishes,

there be an understanding between us, that you shall be ready, to perform the Survey &c at Newcastle, whenever the Government shall enable the Company to do so. In this case, it would of course, be understood, that your reasonable travelling Expenses would be paid by the Company, just as if you still remained inn their Service. Upon this understanding I consent to your leaving Port Stephens (with six Months Salary from the 4th current) so soon as you may have completed the other duties above mentioned.

With reference to your being entitled to a Passage to England, I need scarcely say that I am ready to provide the same for you, at the Company's Expense should you require it; but, as you express a doubt as to your future views in this respect, intimating that your movements will depend on any allowance which may be made you on this score, I would venture (tho' not without some doubts of the propriety of my doing so) to pay you on quitting Port Stephens the further Sum of One Hundred Pounds on this amount, should you decide on remaining in this Colony.

Having thus candidly stated to you the extent to which it is in my power to accede to the Claims, which you have urged upon my Notice, I need only add that I shall make a point of transmitting to the Court of Directors a Copy of your Letter and of this Communication by the earliest opportunity.

Letter No. 841

Port Stephens
11th March 1833

To The Honorable Colonial Secretary

Sir,

1. I do myself the Honor to acknowledge the receipt of your Letter of the 31st of January last, acquainting me, by the Governor's Commands, that His Excellency declines acceding to the proposals contained in my Letter addressed to you on the 22d December last; and also communicating to me His Excellency's Recommendation that I should take, for the Australian Agricultural Company, on and near Peel's River, what is wanting to complete their whole Quantity of Land.

2. I regret that it will not be in my power to adopt His Excellency's Recommendation in this respect, for the reasons already very fully detailed in my former Communications, some of which reasons are again stated in the Enclosure to this Letter.

3. It is also a matter of sincere regret to me, that I cannot consent to the Second of His Excellency's Proposals, and this for the following reasons. If I could conscientiously consent to take the whole tract (**A B C D**) of 481,456 Acres on the left Bank of the Peel, as one Location, there would remain only about 60,000 Acres to select elsewhere. If even these sixty thousand Acres were to be all good, or at least available, land, it would become a question whether so small a portion of the Company's whole Grant would be worth the expence of forming a third and very distant Establishment. But to this consideration must be added the important fact, well known to any person

acquainted with the nature of that Country, that if these 60,000 Acres were selected in the manner His Excellency proposes, namely "from the Dividing Range downwards along the streams" towards Liverpool Plains, fully <u>one half</u> of any such tract would be <u>utterly useless.</u> Whatever appearance, therefore, such an arrangement might make on paper, His Excellency will, I trust, perceive that I cannot accede to a proposal, which, if adopted, would, in fact, amount to a mere nominal possession of two new Locations. Indeed I cannot persuade myself that the granting of so small a portion of land to constitute a third location, separated 40 miles from the other, is in accordance with the spirit of the intentions of His Majesty's Home Government, in granting to the Company the indulgence of making two fresh Selections.

4. Your letter having informed me that the Governor's refusal to comply with my request is grounded on the reasons given by the Surveyor – General in the Extract from that Officer's Communication which you have enclosed for my information, it has become my duty to offer some Remarks thereupon. To these, which form a part of the Enclosure to the present Communications, I respectfully solicit the Governor's attention, and, through His Excellency, that of His Majesty's Home – Government.

5. Anxious as I am to bring this matter to a conclusion, I cannot, for the reasons now fully stated in my various Communications to His Majesty's Government, consent to betray my trust by accepting for the Company a Grant, in which the quality of the land and a supply of water are, in my opinion, made to yield, as matters of comparatively light moment, to the convenience of adopting certain natural boundaries; the acceptance of which Grant would, therefore, according to my judgment, be committing a second error; similar to that which had nearly involved the Company in ruin at the outset.

6. Having given to this important subject the most mature consideration, it appears to me that, His Majesty's Local Government having virtually declined allowing me to select the Lands required to complete the Company's Grant I have no power to proceed any further, and shall, therefore not be justified in incurring more expence on the Selections now refused. Much less can I venture to commence afresh, by exploring some still more distant parts of the Colony, or rather out of the Colony, under the apprehension which I cannot but entertain that any fresh Selection might be met by a similar refusal.

7. I have, therefore, respectfully to request that His Excellency will be pleased to transmit to His Majesty's Secretary of State for the Colonies, Copies of the several Communications I have had the Honor to make to His Majesty's Local Government on this subject. And, in compliance with the tenor of Lord Goderich's Letter to His Excellency, dated the 3^d of March 1832, I beg to acquaint you that I am about to transmit to the Directors of the Company Copies of the same Communications, for the purpose of enabling them to address His Majesty's Home Government on this question.

8. As, under these circumstances, the prospect appears a distant one of any final Settlement of this Question, I would also respectfully request that His Excellency will be pleased to grant to the Company, during this interval,

temporary occupation of such further portions of land near Liverpool Plains, as may, from time to time, be absolutely necessary for the support of their increasing and valuable Flocks.

9. And as I have given Mr Dangar notice of my intention to discharge him almost immediately from the Company's Service, I trust His Excellency will be pleased to direct that the Company's Grant at Newcastle be decided on and finally marked out without delay, in the situation requested by my Letter addressed to you on the 18th of October last, to which I have not yet received a Reply.

Remarks by Sir Edward Parry upon an Extract of a Letter from the Surveyor – General to the Honorable the Colonial Secretary dated 22d January 1833.

A

It is true that there are at some Seasons, Water Holes in the extensive Tract of Land here alluded to; but they are only such as must be dried up during the Summer Months. The Autumnal rains had commenced at the latter period mentioned by the Surveyor General, namely, in March 1832. And the expression of having "found water" 2 Months before implies the difficulty which there really was in finding it. If any portion of this Tract of 100,000 Acres could be advantageously occupied by Stock during some part of the year, they must at least be removed every Summer. It follows that, even on this most favorable Supposition this Tract is virtually a mere waste as I described it. No man would be unwise enough to form Sheep Stations on such a Tract.

Note. The Letters A, B, C &c are merely inserted for the sake of reference.

B

It is true that I included a very considerable portion of this land in my first Selection because I never have been so unreasonable as to expect that I could select the whole quantity good, and I therefore consented to include this very large portion of waste land. – But this is a strange Argument to use, as it here seems to be used against the Company's Claims.

C

The distance of Six Miles from Peel's River is too great, by at least two Miles, or one-third of the whole, for Stock to feed from water. This circumstance, therefore, is nothing in favor of the Tract. What advantage the Surveyor General expects the Company to derive from the fact that "no part of this ground is distant above six miles from the bold hills in one side", I am quite at a loss to conceive.

D

I appeal to the Maps of the Colony, & to the experience of the Settlers generally, whether this reasoning will not equally apply to any other unappropriated land in N. S. Wales. On three-fourths of the Grants on the Hunter River, for instance the Proprietors enjoy the advantage of what is called a "back-run" for their Cattle &c, namely, land not appropriated, nor ever likely to be appropriated as separate Farms, being only useful in connection with the neighbouring Estates, which latter must, in a multitude of instances be passed thro', to arrive at the unappropriated land. But the Company desire no such advantage, & I particularly solicit the attention of H. M. Government to the following observations. If these 100,000 Acres do really constitute so very desirable a Tract, what is to prevent its being occupied by other Colonists? The Surveyor General says, because "it could in fact only be entered by the side of the Company's Grant". If Major Mitchell has occasion to go to Port Macquarie by land or to visit the Grants on the Manning River he would have to ride some fifty miles thro' the Company's present Grant. And why not? Has the Company ever objected, or if they did, would the objection be held valid for one moment, to roads being made & frequented thro' their Grants in any direction necessary to the Public Convenience. The Objection raised by the Surveyor General on this head might indeed startle an English Gentlemen through whose Park or Game Reserve a Public Road was about to be made, but, in this Country such an objection is never thought of, and it must be a weak cause, that, in N. S. Wales, requires such an objection to support it.

E

If I understand these Remarks aright they amount to an admission that the Tract in question is, as I described it, little better than waste land. It is true that it is only a "small proportion" of the whole; but I only described it of its proper extent. The facts that "inequalities are necessary to supply Streams, and that a dead flat would be without water" are truisms which cannot be denied; but they have nothing to do with the one only essential fact that the Tract in question is principally bad.

F

The theoretical "conclusion" on which the Surveyor General has ventured, is erroneous. I, who have seen the portion of Land in question, know that it is not of the description "so much desired" by me elsewhere. The Surveyor General's assertion that it probably is so, seems to convey rather an insulting insinuation. If, however, this Tract be really so desirable to the Colonists as is here represented, it will most certainly be occupied by them whenever Colonization naturally extends so far. The Company know, to their Cost, that their neighbourhood is more sought after than is consistent with their interests; and with respect to Roads see my Remarks above, on this subject.

G

This question appears to turn on the meaning of the word "precipitous". My meaning was hills too steep for Sheep or Shepherds to climb without difficulty, which is the case generally with the Hills to which I allude.

H

This is a very fallacious, & therefore a very unfair point of view to put it in. The Question is, not what is "the average of good or available "land in the whole Colony" – but, what is the average of good or available land in the Tracts appropriated to the usual order of Grants in the Colony? There are Tracts of immense extent in N. S. Wales, not worth one farthing, but nobody has ever thought of including these in any Grants at all. I claim then for the Company, only the usual method of giving Grants, that is, the usual proportion of good to bad land in the Grants of the Colony generally; & every Surveyor who knows the Colony is aware that, had the Question been put in this the only fair point of view, & the Hunter River District, for instance, taken as a guide, the proportion of bad land would not be found to exceed One Eighth instead of Six Sevenths, as the Surveyor General's observations appear to intimate. I earnestly request the attention of H. M. Government to the fallacy which is, at least implied in the Surveyor General's Statement on this most important part of the Subject.

I

I have before admitted that strong natural boundaries are extremely desirable to all parties; but if 100,000 Acres in one place, & half as much in another are to be sacrificed to this consideration it would be purchasing boundaries much too dearly.

K

The insinuation that the Company, or I as their Agent, desire to have "unauthorized possession" of any portion of Land, merits no reply on my part.

L

The real facts respecting Surveys are these. The Company has been engaged for three years, at an Expense considerably exceeding £2,000 in endeavouring to complete their Grant, extending their researches even beyond the proclaimed limits of the Colony for this purpose. Their Selection is refused, and the expense, therefore, probably in great part thrown away. H. M. Government has made one Survey, occupying a Surveyor from 4 to 5 Months, embracing some material points calculated (as His Excellency justly observed) to be of great Service to the Geography of the Colony, even independently of the question relative to the Company's Lands. Is it anything new or unreasonable that the Government should survey Lands proposed to be granted? Indeed – can Lands be sold or granted without a Government Survey? And yet the Surveyor General speaks of this Survey as some great & unusual boon conferred upon the Company.

I respectfully solicit the attention of H. M. Government to this instance, among many others, of the want of candour which characterizes the Surveyor-General's Statements in opposition to the Company's just Claims.

Letter No. 842

Port Stephens
11th March 1833

The Honorable The Colonial Secretary

Sir,

Having, by letter of this day's date, communicated to you my request that the Governor will be pleased to transmit to His Majesty's Secretary of State for the Colonies Copies of the various documents relative to the unlocated lands which His Excellency has declined allowing me to select for the Australian Agricultural Company; I feel called upon to endeavour to exculpate myself in the eyes of the Governor, and of His Majesty's Home Government, from the charge of "commenting with uncalled-for asperity" on the conduct of the Surveyor General in this business; and to express my deep regret at the reproof which His Excellency has been pleased to convey to me on this account in your letter of the 27th of July last.

Upon this subject I would beg leave to observe that no man can detest & deprecate more than I do, those licentious expressions of republicanism, & that indiscriminate & unmerited abuse of the Officers of Government, tending to subvert all Government in Church & State, which are unhappily too prevalent in these times and in this Colony. I trust I may be permitted to say that my disposition, and the habits of a life spent chiefly in the service of the King, make me equally averse to such expressions of disloyalty & misrule, under the specious garb of public spirit. But, Sir, when an Officer of His Majesty's Government, behaves, in a matter which seriously & deeply concerns me, as I believe the Surveyor General has in this instance behaved, I would respectfully appeal to His Excellency whether, in such a case, remonstrance is to be denied me; whether I am silently to submit to that entire want of candour & consideration for the Company's Claims which, as I conceive, so glaringly appears in that officer's conduct and statements on this occasion. I cannot believe that His Excellency would thus wish to exclude me from what I understand to be the common right of the meanest British Subject, who feels himself aggrieved and injured. That I, on behalf of the Company, have thus been aggrieved and injured, and that I have thus a just cause of serious complaint, I conceive that I have fully shewn. I consider that I have proved the Arguments of the Surveyor-General to be in some cases frivolous, in others fallacious; that they abound in theory, where practice alone can be a safe & fair guide; that they substitute speculation for experience & fact; and that they are not always in accordance with ordinary usage, but in many very essential points directly opposed to that usage. I have likewise shewn that all this opposition arose from a predetermination on the part of the Surveyor-General to oppose any Selection I might make, that predetermination having been expressed in the strongest & most unwarrantable terms long before I had even seen the land which I have since selected.

These, Sir, are the facts on which I grounded my remonstrance to the Governor. If, in making that remonstrance, I was so unfortunate as to express myself in a manner which could be construed into the most distant appearance of want of respect to His Excellency, most heartily do I regret it, and most earnestly do I disavow any such intention. But to the Surveyor-General I am not aware that I owe any such respect – much less any such apology and I therefore once more most respectfully appeal to the Governor, and, through His Excellency, to His Majesty's Secretary of State, against a decision based on the arguments of which I complain, and coming from an Officer so prejudiced as the Surveyor-General.

Letter No. 843

Port Stephens
14th March 1833

R. Stubbs Esq.
Carrington

Sir,

I beg to draw your attention to the subject of the Rent payable by you for the Premises you hold under the A. A. Company.

Agreeably to the recommendation of a Committee appointed to consider & report upon this subject in June 1831. I consented that no Rent should be chargeable to you prior to the 11th May 1832, being two years from your first occupation, in consideration of certain Expenses which you had incurred to render the Premises suitable for carrying on your business. In conformity also with a suggestion from that Committee the Premises were completed for your better accommodation at the Company's Expense.

I am now desirous of making some arrangement which shall be satisfactory to both parties, - and for this purpose beg to propose that Rent should be paid by you at the rate of £40 per Annum from the 11th May 1832 for the whole of the Premises in your occupation, namely:

for the Cottage inhabited by your family	£20 per Annum
for the Tenement used as a Store-House at Carrington	£17 per Annum
for do do do at Stroud	£3 per Annum
and that in future such Rent be paid quarterly. –	

I request you will forward to me as early as possible your account against the Company for Articles supplied up to the 31 January 1833 for examination & settlement, and I now transmit an Account for Medicines &ea? furnished by the Company on your account prior to that date, amounting to £8.16.3.

I beg you will favor me with an early reply to this Communication to enable me to arrange your Account to the present time in the Company's Books.

Letter No. 844

Port Stephens
14th March 1833

Henry Dangar, Esq.

Sir,

In reply to your Letter of this day's date, I beg to acquaint you that I consider the proposed understanding of your Surveying the Company's Grant at Newcastle, to extend no further than the 4th day of September next; that I have no objection to allow you, for determining the question of your going to England, the interval proposed to be occupied in the completion of the Surveying duties to which I have alluded in my Letter of the 6th current; and that I consider you fully entitled to the Gratuity of £50 authorized by the Court of Directors on the completion of the Selections of Land for their Grant.

Letter No. 845

Port Stephens
15th March 1833

Honorable Colonial Secretary
Sydney

Sir,

The deficient Certificate referred to in the 2d Paragraph of the Letter I had the Honor to address to you on the 5th instant, having since been received from the Master Attendant I now beg leave to enclose the same as a Voucher for the Account transmitted in that Letter.

Letter No. 846

Port Stephens
15th March 1833

James Laidley Esq.
Deputy Cy. General
Sydney

Sir,

I have the Honor to acknowledge the receipt of your two Letters dated the 15th current enclosing for my signature Cash Vouchers (in duplicate) for the following Amounts due to the A. A. Company, - namely:

For Coals supplied to H. M. Commissariat from 1st July to 30th September 1832	£126.2.5
For Do Do from 1st October to 31st December 1832	£92.14.0
For Provisions supplied to the Military Detachment at Port Stephens from 1st October to 31st December 1832	£34.2.3¼

Letter No. 847

Port Stephens
20th March 1833

Honorable Colonial Secretary

Sir,
   The A. A. Company having formed an Establishment upon the Land near Warrah, Liverpool Plains, of which temporary occupation has been granted to them by H. M. Local Government
   I request you will inform me whether the Act of 3d Wm IV (No 5) dated 31 August 1832 entitled "An Act for preventing the extension of the infectious disease commonly called the Scab in Sheep or Lambs" extends to the Land thus occupied by the Company, so as to authorize the Company to prosecute any person infringing the same.
   And I also request to be informed whether Magistrates of the Territory, Constables or other Officers of Police, can legally act in cases of offences, & especially whether a Magistrate may try such cases upon the spot.

Letter No. 848

Port Stephens
20th March 1833

John Paul, Esq.
Sydney

Sir,
   I beg to acknowledge the receipt of your Letter dated the 2d current, addressed to Mr J. Edward Ebsworth forwarding Account Sales of Sundry Goods sold by you at Auction on account of the A. A. Company.
   The Net Proceeds £63.15.8 (Sixty three Pounds fifteen Shillings & eight Pence) has been placed to my credit at the Bank of Australia, as advised by you.

Letter No. 849

Port Stephens
20th March 1833

F. A Hely Esq.
Sydney

Sir,
    With reference to your Letter addressed to me on the 7th current I have the Honor to acquaint you that the Bearer James Goodwin (*Guilford* 7) is the Prisoner alluded to in your Communication, to whom His Excellency The Governor has been pleased to grant the Indulgence of receiving the Amount deposited in the Savings Bank to his Credit.

Letter No. 850

Port Stephens
21st March 1833

To George Bunn Esq.

Sir,
    Herewith I enclose, for your information, a Memorandum from Mr Ebsworth, relative to your a/c with the Company; to which I beg to draw your attention.
    I likewise enclose the Account you requested, of the Iron & Steel deficient ex *Renown*, amounting to £9.12.6.
    Herewith you will receive a draft on the Bank of Australia for (£15) Fifteen Pounds, to meet the Current Expences on account of the Company.
    I request you will be so good as comply with the enclosed Requisition, and that you will endeavour to expedite as much as possible the delivery on board the *Lambton* of the Goods belonging to the Company per *Prince Regent*.

Letter No. 851

Port Stephens
21st March 1833

John Terry Hughes Esq.
Sydney

Sir,
    I herewith hand you the Account of the A. A. Company against you for £6.16.- (Six Pounds & Sixteen Shillings) with a Copy of the Voucher for the Same, which I request you will be good enough to pay into the Bank of Australia to the credit of the Company.

Letter No. 852

Port Stephens
23rd March 1833

R. Stubbs, Esq.
Carrington

Sir,
    Understanding that Mrs Poole has lately received from India a quantity of Goods some of which she does not require for her own use & was about to offer for sale on the Company's Estate, I have desired that she will not part with any, without first offering them to you; for which purpose she is to furnish you with an Invoice, with the Price she wishes to affix to each Article.

Letter No. 853

Port Stephens
28th March 1833

L. Myles Esq.
Williams River

Sir,
    I have deferred replying to your Letter of the 6th ultimo, until Mr Dangar was at liberty to investigate & report upon the circumstances of which you complain relative to the Road through your property.
    Mr Dangar has now my instructions to proceed on this service; & it will give me pleasure to find that some arrangement can be made to secure you from the inconveniences to which you allude. With respect to any insolent or improper language by the Company's Servants towards you, I need scarcely assure you that I shall use my best endeavours to punish any such offence, if you will point out the individuals you have been guilty of it.

Return of Land in Cultivation
On the Estate of the Australian Agricultural Company;- with an Estimate of the Produce for Season 1832-3.

TABLE 1 1832-33

ACRES	WHEAT ACRES	BARLEY ACRES	OATS ACRES	PEASE ACRES	MAIZE ACRES	TOBACCO ACRES	TURNIPS ACRES	ARTIFICIAL GRASSES ACRES
NO 1 FARM								32
BOORAL	160	10	2	1		9	4	5
STROUD	87							68
GLOSTER					50			
TOTAL	247	10	2	1	50	9	4	105

continued

WHEAT BUSHELS	BARLEY BUSHELS	OATS BUSHELS	PEASE BUSHELS	MAIZE BUSHELS	TOBACCO TONS	TURNIPS TONS	ARTIFICIAL GRASSES 18 TONS OF HAY- THE REMAINDER FED OFF, OR USED AS GREEN-FOOD	LAND IN FALLOW ACRES
1,800	200	60	12		7	40		
700				1,500				66
2,500	200	60	12	1,500	7	40		66

N.B There are no Mines or Quarries on the Company's Estate, nor any Manufactories, Mills, or other Machinery or Works but such as are intended for private use.

Letter No. 854

Port Stephens
29th March 1833

Mr T. A. Meyer
Care of Mr T. Lindinger at George Bunn Esq.
Sydney

Sir,
   I beg leave to acknowledge the receipt of your Letter of the 26th instant offering your Services to the A. A. Company as a Cultivator of the Vine on their Estate
   In reply, I regret to inform you that it will not be in my power to avail myself of your offer, one of the Company's present Servants being already engaged in that Capacity.

Letter No. 855

Port Stephens
2nd April 1833

Dr Mitchell
General Hospital
Sydney

Sir,
   I have the Honor to enclose to you the Case of the Prisoner of the Crown named in the margin an assigned Servant of the A. A. Company, whom I request you will receive into the General Hospital,
   Mr George Bunn George St– Sydney will receive him, when cured, on the part of the Company.

Margin: James Cockayne *Leyton*, Life

Letter No. 856

Port Stephens
2nd April 1833

Principal Superintendent of Convicts
Sydney

Sir,
    The Men named in the Margin applied to me to obtain for them the Sums placed against their respective names, which were deposited in the Savings Bank at the periods mentioned, and these Men being highly deserving of this Indulgence,
    I request you will obtain the Sanction of His Excellency The Governor, to their with-drawing their Monies.

[Margin:] Samuel Leman, *Marquis of Hastings*, 7 years (just Free) £1.10.6 in 1827

William Constable, *Marquis of Huntly*, Life (due for a Ticket of Leave) £7.1.- in 1826

Letter No. 857

Port Stephens
2nd April 1833

George Bunn Esq.
Sydney

Sir,
    I beg leave to enclose to you herewith a Draft on the Bank of Australia (No. 1634) for the Sum of (£55) Fifty-five Pounds, to meet the Current Expences on account of the Company.
    With reference to a Voucher, herewith returned, for freight of a Cask of Oil, I request you will insert by what vessel & to what place, and obtain the signature of the party.
    I enclose a Requisition for Stores, with which I request you will comply by return of the *Lambton*.

Letter No. 858

Port Stephens
2nd April 1833

James Laidley Esq.
Deputy Commissary General
Sydney

Sir,
    I have the Honor to transmit to you herewith an account (in Triplicate) amounting to Thirty Three Pounds, Nine Shillings & Eight pence (£33.9.8) for Supplies to the Military Detachment stationed at Port Stephens, between

the 1st of January & 31st March 1833 – together with the Vouchers complete for the same.

I also transmit herewith an Account (in Triplicate) amounting to Six Pounds Seven Shillings & Ten Pence (£6.7.10) for Supplies to sundry Persons on account of His Majesty's Government to the 31st of March last with the Vouchers complete.

Letter No. 859

Port Stephens
2nd April 1833

Mr Thomas N. Tozer
Stroud

Sir,

In reply to your Letter of the 30th ultimo, informing me that you are ready to negociate with me on the subject of the Cancelment of your Agreement with the Australian Agricultural Company,

I beg to acquaint you that any proposal of this kind must come from yourself, and that I am ready to take into consideration any such proposal which you may be disposed to make.

It may be necessary, however, to add that your application must be made without delay.

Letter No. 860

Port Stephens
3rd April 1833

Principal Superintendent of Convicts.
Sydney

Sir,

The Prisoner of the Crown named in the Margin an assigned Servant of the A. A. Company having applied for a Ticket of Leave & being desirous of remaining in the Company's Service, I have to request you will be pleased to move H. E. the Governor to allow his Ticket of Leave to be changed from Maitland, (for which place he originally applied) to Port Stephens, should this Indulgence be granted to him.

*[Margin: William Constable. *Marquis of Huntly*. Life]*

Letter No. 861

**Port Stephens
3rd April 1833**

Richard Stubbs Esq.

Sir,
    With reference to the last Paragraph of one of your two Letters of yesterday's date received this day, I am much surprized at your intimation that retail dealing is carried on by several other persons besides yourself on the Company's Estate, as I was not aware that any Article whatever was sold on this Estate by any but yourself except in the single Case of Mrs Pool's Goods, of which you have had the refusal.
    If by this intimation you allude to the retailing of Spirits, it will become my duty as a Magistrate, in conjunction with the other Magistrates of this Bench, to investigate so unlawful a proceeding.
    But if your allusion is confined to the retailing of other Articles, I can only say, so far as regards the Company's Servants, that no endeavour of mine shall be wanting to prevent a practice which I conceive to be highly injurious to the Interests of the Company, altho' I am not aware whether I have any <u>legal</u> power to prevent it.
    In either case, I consider it due to myself, and to the Company's Servants generally, to request you will furnish me with the names of the several persons alluded to in your Communication.

Letter No. 862

**Port Stephens
3rd April 1833**

**Lieutenant Caswell, Retired
Tanilba
Port Stephens**

Sir,
    The House formerly occupied by Mr William Barton, at Carrington, & at present inhabited by Mr Ebsworth, being about to become vacant on and after the 15th instant by Mr Ebsworth's removal, I beg to acquaint you therewith, as one of Mr Barton's Attorneys in this Colony; there being as you are aware, in one of the Closets of that house, (of which you have the key,) certain Articles the property of Mr Barton, which you will perhaps agree with me in thinking not perfectly secure in an uninhabited house.

Letter No. 863

Stroud
8th April 1833

Mr Thomas N. Tozer
Stroud

Sir,

In reply to your Letter of the 6th instant I beg to acquaint you that it is entirely out of my power to accede to the extravagant demands contained in that Communication.

It may save trouble for me to add that the utmost allowance I can make you, should you wish to leave the Company's Service, is One Year's Salary (vizt £80) with the Entire Cancelment of your Agreement. But this it will not be in my power to offer to you in a short time; an arrangement being in progress for transferring your Services to another Station.

Letter No. 864

Port Stephens
8th April 1833

George Bunn Esq.
Sydney

Sir,

In the absence of Sir Edward Parry – I have to request you will cause the several Letters herewith forwarded to be distributed as early as convenient according to their respective addresses.

I am &c &c &c
(Signed) "J. Edward Ebsworth"

-oOo-

Australian Agricultural Company

Persons desirous of Contracting to supply the Servants of the A. A. Company employed at Newcastle with Rations from the 1st June 1833 to 1st June 1834 are requested to address Tenders to me under Cover to John Henderson Esq., Newcastle on or before the Fourth day of May next

The Articles required are

Good Fresh Beef or Mutton	about 350 lbs per Week, more or less.
Good Seconds Flour – from which [ ] per cent has been extracted for Bran	about 600 lbs per Week, more or less
Sugar	about 50 lbs per Week, more or less
Tea	about 7 lbs Week, more or less

    Tenders accompanied by Samples may be made for all or any part of the Articles required but they must specify in words, the price per pound at which the several Articles will be supplied, and all or any of the Articles will be taken at the prices tendered at the option of the Company.

    The Contracts to be signed & sealed on or before the 22^d May 1833.

    The Rations are to be delivered to the Company's Servants in such Quantities & at such times as the Company shall appoint.

    The Contractor will be required to leave in the hands of the Company the Amount of Two Months Supplies as Security for the due performance of his Contract; in default of which the Amount so retained shall become forfeited to the Company.

    Payment to be made Monthly in Cash, or by Drafts of the Company on the Bank of Australia (subject to the last-mentioned condition) on the delivery of an Account in such form as the Company may prescribe. –

W. E. Parry Commissioner to the A. A. Company.
Port Stephens.
8th April 1833

One Insertion in the
  Sydney Gazette
  - do – *Herald*
  - do – *Monitor*

-oOo-

Unfurnished Cottages to be Let

    To be let several neat & convenient Cottages with Offices and Gardens attached – situate at Carrington – Port Stephens – well adapted for the residence of Settlers on their first arrival in the Colony; or for Persons desirous of residing near the sea during the Summer Months – applications to Sir Edward Parry Port Stephens – to be left at the Office of George. Bunn Esq. Sydney. –

Port Stephens
8th April 1833

Two insertions in the
  Sydney Gazette
  - do – *Herald*
  - do – *Monitor*

Letter No. 865

Port Stephens
9th April 1833

Lieutenant Caswell, Retired

Sir,
With reference to the subject of my Letter addressed to you on the 3d instant & your reply of the 4th instant – I beg to propose that you should be present, on any day this week most convenient to you, while an Inventory is taken of Mr Barton's property now in the House occupied by Mr Ebsworth, preparatory to being removed to the Company's Stores for better Security.

Letter No. 866

Port Stephens
9th April 1833

W. H. Mackenzie Esq.
Bank of Australia

Sir,
I beg leave to enclose to you herewith a Draft on the Bank of Australia for (£117.6.-) One Hundred & Seventeen Pounds & Six Shillings, endorsed to your Order, to be placed to the Credit of the A. A. Company at the Bank.

Letter No. 867

Port Stephens
13th April 1833

Messrs George Bunn & Co
Sydney

Gentlemen
I beg to acknowledge the receipt of your Circular of the 1st current to which due attention shall be paid.
Herewith you will receive a Draft on the Bank of Australia for (£10) Ten pounds to meet the Current Expenses on account of the Company.
I request you will comply with the enclosed Requisition, & remain

Letter No. 868

Port Stephens
18th April 1833

L. Myles Esq.
Williams River

Sir,
   In reply to your Communication of the 10th instant I shall be much obliged by your allowing the Drays and Servants of the A. A. Company to pass thro' the Private Road upon your property when they require to go to or from Maitland; and this Letter will be a sufficient acknowledgment that this accommodation is not claimed as a right by the Company, but allowed on your part as a matter of courtesy. I enclose a copy of an Order I have issued to the Company's Servants on this subject.

Letter No. 869

Port Stephens
18th April 1833

John Larnack Esq.
Castle Forbes – Patrick's Plains

Sir,
   Mr Helenus Scott having informed me that you had obligingly communicated to him the fact of there being in the possession of several Individuals in your neighbourhood Sacks bearing the usual mark of the A. A. Company.
   I take the liberty of requesting that you will further oblige me by communicating the names and Residences of the persons to whom you allude; in which case I pledge myself not to take any steps against them without first obtaining your consent.

Letter No. 870

Port Stephens
25th April 1833

W. Wetherman Esq.

Sir,
   With reference to your Claim for £20 per Annum, as an Extra Allowance; which Claim I submitted to the Court of Directors for their decision, I beg leave to transmit to you herewith an Extract from their Despatch No 27 lately received.

Letter No. 871

Port Stephens
30th April 1833

Colonial Secretary

Sir,

I have the Honor to enclose to you herewith an Account in Triplicate amounting to (£22.4.-) Twenty-two pounds Four Shillings for Coals supplied by the A. A. Company to the Department of the Master Attendant between the 1st of January & 31st of March last together with the requisite Vouchers.

I request you will be pleased to obtain the Sanction of H. E. The Governor to the payment of this Account, with as little delay as possible.

I also enclose for your perusal an open Letter to the Deputy Commissary General, transmitting a similar Account amounting to (£18.12.-) Eighteen Pounds, Twelve Shillings for Coals supplied to the Commissariat Department of H. M. Colonial Government, during the same period which I request you will forward to the Deputy Commissary General.

You will observe, with respect to both these Accounts, that the usual Affidavit of the Manager of the Coal-Mines is not required – the whole supply to H. M. Government not exceeding one fourth part of the Entire quantity disposed of – and therefore being charged at 6s/- per Ton – the price agreed to be paid on account

---

Letter No. 872

Port Stephens
30th April 1833

James Laidley Esq.
Deputy Commissary General

Sir,

I have the Honor to enclose to you herewith an Account, in Triplicate, amounting to (£18.12.) Eighteen Pounds, Twelve Shillings, for Coals supplied by the A. A. Company to the Commissariat Department of H. M. Colonial Government – between the 1st of January & 31st of March last – together with the requisite Vouchers – and I request you will have the goodness to pay the Amount into the Bank of Australia, to my Credit, as Commissioner, to the Company with as little delay as possible.

Letter No. 873

Port Stephens
30th April 1833

Messrs George Bunn & Co
Sydney

Gentlemen,
    I beg leave to enclose to you herewith a Draft on the Bank of Australia, No 1717, for Ten Pounds – to meet the Current Expenses on account of the A. A. Company.
    I likewise enclose Bills on the Governors & Directors for One Thousand Pounds drawn to the order of Mr Bunn, which I request that Gentlemen will endorse & lodge at the Bank of Australia to my Credit as Commissioner to the Company.

Letter No. 874

Port Stephens
2nd May 1833

George T. Palmer Esq.
Parramatta

Sirs,
    In reply to your letter of the 20th ultimo I beg to acquaint you that, under the circumstances detailed in that communication, I am induced to depart from the usual custom in such cases, by allowing a deduction from your Account of £12.10.- & I request you will pay the Balance (£25) Twenty five Pounds into the Bank of Australia to my Credit as Commissioner to the Company with as little delay as possible.

Australian Agricultural Company.
Established and Incorporated by Act 5 Geo IV. Cap 86 and by Royal Charter.

    Notice is hereby given that a further Call of One Pound, ten shillings per Share has been made by the Governors & Directors upon the Proprietors of Stock in this Company.
    The Proprietors resident in New South Wales and Van Diemen's Land are requested to cause the Amount upon their respective Shares to be paid on or before the 15th day of July next, into the Bank of Australia, where Receipts will be given for the same.

W. E. Parry, Commissioner for managing the Affairs of the A. A. Company In New South Wales

Port Stephens.
7th May 1833.

| *Sydney Gazette* *Sydney Herald* *Sydney Monitor* | One Insertion each |

Letter No. 875

Port Stephens
7th May 1833

George Bunn & Company
Sydney

Gentlemen

Enclosed you will receive 21 Letters addressed to some of the Colonial Proprietors of Stock in the A. A. Company respectively, which I request you will cause to be forwarded to them without delay.

With reference to any further Proceedings which the Governors & Directors may institute on this head, I request you will insert opposite each name in the accompanying List, the manner in which you have disposed of the respective Letters, & that you will return the List to me, signed by yourselves for transmission to the Court of Directors.

-oOo-

List of 21 (Twenty-One) Proprietors of Stock in the A. A. Company to whom Circulars are addressed announcing the Fourteenth Call – One Pound ten Shillings per Share.

Name	Addresses	How disposed of
The Honorable A. Berry Esq. M. C	Sydney	
George Bunn Esq.	do	
The Executors of the late J. T. Campbell Esq.	do	
The Honorable R. Campbell Esq. M. C.	do	
Mr D. G. Forbes	do	
Mr T. W. Forbes	do	
T. A. Hely, Esq.	do	
Patrick Hill, Esq.	Liverpool	

Rev R. Hill	Sydney
The Executors of the late Thomas Macvitie Esq.	do
Rev Samuel Marsden	Parramatta
James Murdock Esq.	
Peter Murdock Esq.	
James Norton Esq.	Sydney
The Executors of the late John Ovens Esq.	do
The Executors of the late John Oxley Esq.	do
G. T. Palmer Esq.	Parramatta
A. B. Spark Esq.	Sydney
John Stephen Esq.	do
The Executors of the late Charles Throsby Esq.	Glenfield
The Executors of the late Edward Wollstoncraft Esq.	Sydney

Port Stephens 7th May 1833

Letter No. 876

Port Stephens
7th May 1833

John Henderson Esq.
Newcastle

Sir,
Enclosed you will receive 3 Letters addressed to some of the Colonial Proprietors of Stock in the A. A. Company respectively, which I request you will cause to be forwarded to them without delay.

-oOo-

List of 3 (Three) Proprietors of Stock in the A. A. Company to whom Circulars are addressed announcing the Fourteenth Call – One Pound ten shillings per Share.

The Honorable E. C. Close Esq. M. C	Hunter's River
John Henderson, Esq.	Newcastle
Robert Scott & Helenus Scott Esq.	Glendon, Hunter's River

Port Stephens 7 May 1833.

Letter No. 878

Port Stephens
9th May 1833

W. H. Mackenzie Esq.
Bank of Australia

    Sir Edward Parry presents his compliments to Mr Mackenzie, & encloses to him herewith a Draft on the Bank of Australia for £97 drawn by Mr Croasdill, & endorsed to Mr Mackenzie's Order; which Sir Edward requests may be placed to the Credit of the A. A. Company.
    A Book of Receipts for the Payment of Calls is also forwarded herewith, together with a List of Colonial Proprietors.

Letter No. 879

Port Stephens
10th May 1833

Thomas Freith, Champion, 14 Years

Charles Berryman, Marquis of Huntly, Life

Principal Superintendent of Convicts
Sydney

Sir,
    I have to report to you the Deaths of the Two Prisoners named in the Margin, Assigned Servants to the A. A. Company, which occurred at the Company's Hospital, the former on the 25th ultimo and the latter on this day.

Letter No. 880

The Editors of the *Australian* Newspaper
    Sir Edward Parry presents his Compliments to the Editor of the *Australian* Newspaper and requests they will direct one copy of that Journal to be furnished to the A. A. Company regularly thro' the Sydney Post Office from its commencement.

Port Stephens 10 May 1833

Letter No. 881

Port Stephens
15th May 1833

William Wetherman Esq.
&c &c &c

Sir,
 I beg to acquaint you that I have received Instructions from the Court of Directors of the Australian Agricultural Company to combine under One Superintendent certain of the Offices hitherto held by more than One Officer in their Establishment; and that these Instructions are accompanied by a Minute directing me to dispense with your future Services.
 In compliance with these Instructions, it becomes my duty to give you notice that your services will not be required by the Company after the 15th July next.
 Altho' you are under no Legal Agreement with the Company, I conceive it to be the intention of the Court of Directors that this notice should be given on the same terms as those expressed in the Agreement of their other Officers; namely, Six Months' notice, or Six Months' Salary, at the option of the Company. I shall, therefore, consider you entitled to Six Months' Salary from the 15th of July, being the day of your quitting the Company's Service.
 In announcing to you this arrangement, I am desirous also of conveying to you my assurance, on the part of the Company, that it is entirely a matter of economy; and that your conduct has been considered in all respects satisfactory during the time you have been in their Service.
 It being intended to appoint Mr White to perform the duties of Store-Keeper, in conjunction with the Superintendence of another Department, I request you will communicate with Mr White, by every convenient opportunity, upon the subject of the duties he is about to undertake, and that you will deliver the Stores into his charge by the 15th July next.

Letter No. 882.

Port Stephens
15th May 1833

Board for Assignment of Servants

Gentlemen,
 Observing, in the List of Prisoners assigned to Individuals, published in the Government Gazette of 3d April last, that the Prisoner named in the Margin was assigned to the A. A. Company, and this Man not having appeared at Port Stephens, nor been delivered to the Company's Agent Mr Bunn, I request you will do me the favor to inform me how I am to obtain information respecting him.

John Mann, a Weaver, Camden 2

Letter No. 883

Port Stephens
16th May 1833

Richard Jones Esq.
Sydney

Sir,
    Understanding that the Elizabeth is shortly expected to arrive at Sydney with Tea, I request you will, on her arrival, be pleased to furnish to the Australian Agricultural Company, the quantity of that Article (Hyson Skin) as undermentioned: namely

If under £4.4.0 per Chest	30 Chests
If between £4.4.0 & £5.5.0	20 Chests
If between £5.5.0 & £6.6.0	10 Chests

Letter No. 884

Port Stephens
20th May 1833

John Smith Esq.
Newcastle

Sir,
    In reply to your letter addressed to me on the 1st current I beg leave to acquaint you that I accept, on the part of the A. A. Company, your Tender for Supplying their Servants at Newcastle with Fresh Beef at One Penny per lb for One Year from the 1st of June next, subject to the Conditions named in my Advertizement.
    And I request you will communicate with Mr Henderson, as to the mode of issuing the same.

Letter No. 885

Port Stephens
20th May 1833

John Reid Esq. J. P.
Newcastle

Sir,
    In reply to your letter addressed to me on the 24th ultimo offering to Supply the Servants of the A. A. Company at Newcastle with certain Articles of Provisions from the 1st June next:

I beg leave to acquaint you that it is not in my power to accept your Tender for any of the Articles, the same having been offered at a lower price.

I beg leave to add that I regret the necessity of declining your Tenders, from the regularity & attention with which your former Contract has been executed.

Letter No 886

Port Stephens
20th May 1833

A. W. Scott Esq.
Newcastle

Sir,

In reply to your letter addressed to me on the 4th current I beg leave to acquaint you that I accept on the part of the A. A. Company, your Tender for the undermentioned Supplies to the Servants of their Establishment at Newcastle for one year from the 1st day of June next.

Good Seconds Flour	at One Penny & three-eighths of a Penny per pound.
Sugar	at Two pence three farthings per pound
& Salt	at One Penny per pound.

subject to the Conditions named in my Advertisement.

And I request you will communicate with Mr Henderson, as to the mode of issuing the same.

Letter No. 887

Port Stephens
20th May 1833

Colonial Secretary.
Sydney

Sir,

I do myself the Honor to acknowledge the receipt of your Letter of the 2d current on the subject of the Company's Coal Grant at Newcastle.

And I request you will convey to the Governor my earnest entreaty that H. Excellency will be pleased to direct that the previous marking out of the Road & the final measurement &ca of the Grant be completed without delay, to prevent the heavy expence to the Company of hiring a Surveyor after Mr Dangar has left their Service. I beg to add that the whole business will not occupy a Surveyor more than one week.

Letter No. 888

Port Stephens
28th May 1833

George Mackenzie Esq. of Craig-darroch
Williams River

Sir,
    Herewith I beg leave to transmit you an Account due by you to the A. A. Company for Two pure bred Rams delivered to your order dated the 8th of April 1833. Amounting to £7 Sterling & I request that you will pay the Same to John Henderson Esq. at Newcastle or into the Bank of Australia to my Credit as Commissioner to the Company.

Letter No. 889

Port Stephens
1st June 1833

Mr Benjamin Singleton.

Sir,
    I herewith hand you an Account of the A. A. Company against you for (£4) Four Pounds, which I request you will be good enough, at your early convenience, to pay into the Bank of Australia to the Credit of the Company.

Letter No 890

Port Stephens
3rd June 1833

Mr P. J. Cohen
Maitland

Sir,
    In reply to your Communication of the 23rd ultimo, I have the Honor to acquaint you that it will not be in my power to accept your obliging offer of becoming a Patron to the Hunter River Jockey Club; but that I shall be glad to subscribe the Sum of £15 on the part of the A. A. Company, on the understanding that two of the Company's Officers be considered as subscribers, & the usual privileges of a Subscriber be allowed to each.
    On your acquainting me that the Committee accede to this proposal, I will cause the Sum of £15 to be paid in any manner you desire.

Letter No. 891

Port Stephens
5th June 1833

James Laidley Esq.
Deputy Commissary General

Sir,

In reply to Mr Miller's letter of the 20th ultimo I have now the Honor to return to you, signed the Documents therewith transmitted – namely two Accounts & Receipts for the respective Sums of £18.12.- and £33.9.8¾; & I request you will cause these Accounts to be paid into the Bank of Australia to my Credit as Commissioner to the Company.

Letter No. 892

Port Stephens
6th June 1833

William Wetherman Esq.

Sir,

I have delayed replying to your Letter of the 15th ultimo in order that I might give full consideration to the subject of it, after collecting every fact respecting the Payment of "Passage & Outfit Money" by the Company to any of the Persons engaged in their Service from the Commencement till the present time

With respect to Passage Money, it appears that no Individual has received anything on this account except those who were engaged in England, and who therefore, bona fide, came to New South Wales in the Company's Service. I should not, therefore, feel myself justified, in making you any money – allowance on this account, since you came to this Country on your private business, without reference to the Company's Service.

As regards "Outfit-Money", I cannot discover that any such allowance has been made. In the Ships chartered by the Company, Cabin-Stores appear to have been found by them, for the use of the Servants they had engaged. But this advantage (to which a person engaged in the Colony can have no claim) was fairly earned by the very responsible & laborious duties they had to perform, during the whole voyage, in the care of the valuable thorough-bred Stock. In this respect therefore, I have no precedent, and consequently no authority, for making you any allowance.

In reply to your Letter of the 25th ultimo, since received, it can only be necessary for me to remark that I cannot in the face of the decision of the Court of Directors (communicated to you in my Letter of the 25th of April) presume to alter that decision upon my own authority.

All I can do, therefore, in addition to what I have already consented to allow you, in accordance with past usage on such occasions, is to forward to the Court of Directors Copies of your several Communications on this subject, and of any other which you may wish to make to them. I feel confident that they will be most ready to give every liberal & indulgent consideration to the Claims of an old & faithful Servant of the Company, consistently with the duty they owe to the Proprietors at large.

I am at a loss to understand what you mean, in remarking that your Services have been brought to a close in a "mysterious" & "unsatisfactory" manner. This must refer either to the Directors' Instructions to dispense with your Services, or to my manner of communicating those Instructions. If to the former, I should think the Directors have a right, and that they will maintain their right, to order the discharge of any of the Company's Servants, whenever they see fit to do so. If to the latter, I am not aware that I have used any "mystery" in this business; nor can I consider that arrangement "unsatisfactory", by which you have received two Months' longer Notice, and therefore two Months' more Salary, than has ever before been allowed to an Officer of the Company under similar circumstances.

Letter No. 893

Port Stephens
6th June 1833

James King Esq.
Sydney

Sir,

I have the Honor to acknowledge the Receipt of your Letter of the 18th ultimo accompanied by Specimens of Cut glass manufactured in England from the Sand which you sent home from this Colony, together with the Letter (& its Enclosures) which you have addressed to the Secretary of the Australian Agricultural Company on this subject.

I beg leave to assure you that I shall have great pleasure in transmitting to the Directors of the Company these very handsome Specimens of the Manufacture to which your Letter refers; and in drawing their attention to the several important points contained in your Communication, with reference to the probable advantages which the Company may hereafter derive from the manufacture of Glass at Newcastle.

As you state your intention of shortly living at your farm, I shall hope for an opportunity of conversing with you on this subject. In the mean time the Glass Articles shall be sent home by my first box to the Directors.

I will take care that you are supplied with Vine-Cuttings, as soon as our pruning commences.

Letter No. 894

Port Stephens
7th June 1833

Messrs George Bunn & Company
Sydney

Gentlemen,
I beg leave to enclose to you herewith a Draft on the Bank of Australia for (£15) Fifteen Pounds to meet the Current Expences on account of the A. A. Company.

Mr Wetherman will deliver to you a Requisition for Stores, and is instructed to determine what quantity of Salt is to be purchased for the Company; also as to a deficiency in the vinegar sent down by the *Lambton*

Letter No. 895

Port Stephens
7th June 1833

Hon. Colonial Secretary

Sir,
I do myself the Honor to acquaint you, for the information of His Excellency the Governor, that I have received from the Directors of the Australian Agricultural Company a Communication on the subject of the Price to be paid for Coals furnished by the Company to His Majesty's Local Government, enclosing a Copy of a Letter addressed to the Governor of the Company by Mr Hay, dated the 12th of April 1832.

As it appears by this latter document, of which I have now the Honor to transmit to you a Copy, that His Majesty's Home Government has referred to His Excellency the proposal made by the Directors of the Company, that the Government should pay, as a fixed price, eight shillings per ton for the whole quantity of Coals supplied to them, I beg leave respectfully to request that this Proposal be acceded to by His Excellency on the part of His Majesty's Government.

In making this request, I am prepared to shew that His Majesty's Government will, under the proposed arrangement, be supplied with Coals on terms highly advantageous to the public, while the confusion arising from the payment of two distinct prices under the present system (according to the quantity furnished) will be altogether avoided.

I beg leave to add that, finding it impossible to go on supplying the Public at the losing Price of eight shillings per ton, I have been under the necessity of raising it to nine shillings; and, unless the demand should increase very considerably, I shall be obliged to return to the Price charged by His Majesty's Government up to June 1831, or three months before the Working of the Mines was transferred to the Company.

Letter No. 896

Port Stephens
14th June 1833

Lieutenant Charlton
Bengal Infantry

Sir,
    Having understood from Mr J. G. Smith, that you are desirous of purchasing some well-bred Stallions to take to India, I beg leave to propose that you should come down to Port Stephens when convenient to you, and inspect the Horses belonging to the Australian Agricultural Company, when I have little doubt of your being able to select the horses you require, out of their Stud, which is upwards of Three Hundred in number.
    As, however, the duties of the Company's Superintendent, as well as my own, often take us to a considerable distance from home, I request you will favor me with a sufficient previous notice of the time of your intended visit, in order to prevent disappointment or loss of time.

Letter No. 897

Port Stephens
17th June 1833

The Principal Superintendent of Convicts
Sydney

Sir,
    The Prisoner of the Crown named in the Margin, has been in the Service of the Australian Agricultural Company since August 1827, being employed as a Clerk of Stores in a situation of very considerable responsibility, as well as laborious exertion, and has, without a single exception, conducted himself, during this period, in such a manner as to gain the respect and good will of, I believe, every individual on the Company's Estate.
    He has just applied for a Ticket of Leave, and I should have been glad to retain him in the Company's Service at the Salary he has already enjoyed for some years – namely Fifty Pounds per annum; but as he considers his Services may be more valuable in Sydney, as no doubt they will, I beg leave respectfully to solicit that His Excellency the Governor will be pleased to make an exception in favour of Jelf by allowing him a Ticket of Leave for the Town of Sydney.

Margin note: Robert Jelf, *Manlius*, 14 yrs

[Letter 897a]

Copy of a Document forwarded to Mr Sempill – 17th June 1833.
See Demi Official Letter Book.
Description of a 4 Horse power high pressure portable beam Engine with Fly Wheel &c

---

1 Fly Wheel – 8 ft 4 in: diameter.
2 Shafts – wrought Iron – connected by 2 cast Iron Cranks each Shaft – 8 feet long & 3 inches square. If applied to a Mill – one of these will be sufficient.
1 Steam Cylinder – 7 inches Diameter – in good order. Length of Stroke – 2 feet 2 inches Cylinder Plate and Top.
1 Steam Boiler – 4 feet 7 inches diameter – 10 feet long with a Tube passing thro' the Centre – 2 feet diameter, all in good condition
4 Cupelo Plates
1 Beam Stand – 1 Piston & Cover. 1 Steam Chest & Cover
1 Engine Beam – 1 Cylinder Bow
3 Columns Screws & Nuts – 2 Radius Bars & Brasses.
1 Gland & Brasses – 4 Centres for Beam.
2 Glands & 4 Brasses for the Centres.
1 Connecting Rod – 3 Glands & 6 Brasses
1 Piston Rod – 1 Steam Valve & Side Rods.
1 Throttle Valve & Nozzle – 1 Hot Water Pump
Connecting Rod & Levers – 2 Iron Stays –
1 Brass Cock in Cylinder Cover –
1 Three flange Nozzle with 1½ inch Flange brass Cock to connect hot water Pump – with Steam Boiler
1 Hot water Cistern, lined with lead with 2 Brass Cocks
9 ft Copper Pipe - 16 ft cast Iron Steam Pipe
1 Safety Valve & Nozzle
4 ft Hot water Pipe – 1 Nozzle for connecting Pump and Boiler - & 1 Copper Smoke Funnel
1 Eccentric Wheel & Eccentric Rod.
1 Traverse Spindle & 2 Brass Brackets.
2 Large Plomer Blocks –

Value of the above Steam Engine – including only One Shaft -   £250.0.0

Apparatus for fitting to a Boat, as under
1 Shaft – 2 small Plomer Blocks and Iron Works for Paddle Wheels   30.0.0
Total Value – <u>deliverable at Port Stephens</u>   £280.0.0

Letter No. 898

Port Stephens
21ˢᵗ June 1833

Committee of the Maitland Jockey Club

Gentlemen,
   With reference to your communication on the subject of the Maitland Jockey Club & my reply thereto, I request that you will communicate to the Bearer Mr Henry Hall, Superintendent of the A. A. Company's Stud any arrangements that may be necessary for the ensuing Races, as I have deputed him to act on behalf of the Company on that occasion.

Letter No. 899

Port Stephens
21ˢᵗ June 1833

Messrs Thomas Dent & Co
Canton

Care of Richard
Jones Esq.,
Sydney

Gentlemen,
   The A. A. Company requiring a Supply of One Hundred Chests of Hyson skin Tea, of the quality usually imported into this Colony for the use of the Prisoner Servants, I request you will ship, by the earliest conveyance to Sydney, that number of Chests, consigning them to me as Commissioner to the A. A. Company, & enclosing the Bill of Lading to Messrs George Bunn & Co Sydney. I shall be further obliged by your causing the Chests to be marked in legible characters A^{co}A- N°s 1 to 100.
   I beg leave to suggest, as the most convenient mode of payment which occurs to me, that, on delivery of the Tea, the amount of your Invoice be paid to your Agent in Sydney; but I shall be ready on receiving advices from you to adopt any other arrangement which may be more agreeable to you. I shall esteem it a favor if you will acknowledge the Receipt of this Communication, acquainting me about what time the Supply above mentioned may be expected to arrive in New South Wales.

Letter No. 900

Port Stephens
24ᵗʰ June 1833

Editor of *Sydney Monitor*
Sydney

   Sir Edward Parry presents his Compliments to the Editor of the *Sydney Monitor*, & observing by his Advertizement that he has ceased to furnish

Accounts to the Subscribers to that Paper, begs to observe that as Agent to the A. A. Company he is at a loss how to pay an Account which has not been regularly rendered, as heretofore; more especially as a part of the Sum due to the *Sydney Monitor* is usually <u>for Advertizements</u> during each Quarter.

Sir Edward Parry requests therefore, that the Editor will direct an Account to be made out for what may now be due by the Company for which the Master of the *Lambton* is directed to call before leaving Sydney.

Letter No. 901

Port Stephens
24th June 1833

Messrs George Bunn & Co
Sydney

Gentlemen,

I request you will do me the favor to inform me, <u>by post</u>, as soon as convenient after receiving this, whether it is now necessary for the Wool Ships from this Country to take in Stone or other Ballast of no value, in addition to any deadweight as Cargo – and if so to what extent this is usually found necessary.

Letter No. 902

Port Stephens
28th June 1833

Honorable Colonial Secretary

Sir,

H. E. The Governor having on his late visit to Newcastle done me the Honor to desire that I would suggest any improvement which might occur to me in the Act of Council "for the better preservation of the Ports, Harbours &c &c" of the Colony more especially as relates to the throwing overboard Ballast in the confined Channels of the Port of Newcastle, I beg leave to inform you, for H. E's information, that altho' the Provisions of that Act, generally, appear sufficient to answer the intended purpose as regards the throwing overboard of Ballast its efficacy is, in practice found to be entirely lost by the circumstance of the whole of the Fine directed to be levied in such cases, being paid to His Majesty, and no part of it to the Informer.

As it must be obvious that the Class of Persons who are most likely to obtain & give information on this subject, are those who will not occupy their time or take any trouble from a mere sense of public duty without the prospect of pecuniary Reward, I beg leave to suggest that a Moiety of the

Fine be given to the Informer in all Cases referred to in that part of the Act in question as in similar cases under the British Laws.

I do myself the Honor to add that the injurious practice of throwing out Ballast still continues unabated at Newcastle, and that I have the Authority of Messrs Brooks & Warner, H. M. Justices of the Peace residing at Newcastle & Lake Macquarie, for saying that they entirely coincide with me in the suggestions I have now made.

[Letter No. 903a]

To His Excellency Major –General Richard Bourke, Governor – in Chief, and the Honorable Executive Council of the Colony of New South Wales

The Humble Petition of Sir William Edward Parry, Knight, Commissioner for managing the affairs of the Australian Agricultural Company in New South Wales, most respectfully sheweth,

That Your Petitioner, as Agent to the said Company, received written Authority A from Your Excellency, dated the 28th August 1832, to occupy, pro tempore, on account of the said Company, a certain Portion of Land to the extent of Forty – Thousand Acres, situated near, and partly upon, Liverpool Plains;

That, in consequence of receiving such Authority, Your Petitioner transferred to the said Land about Six Thousand Sheep belonging to the said Company, together with the requisite number of men, both free and bond; that several buildings have been there erected, and others, together with a wool – press, are now in course of erection; the whole property thus situated amounting in value to not less than twelve thousand pounds, and likely to increase in value very considerably before the *close of the current year*,

That Your Petitioner, being, as he believes, the first Person to whom occupation of any Land on the Western side of the Great Dividing Range has been granted, and therefore considering the case as a novel one, on which His Majesty's Government was alone competent to decide, was anxious to ascertain to what extent the Laws of the Colony could protect the Persons & Property placed upon the said Land; and for that purpose Your Petitioner addressed to he Honorable Colonial Secretary a letter B, dated 20th March 1833 (of which a Copy is annexed to this Petition) requesting to be informed on this subject; more especially as relates to the operation of the Scab – Act; and also, as a general & most important question, whether Magistrates, Constables, and other Officers of Police could legally act in cases of Offences committed upon the Land thus occupied;

That Your Petitioner received in reply a Letter C from the Honorable Colonial Secretary, dated 15th May 1833 (of which a Copy is hereunto annexed) acquainting him, by Your Excellency's Command, that "the Government cannot be called upon to answer questions of the nature contained in Your Petitioner's Letter, which are usually transmitted through the Colonial Secretary's office for reference to the Attorney General, when

Magistrates find themselves under any difficulty as to the meaning of an Act, at the time they are called upon to decide, in a case affected by it"; but that, in this instance, the questions had been referred to the Attorney General for his opinion thereon;

That Your Petitioner has since received from the Honorable Colonial Secretary, a Letter **D** dated 21st June 1833, (of which a Copy is hereunto annexed) acquainting him, by Your Excellency's Command, that it is the opinion of the Attorney General that the Scab Act "is restricted to the part of the Colony prescribed for the Location of Settlers", by which Your Petitioner understands that it does not extend to the Land in question;

That, altho' Your Petitioner has not been favoured with any Reply to the general question upon which he solicited information – namely, whether the Magistrates & Constables &c of the Territory of New South Wales can legally act in cases of offences committed upon the Land in question, yet Your Petitioner cannot but infer, from the reply already alluded to, that no such authority can legally be excercised; and Your Petitioner feels confident that, in the face of the Attorney General's opinion, no Magistrate of this Territory will venture to act against an Offender in such cases;

Your Petitioner is therefore unavoidably led to the conclusion that the Servants & Property of the Australian Agricultural Company, situated as before described, are virtually not within the pale of the Laws of New South Wales, and consequently have not the advantage of the protection of His Majesty's Government, by whose authority alone Your Petitioner, on behalf of the said Company, occupies the said Land.

Under these very alarming circumstances, Your Petitioner respectfully entreats that Your Excellency and Your Honorable Council will be pleased to take this subject into your early consideration, and adopt such measures as may afford due protection to the Persons & Property belonging to the Australian Agricultural Company, occupying the said Land by authority from His Majesty's Government.

And Your Petitioner, as in duty bound, will ever pray &c &c &c

W. E. Parry. Commissioner for managing the Affairs of the Australian Agricultural Company in New South Wales.
Port Stephens June 28th 1833

Letter No. 903

Port Stephens
28th June 1833

Alexander McLeay Esq.

Sir,
I have the Honor to request that you will do me the favor to present the enclosed Petition to His Excellency the Governor and the Honorable Executive Council.

Letter No. 904

Port Stephens
28th June 1833

Mr Robert Jones
Tailor
Sydney

Sir,

In reply to your communication of the 11th current, requesting me to return to Government on your behalf, the Prisoner of the Crown named in the Margin who was transferred by H. M. Government from your Service to that of the A. A. Company.

I beg leave to acquaint you that Phillips having become an Assigned Servant of the Company, I cannot return him to the Government:, without incurring the imputation of doing an improper thing; especially as the Company is in absolute distress for Men; but that, under the circumstances you describe, I have no objection to do so, provided H. M. Government be pleased to sanction the transfer in consideration of any representation you may make to that effect.

For this purpose, you are at liberty to make use of this Communication as you please, and I am ready to further your wishes by any means in my power, whenever I am assured that I can do so without impropriety.

William Phillips, Countess of Harcourt, Life

Letter No. 905

Port Stephens
1st July 1833

Messrs George Bunn & Co
Sydney

Gentlemen,

I beg leave to acknowledge the receipt of? Your favor of the 27 ultimo & also of the Invoice per *Lambton* with an unsigned Bill No. 1732, I herewith enclose to you a Draft (No 1740) on the Bank of Australia for the Sum of £75, to meet the Current Expences on account of the A. A. Company – also the Draft No 1732 for £15 which is now duly signed

I likewise forward to you herewith a Memorandum of the deficient Articles per *Lunar*, with the Invoice Prices thereof; but I beg to observe that should the Articles be found unfit for the Company's use, the Invoice Price together with the usual allowance for Freight will by no means cover the damage, as I shall be obliged to purchase similar Articles in Sydney, at a much higher price.

With reference to Mr Macpherson's Note on the subject of Four Miners, which you obligingly forwarded to me, I beg to acquaint you that the Company does not at present require the Services of Men of that trade.

I beg leave to remark that you have inadvertently inserted in your A/C the Sum of 19/- for Hospital Expenses for Ellen Dormer, for which item I hold your receipt on my <u>Private Account</u>. I request you will favor me with a Memorandum to enable Mr Ebsworth to rectify this inadvertency, & to agree your Account by Post, the receipt of this Communication with the Drafts &c herein contained

Letter No. 906

Port Stephens
8th July 1833

J. E. Manning Esq.
Registrar of the Supreme Court.
Sydney

Sir,
 I have the Honor to enclose to you a List of the Property belonging to the late James Henderson, Overseer (Free by Servitude) in the Service of the A. A. Company, who was murdered by the Natives on or about the 6th ultimo – I likewise transmit to you a Letter from Henderson's Father dated the 26th February 1831.
 I request you will inform me what is to be done with the Property in question.

Letter No. 907

Port Stephens
8th July 1833

Principal Superintendent of Convicts, Sydney

Sir,
 As it frequently occurs that the Assigned Servants of the A. A. Company become free before their Certificates of Freedom are transmitted to the Resident Magistrate at this place I request you will inform me whether I am justified in granting to Men declaring themselves to be free, Passes in the usual form for 14 days to enable them to proceed to your Office to obtain their Certificates. If not I request you will inform me what it is proper for me to do in such cases.

Letter No. 908

Port Stephens
11th July 1833

James Laidley Esq.
Deputy Commissary General
Sydney

Sir,
    I have the Honor to transmit to you herewith an account (in Triplicate) amounting to Thirty two pounds, six shillings and three pence (£32.6.3) for supplies to the Military Detachment stationed at Port Stephens – between the 1st of April and 30th of June 1833. Together with the Vouchers complete for the same.
    I also transmit herewith an Account (in Triplicate) amounting to One pound seventeen shillings and eleven pence (£1.17.11) for Supplies to Sundry Persons on account of His Majesty's Government to the 30th of June last with the Vouchers complete.
    And I beg leave to remind you that several Accounts of the A. A. Company against H. M. Government similar to that last mentioned still remain unpaid.

To be sold

    A Four horse Power high pressure Steam Engine complete for immediate use, with or without the Apparatus for applying it to a Vessel.
    For a particular Description and Terms apply to Messrs George Bunn & Company, Sydney

Sydney 18th July 1833.

Letter No. 909

Port Stephens
17th July 1833

Messrs George Bunn & Co
Sydney

Gentlemen,
    I herewith enclose to you a Requisition for Stores, which I request you will forward to Mr Henderson by the first opportunity.
    I likewise enclose herewith a Description &c, of a Steam Engine to be sold, which Description I request you will shew to any person applying to see the same, in consequence of an Advertizement about to be inserted in the Sydney Newspapers.

I request you will cause the enclosed Letters to be delivered according to the respective addresses as soon as possible.

Letter No. 910

Port Stephens
29th July 1833

A. B. Spark Esq.
Treasurer to the Maitland Jockey Club
Sydney

Sir,
I am requested by Mr P. I. Cohen, Secretary to the Maitland Jockey Club, to transmit to you the enclosed Sum of £15. Being the Subscription of the A. A. Company to that Institution – I request you will give Captain Corlette a Receipt for the same – which is likewise enclosed.

Letter No. 911

Port Stephens
29th July 1833

To Mr Jnº Paul
Sydney

Sir,
I herewith hand you an Invoice of 75 Cheeses weighing cwt 10.2.10 shipped to your Address on board the Cutter *Lambton*, and request you will cause the same to be sold on account of the A. A. Company forwarding me the A/C Sales as soon as possible (and lodging the Amount in the Bank of Australia to the credit of the Company). *not included*

I also request when you will pay the Proceeds of the last A/C Sales of Cheese when due into the Bank of Australia to my credit as Commissioner to the Company.

Letter No. 912

Port Stephens
29th July 1833

Messrs G Bunn & Co

Gentlemen,
Herewith you will receive a Draft on the Bank of A. for £70. Seventy Pounds to meet the Current Expenses on account of the A. A. Company.

I likewise enclose to you herewith, Bills on the Governors & Directors of the Company to the Amount of (£1000) One Thousand pounds, which I request Mr Bunn will endorse as usual and lodge the same in the Bank of Australia, to my credit as Commissioner to the Company.

Letter No. 913

Port Stephens
31st July 1833

George. Bunn Esq.

Sir,
In reply to your Letter of the 29th current, enclosing one from Mr Manning, I beg leave to acquaint you, for that gentleman's information, that I accept his offer for the Steam-Engine belonging to the A. A. Company; namely that the Price be (£280) Two Hundred and Eighty Pounds, deliverable at Port Stephens; and that Mr Manning give his Bills for the several sums of £93.6.8 at six, nine & twelve months respectively, the two latter bearing interest (at the rate of eight per cent per annum) from the end of the six months.

Letter No. 914

Port Stephens
1st August 1833

The Honorable Colonial Secretary,

Sir,
His Excellency the Governor having been pleased to accede to the proposal made by the Directors of the A. A. Company to H. M. Home Government to fix the price to be paid to the Company for Coals furnished by them to the Local Government at Eight Shillings per Ton, as notified to me by your Letter of the 27th ultimo,

I have the Honor to inclose to you herewith an Account in Triplicate, amounting to (£25.10.8) Twenty five Pounds ten Shillings and Eight pence, for the arrears due to the Company upon the several quantities of Coals furnished to the Colonial Department, and for which the Sum of Six Shillings, only, per Ton has before been charged on account and I request you will obtain the Sanction of H. E. the Governor for the immediate payment of the above Sum.

Letter No. 915

Port Stephens
1st August 1833

To James Laidley, Esq.
Deputy Commissary General, Sydney

Sir,

H. E. the Governor having been pleased to accede to the proposal made by the Directors of the A. A. Company to H. M. Home Government, to fix the price to be paid to the Company for Coals furnished by them to the Local Government at Eight Shillings per Ton, as notified to me by a Letter from the Colonial Secretary dated 27th ultimo.

I have the Honor to inclose to you herewith an account, in Triplicate, amounting to (£159.10.9) One hundred & fifty nine Pounds ten Shillings and nine pence, for the arrears due to the Company upon the Several Quantities of Coals furnished to the Commissariat Department, and for which the Sum of Six Shillings only per Ton has before been charged on Accounts and I request you will pay the above amount into the Bank of Australia to my Credit as Commissioner to the Company.

Letter No. 916

Port Stephens
3rd August 1833

To James King Esq.
Sydney

Sir,

I beg leave to offer you my best acknowledgements for the favor of your Communication enclosing Copies of your Printed Letter addressed to Lord Goderich; which I shall take an early opportunity of transmitting to my friend Mr Barrow, Secretary to the Admiralty, requesting him to circulate them among his Scientific Friends, which I am sure, from his love of Science, as well as the kindness of his disposition, he will gladly do. I shall esteem it a pleasure if I can be in any way instrumental in furthering your Views on this important and interesting subject – I cannot doubt that your Representation will meet from Lord Goderich the consideration to which your discovery appears so justly entitled.

Letter No. 917

Port Stephens
5th August 1833

William Wetherman Esq.

Sir,

I received, on the 3d current, your two Letters dated the 29th ultimo, and the 4th current – the latter date probably intended for the 3d

With respect to the first of these Communications, it will be my duty to transmit a Copy of it, by an early opportunity, to the Court of Directors (as I have already transmitted the former Correspondence on the same subject) for their decision.

In replying to the question with which your Letter dated the 4th current commences, I beg to remark that I have neither the power nor the wish to "compel" you to remain one moment longer here than suits your own convenience, after your accounts to the 15th July have passed. The whole arrangement has been made by me with a view to your accommodation; as I conceived it must be equally important to you and to the Company, that the Accounts relating to Stores in your charge, valued at six to seven thousand Pounds, should be satisfactorily closed before your departure.

But I must also remind you that, in asking this ungracious question, you seem to have forgotten that you have lately been absent sixteen days on your private affairs (for which period you have received your full salary) and that another officer was doing your duty all that time, at a very considerable inconvenience to the Company, as well as to himself!

With respect to the payment of the Sum alluded to in your Communication dated the 4th current, I believe that, in withholding it for the present, I am acting in strict accordance with the universal usage in the public Service in such cases. In my own profession, and in the public offices in London, I know it to be so; and I believe it to be the same in the Commissariat Department of His Majesty's Government. But, if you think otherwise, I am willing to refer the whole of the facts of the case to Mr Laidley and any second person to be named by yourself, and shall cheerfully abide by their decision, whatever it may be.

I was not aware, however, till the receipt of your two Letters, that your Accounts to the 15th of July <u>had yet been sent in</u>, having received no Communication from you to that effect. I cannot, therefore, form any idea when the Audit of those Accounts can be closed – that is, when the Accountant's part of this duty can be completed.

For the same reason, I am of course unable to judge of the justice of the insinuation against Mr Ebsworth contained in your Letter dated the 4th current; upon this, therefore, I can only remark that I should hope your better judgment will disapprove of the terms in which this insinuation has been conveyed to me, and that I shall refer it to Mr Ebsworth for his explanation.

Letter No. 918

Port Stephens
7th August 1833

James Scott Esq.
Stonehenge

Sir,
I beg leave to acknowledge the receipt of your Letter of the 14th ultimo, offering to supply the Establishment of the A. A. Company at Liverpool Plains with any Articles they may require. I am not at present aware of any supplies which we are likely to require, but should any be wanted, I shall be glad to avail myself of your offer. –

(forwarded via Newcastle per *Lambton*)

Letter No. 919

Port Stephens
9th August 1833

Colonial Secretary

Sir,
I have the Honor to enclose to you herewith an Account in Triplicate amounting to (£38.8.-) Thirty Eight Pounds, Eight Shillings, for Coals supplied by the A. A. Company to the Department of the Master Attendant between the 1st of April and 30th of June last, together with the requisite Vouchers.

I request you will be pleased to obtain the sanction of H. E. The Governor to the payments of this Account with as little delay as possible.

As great delay is incurred every quarter in the transmission of these Accounts in consequence of the difficulty of obtaining the Master Attendant's Voucher I shall be obliged by your making some arrangement with Mr Nicholson which may obviate this difficulty in future.

(per Post – via Newcastle per *Lambton*)

Letter No. 920

Port Stephens
9th August 1833

James Laidley Esq.
Deputy Commissary General

Sir,
 I have the Honor to enclose to you herewith an Account in Triplicate amounting to (£120.8.-) One Hundred & Twenty Pounds and Eight Shillings for Coals supplied by the A. A. Company to the Commissariat Department of H. M. Colonial Government between the 1st of April and 30th of June last, together with the requisite Vouchers, and I request you will have the goodness to pay the Accounts into the Bank of Australia, to my Credit as Commissioner to the Company, with as little delay as possible.

(per Post – via Newcastle per *Lambton*)

Letter No. 921

Port Stephens
9th August 1833

A. B. Spark Esq.
Managing Director of the Bank of Australia

Sir,
 I herewith have the Honor to enclose to you two Drafts on the Bank of Australia for the Sums of £106.9 – and £27.6 – respectively both being endorsed to your order.
 I request you will place the former Amount to the credit of the A. A. Company and the latter to the credit of Colonel Dumaresq in the Bank of Australia.

(per post via Newcastle per *Lambton*)

Letter No. 922

Port Stephens
12th August 1833

Colonial Secretary
Sydney

Sir,
 The Survey of the Lands intended to be granted to the A. A. Company at & near Newcastle having been completed, in accordance with the Proposal

contained in my letter addressed to you on the 18th of October 1832, & acceded to by H. E. the Governor as communicated to me by your letter dated the 2d May 1833,

I have the Honor to request that His Excellency will be pleased to cause the requisite Description of the said Lands to be transmitted to H. M. Principal Secretary of State, for the purpose of obtaining the necessary Warrant under the Royal Sign Manual for passing the Grant under the Great Seal of the Colony, as provided by the First Condition of the Company's Charter.*

* The following Paragraph added to the above.

And, in the mean time, I request that His Excellency will be pleased to grant me, on behalf of the Company, a Licence of Occupation for the same.

Letter No. 923

Port Stephens
19th August 1833

Alexander McLeay Esq.

Sir,

In consequence of the Two Prisoners of the Crown named in the Margin (now employed at the Coal Mines at Newcastle) expecting to receive Tickets of Leave immediately, I have applied this day to the Board for the Assignment of Servants for a Bricklayer & a Sawyer to supply their places.

I beg leave respectfully to request that H. E. the Governor will be pleased to direct two Men of the above description to be assigned to the Company for the Colliery, their Services being constantly required in the necessary repairs of the Works.

Thomas Bridges (a bricklayer)

James Wells (a sawyer)

Letter No. 924

Port Stephens
19th August 1833

Board for the Assignment of Servants

Gentlemen

In conformity with the Regulations I request One Sawyer & One Bricklayer for keeping in repair the Coal Works of the A A. Company now employ 5 Free & 43 Convict Servants at the Colliery of the Company at Newcastle

I now employ 5 Free & 43 Convict Servants at the Colliery of the Company at Newcastle

Letter No. 925

Port Stephens
21st August 1833

To Lieutenant Colonel Dumaresq
St Helier's, Hunter's River

Sir,
    Having just received from the Court of Directors of the Australian Agricultural Company an intimation of your appointment as my Successor in the Management of their Affairs in this Colony, accompanied by a request that I would invite you to Port Stephens for the purpose of being in communication with you as much as possible, relative to the Company's Affairs, before I leave the Colony,
    I do myself the honor to request that you will, at your earliest convenience, favor me with your Company at Port Stephens for that purpose.
    The most convenient method of coming, is by Steamer from Maitland on Tuesdays or Thursdays, as far as Mr Graham's Farm (Kinross) about half way down the Hunter River; where, by previous arrangement I shall send horses to bring you over; the distance being only 18½ miles of good bush road. By way of saving time, in receiving your reply, I beg leave to acquaint you that I shall send horses for you on Tuesday the 3^d proximo, and on each succeeding Tuesday till you arrive, or till I hear from you.

Letter No. 926

Port Stephens
21st August 1833

Mr Thomas Barker
Sydney

Sir,
    I request you will ship on board the Cutter *Lambton* on account of the A. A. Company Five Tons of good fine Flour with your Account for the same.
    A Draft for the amount shall be forwarded by return of the *Lambton* to Sydney

(One Hundred Bags sent herewith by the *Lambton*)

Letter No. 927

Port Stephens
21st August 1833

Colonial Secretary

Sir,
    Mr Laidley the Deputy Commissary General having informed me by Letter dated the 15th current that he cannot entertain the charge of Eight Shillings per Ton to be paid by H. M. Local Government to the A. A. Company for Coals furnished by them, until he receives a Communication from you to that effect
    I have the Honor respectfully to request that the necessary Instructions may be given to Mr Laidley, to authorize him to make payment for the same.

Letter No. 928

Port Stephens
21st August 1833

W. Wetherman Esq.

Sir,
    I enclose to you herewith Mr Ebsworth's Memorandum relative to your Store Accounts, and I request you will favor me with any Explanation you may wish to offer relative to the deficiencies in Slop Clothing.

Letter No. 929

Port Stephens
22nd August 1833

Principal Superintendent of Convicts
Sydney

Sir,
    The Prisoner of the Crown named in the Margin holding a Ticket of Leave for the District of Port Stephens being desirous of leaving the Service of the A. A. Company, I have to request that his Ticket of Leave may be changed to Parramatta.

James Goodwin, Guilford, 14 Years

Letter No. 930

Port Stephens
27th August 1833

James Laidley Esq.
Deputy Commissary General

Sir,
    I have the Honor to return to you herewith (duly signed) the Account in Duplicate transmitted to me with your Letter of the 15th current for Provisions supplied by the A. A. Company to the Military Detachment at Port Stephens, amounting to £32.6.3½; and I request you will pay the same into the Bank of Australia to my Credit as Commissioner to the Company.

    With reference to your Second Communication of the same date, I have the honor to acquaint you that I have requested the Honorable Colonial Secretary by letter dated 21st current to furnish you with the requisite authority for the payment of the Company's Accounts against the Commissariat Department for Coals supplied by the A. A. Company.

Letter No. 931

Port Stephens
28th August 1833

Honorable Lieutenant Colonel Snodgrass CB
Brigade Office – Sydney

Sir,
    I do myself the Honor to acknowledge the receipt of your letter of the 23d current & in reply beg to acquaint you that I had already, before the receipt of your Communication made an arrangement with Captain Moffatt for the exchange of the Military Detachment at Port Stephens by conveyance in the *Lambton*, the Commander of which Vessel was directed to communicate with you on this subject.

    I beg to add that every facility in my power shall be given to Captain Moffatt for removing the present Detachment to Sydney on the arrival of the other Men.

[Letter No. 931a]

Shearers wanted

    Wanted by the Australian Agricultural Company at Port Stephens Ten good Shearers to commence Shearing on the 15th of October.

Application to be made to Mr James Corlette on board the *Lambton* – or to me at Port Stephens.
W. E. Parry, Commissioner to the Company
Port Stephens 2ᵈ September 1833.

Letter No. 932

Port Stephens
2ⁿᵈ September 1833

**Henry Dangar, Esq.
Neotsfield – Hunters River**

Sir,
By command of the Court of Directors I beg leave to enclose to you herewith a Letter addressed to you by Mr Henry T. Ebsworth, their Clerk, in reply to your Communication made to them on the 18ᵗʰ June 1832.

I request you will do me the favor to acknowledge the receipt of this Communication.

Letter No. 933

Port Stephens
4ᵗʰ September 1833

**Dr Mitchell
General Hospital Sydney**

Sir,
I have the Honor to enclose to you the Case of the Prisoner of the Crown named in the Margin an Assigned Servant of the A. A. Company, whom I request you will receive into the General Hospital. *James Cockayne Leyton, Life*

Mr George Bunn – George Street – Sydney will receive him, when cured on the part of the Company.

Letter No. 934

Port Stephens
4ᵗʰ Septermber 1833

**George Bunn Esq. J. P.
Sydney**

Sir,
I beg leave to enclose to you herewith by command of the Court of Directors of the A. A. Company a Copy of a Statement of Interest due by

you on Arrears of Instalments upon Ten Shares, in the Joint Stock of the Company, amounting to the Sum of (£5.10.7) Five Pounds-Ten-Shillings & Seven pence.

Letter No. 935

Port Stephens
4th September 1833

J E Manning Snr Esq.
Ultimo

Sir,
I have the Honor to acknowledge the receipt by the hands of Messrs Bunn & Co of your Three Promissory Notes for the Sum of £100 - £102.10 - & £105 respectively on account of the Steam Engine and Models sold to you by the A. A. Company.

And I likewise beg leave to acquaint you that Messrs Bunn & Co have advised having received from you on account of the Company the Sum of £16.-.6 for freight & Iron.

Letter No. 936

Port Stephens
4th September 1833

Messrs George Bunn & Co
Sydney

Gentlemen,
I beg leave to acknowledge the receipt of your favor of the 29th ultimo & of Mr Manning's Three Promissory Notes for £100, £102.10 & £105 respectively as therein mentioned.

I herewith enclose to your order a Draft on the Bank of Australia for £25 to meet the Current Expenses on account of the Company.

In pursuance of Instructions received from the Court of Directors of the Company, I beg leave to acquaint you that their Quarterly Accounts are in future to be made up to the 31 of March – 30 of June 30 of September & 31 of December respectively, and their Annual Accounts to the 31 of December instead of 30 of April as heretofore.

With reference to these Instructions I request you will in future transmit your Accounts in accordance with the new Arrangement; commencing on the 30 Instant. But I request that you will <u>also</u> favor me, as early as possible with your A/C to the <u>31 July last</u>, to enable me to close the Company's Books up to that period.

I beg your attention to the accompanying Requisition for Supplies, &

especially to the Memorandum in Red ink, relative to the three Articles to be sent direct to Mr Henderson per Steamer.

Some of the Company's Goods ex *Richard Reynolds* by the *Lambton* being entirely destroyed by Salt-water occasioning a very serious loss to the Company, I request you will, in such cases, cause a Survey to be held on the Goods before they are delivered to the *Lambton*, with a view to obtain compensation for the damage.

I have desired Captain Corlette not to receive any damaged Goods in future without your Certificate that they have been duly surveyed, or otherwise dealt with as may be necessary & usual in such cases.

Letter No. 937

Port Stephens
9th September 1833

Joseph Watson

In reply to your letter of the 6th current just received, I have to acquaint you that it is not true, as therein stated, that you ever asked my permission to go to Sydney until now.

And I have further to acquaint you that, whenever you ask me in a proper manner for this indulgence I will give your request due consideration.

Letter No. 938

Port Stephens
9th September 1833

John Reid Esq. J. P.
Newcastle

Sir,
I have the honor to acknowledge the receipt of your letter of the 2d current requesting that payment may be made to you of an Account furnished on the first of June for Supplies to the A. A. Company.

In reply I beg to acquaint you, that on the 17th of June a Draft (No 1735) for £8.19.3 was drawn by me to the Order of Mr Henderson for the payment of your Accont above alluded to; and that this Draft was paid at the Bank of Australia on the 3d of July.

I have communicated with Mr Henderson on this subject, requesting him to explain to you, as well as to me, how it is that the Draft was not endorsed to you as intended, & I request that you will do the Same, as I am unable to offer any further explanation until the Draft is returned from the Bank & the endorsement ascertained.

I regret that, by some unaccountable mistake, the payment of your Account should have been thus delayed, which, however, as you will perceive from the above Statement, has not been occasioned by any neglect of mine.

Letter No. 939

Port Stephens
9th September 1833

William Dangar Esq.r
Neotsfield – Hunter River

Sir,

In reply to your letter of the 22d August, lately received I beg leave to acquaint you that there appears to have been some misunderstanding as to the information given by Mr Charles Hall to your Brother, relative to the price of the A. A. Company's Rams, Mr Charles Hall having acquainted me that he did not mention so low a price as that named in your communication.

I am willing to sell you any number of French Merino or Saxon Rams, on the following terms, deliverable on the Company's Estate, at or near Stroud, on or before, the 31 of October next, to be selected by yourself out of a Flock of 300.

If under 10 be purchased	£3.15.- each
above 10 & under 30	£3.10.- each
above 10 & under 60	£3.5.- each
above 60	£3.- each

Payable by your Bill at 6 Months date.

The very great inconvenience attending the delivery & conveyance of Wheat, and the difficulty of fixing the price at the time of delivery will prevent my acceding to your proposal of receiving this article in payment.

Letter No. 940 (a)

Port Stephens
9th September 1833

Joseph Watson

In reply to your Letter of this days date requesting permission to go to Sydney on your private business.

I have to acquaint you that you have my permission to be absent from your duty for Fourteen days, and that you can have a passage in the *Lambton* when she next sails for Sydney.

Letter No. 940 (b)

Port Stephens
11th September 1833

R. Stubbs Esq.

Sir,

In reply to your Application to me to have your Rents lowered, in consequence of the houses you occupy being no longer licensed,

I beg to acquaint you that I propose fixing the Rent at £30 for the Quarter ending the 11th August last & at £25 per Annum subsequently to that period.

[Letter No. 940c]

Shearers Wanted

<u>In addition</u> to the Shearers advertized for on the 2d instant, for Port Stephens, the Australian Agricultural Company will also require Four Good Shearers at Warrah, Liverpool Plains, to commence shearing on the 1st November next.

For terms &c, apply to me at Port Stephens or to Colonel Dumaresq at St Helier's Hunters River

W. E. Parry Commissioner to the Company
Port Stephens
16 September 1833.

Sydney Gazette	
-------- *Herald*	Two insertions each
-------- *Monitor*	
-------- *Australian*	

Illustration 4: *Sydney Herald*, 19 September 1833 (Letter No. 940c) ←

Illustration 5: *Sydney Herald*, 19 September 1833 (Letter No. 940d) →

[Letter No. 940d]

To Cover this Season.

At the Australian Agricultural Company's Stud Establishment at Alderley – Port Stephens

The Blood Horses
'Courier' and 'Shark'

Clevelands
'Noble' and 'Granby'

Welch Ponies
'Spangle' and 'Marquis'

Terms
Blood Horses £4 - Clevelands £3 - Welch ponies £1-10 Groomage 5/-

No charge for Paddocks – and a liberal allowance to persons sending more than one Mare according to the number sent.

All Expenses to be paid before the Mares are removed.

W. E. Parry. Commissioner to the Company
Port Stephens.
16 September 1833.

Sydney Herald	
-------- *Gazette*	Two insertions each
-------- *Monitor*	
Australian	

Letter No. 941

Port Stephens
11th September 1833

Principal Superintendent of Convicts
Sydney

Sir,
   In reply to your letter of the 3^d instant, I beg to acquaint you that on enquiry I find that the Man who died at Port Stephens as reported to you in my Communication of the 10 May last, appears to be Samuel Berryman Ship *Burrell* – Life.

Letter No. 942

Port Stephens N. S. Wales
12th September 1833

Right Honorable E. G. Stanley
His Majesty's Principal Secretary of State
for the Colonies

Sir,
    As Commissioner for managing the Affairs of the A. A. Company in N. S. Wales, I do myself the honor to submit to your consideration the following Statement,
    The Company has, under certain Conditions, agreed upon with H. M. Home Government, erected very complete Coal Works at Newcastle, in this Colony, at an Expense of between Sixteen & Seventeen Thousand Pounds.
    One of the Conditions on which the exclusive right to work the Coals was granted to the Company, as stated in Mr Twiss' Letter to Mr Brickwood (the Company's Secretary in London) dated 31st July 1828, is as follows: "that Government shall be entitled in perpetuity to all Coal wanted for its own consumption not exceeding in any case one fourth of the average annual produce of the Mines, to be delivered at the Pits Mouth, at <u>Prime Cost</u>".   *See Mr Twiss' Letter to Mr Brickwood 31 July 1828*
    In recapitulating these Conditions, in a letter addressed to me on the 25th June 1830, the Colonial Secretary confirmed the above Stipulation.
    On the 29th of September 1831, being two days after the Working of the Coal Mines had been transferred by the Local Government to the Company, I addressed a letter to the Colonial Secretary (of which I now annex a copy for your information) requesting to be informed on what <u>data</u>, or according to what principle His Excellency the Governor conceived the <u>Prime Cost</u> of the Coals ought to be computed. I received no reply to this Communication; & have only mentioned it here, in order to shew that from the beginning I was desirous of having this question decided.   A
    On the 15th February I transmitted for payment the Company's first Account for Coals supplied to H. M. Local Government. This Account it was necessary to divide into two parts; 1st for a Supply of Coals amounting to one fourth part of the whole quantity disposed of during the period, and to be charged at Prime Cost; 2dly for the Remainder of the Quantity furnished to the Government, to be charged at the price paid by the Public. – The former of these two Accounts was accompanied by the Manager's Affidavit of the whole quantity disposed of by the Company.
    These Accounts were accompanied by a letter from me to the Colonial Secretary (of which I annex an Extract) suggesting that, <u>pending the settlement of the Question respecting Prime Cost,</u> the Government should pay to the Company "a certain portion of the price say six Shillings per Ton for that Quantity of Coal which is chargeable at Prime Cost;" as it would appear to be only equitable that the Company should not be kept entirely out of their Money until this Question could be settled.   B
    I received no reply to this Communication 'till, having occasion on the 16 May 1832 to transmit a <u>Second</u> Quarter's Accounts against the

C

D

Government, made out in a similar manner, I repeated my request that payment might be made.

Shortly afterwards, I received a Communication from the Colonial Secretary dated 7 June 1832 (a copy of which is annexed) acquainting me that the Governor had directed the above-mentioned Accounts to be discharged "in conformity with the proposals contained in my letter of the 15 February 1832". (**B**, above)

Subsequently to that time the Accounts were regularly made out & transmitted in a similar form, every Quarter, accompanied by the Manager's Affidavit, it being expressly stated in those Accounts in which only Six Shillings per Ton was charged, that this Sum was "<u>on account</u>," – that is, in part payment only, pending the settlement of the Question of "Prime Cost".

It may further be of importance to remark that, so cautious have I been in not admitting this amount of Six Shillings to be anything but <u>a part</u> of the payment, that, even in the printed Receipts for the Money, sent from time to time by the Deputy Commissary General for my Signature, I have myself caused to be inserted the words "on account" or to that effect, before I would attach my Signature to them.

See Mr Smith's Letter to Viscount Goderich 6 April 1832

As however, this mode of rendering the Accounts was attended with great practical inconvenience, and as it plainly appeared that the Prime Cost could never be fixed at a particular Amount, but must continually fluctuate according to the actual Quantity of Coals disposed of, it was suggested by the Directors of the Company in London, in a Letter addressed by their Governor, Mr Smith, to Viscount Goderich dated the 6th April 1832 that the whole of the Coal furnished to the Colonial Government should be charged at the fixed rate of Eight Shillings per Ton.

See Mr Hay's Letter to Mr Smith 12 April 1832

Mr Hay's reply to this communication dated the 12th April 1832, acquainted Mr Smith that Viscount Goderich could only authorize General Bourke to accede to the proposed price "provided he saw no reason to question the reasonableness of that amount."

E

I, therefore, applied to the Colonial Secretary by letter dated the 7 June (of which an Extract is annexed) requesting, with reference to the above Correspondence with the Home Government, that the Governor would be pleased to accede to the proposal of paying Eight Shillings per Ton for the whole quantity of Coals furnished to H. M. Local Government.

F

The Colonial Secretary informed me, by letter dated the 27 July 1833 (an extract from which is annexed) that His Excellency "acceded to the proposal that the Government shall be furnished at the Pit's Mouth with all the Coal wanted for its' own Consumption at the rate of Eight Shillings per Ton".

This long-pending Question being now, as I conceived, finally settled, I transmitted to H. M. Local Government on the 1st of August last, the Company's Accounts against them for the arrears of two Shillings per Ton due upon those quantities of Coals which had from time to time been paid for in part at Six Shillings. These Arrears amount to £25.10.8 due by the Colonial Department of H. M. Government, and £159.10.9 due by the Commissariat Department making a Total of £185.1.5. –

G

The Colonial Secretary's Reply dated the 6th of the present Month (of which a Copy is hereunto annexed) informs me, to my great Surprize, that

H. E. The Governor declines paying these Arrears, on the grounds that the Arrangement to which he has agreed was "intended to be prospective only", and that it is inconsistent with the usual practice to open out Accounts previously adjusted & paid.

Under the circumstances of this refusal, my duty to the Australian Agricultural Company compels me to appeal to your decision, whether, in making the above claim, I have not acted in strict accordance with the Spirit of Viscount Goderich's just instructions towards the Company, I submit to you Sir, with the utmost confidence as to the result, whether the arrangement of paying Eight Shillings per Ton was not bona fide intended by H. M. Government <u>as a substitute for the original Stipulation respecting the Prime-Cost</u>; and therefore whether the Company can be denied payment according to the terms of their Agreement, for any period of the supplies, without a direct breach of Faith on the part of H. M. Government.

It can scarcely be necessary for me to draw your attention to the obvious fact that the Company must be entitled to payment according to <u>one or the other</u> of the two arrangements – that is, either at prime-cost, <u>or</u> at Eight Shillings per Ton; whereas, according to General Bourke's present view of the matter they would appear to be entitled neither to the one nor the other. But it may be necessary for me to apprize you that, if His Excellency prefers the former of these two, the Directors of the Company can easily prove to you that H. M. Government would have to pay at least two or three Shillings <u>more</u> than Eight, as the Prime Cost of every Ton of Coals furnished during the period in question.

I beg leave further to submit to you whether one of the reasons given by the Governor for the non payment of this Claim, - namely, that it is inconsistent with the usual practice to open out Accounts previously adjusted & paid, can apply, with any propriety or justice, to the present case. It can hardly be necessary for me to appeal to your decision in this particular instance, whether it be consistent with justice, in <u>any</u> case for H. M. Government to refuse the payment of a just debt to a large Amount, merely because some forms of Office might suffer inconvenience or derangement by the payment; but, Sir, I think it will appear to you sufficiently clear from the foregoing statement that the Accounts for which I now claim payment, have <u>not</u>, in any legitimate sense of the words, been "adjusted and paid" at all.

Having thus laid before you a correct Statement of the facts of this Case, I do myself the Honor respectfully to request that instructions more explicit than His Excellency appears yet to have received may be given to General Bourke to pay these Amounts without further delay.

And I am also desirous of submitting to your consideration whether, as a part of this debt has already been due nearly Two Years, and a large portion of another year may probably elapse before your Instructions can be received, the Company will not be entitled to a reasonable allowance for Interest; H. M. Government being the only purchasers who have not paid <u>Cash</u> for Coals supplied to them by the Company, & the Company being obliged to pay Cash for all <u>their</u> expenses in maintaining the Colliery.

Letter No. 943

Port Stephens
12th September 1833

The Honorable The Colonial Secretary

Sir,
 Having received a Copy of Viscount Goderich's Despatch (No 153) dated Downing Street March 1833, & addressed to the Governor, directing His Excellency with as little delay as possible after the receipt of that Despatch, to place me in possession of the Two Locations which I selected for the A. A. Company as intimated to you in my letter of the 5th of May 1832, accompanied by a Map in illustration of my selections.
 I have now the Honor respectfully to request that His Excellency will be pleased to take the necessary steps for putting me in immediate possession of the same, and more especially of the whole of the Green Shaded Portion in the above-mentioned Map where the encreasing quantity of Scabby Sheep is becoming a very serious evil likely to affect the best interests of the Company, if suffered to proceed further for want of due authority to remove them.
 I have the honor to add that I am ready in compliance with Lord Goderich's desire to enter into any reasonable arrangement for securing proper Roads, to be made at the Expense of the Government, wherever they may be requisite for public benefit, through either of these Portions of the Company's Estate, as well as to secure to the Settlers on the Lands adjoining the Company's Tracts, the use of those Streams which may be available for the fertility and cultivation of their Land, as well as afford Water-Carriage for their produce.

Letter No. 944

Port Stephens
12th September 1833

To The Honorable Colonial Secretary

Sir,
 I do myself the honor to acknowledge the receipt of your Letter of the 6th instant, and, with reference to the subject of that Communication, I respectfully request that His Excellency the Governor will be pleased to forward the enclosed Letter to the Right Honorable the Secretary of State for the Colonies, which is left open for His Excellency's perusal and information.

Letter No. 945

Port Stephens
13th September 1833

To The Honorable Colonial Secretary

Sir,
On the 28th of June last, I had the Honor to address a Letter to you, enclosing a Petition to His Excellency the Governor and the Honorable Executive Council.

I request you will have the goodness to inform me whether these Documents have been received.

Letter No. 946

Port Stephens
14th September 1833

Messrs George Bunn & Company
Sydney

Gentlemen
By the *Lambton* which is about to proceed to Newcastle, I forward a Box for the Governors and Directors of the A. A. Company, which Captain Corlette is instructed to send to your address by the Steamer which will arrive in Sydney on Tuesday night next;, should he miss that opportunity, he will send it by the other Steamer on Thursday.

I request you will be so kind as to enquire for the Box accordingly, and forward it to England by the first opportunity, enclosing to the Governors and Directors a Bill of Lading of the same; transmitting to me the Duplicate and Triplicate; and favouring me with a line by post informing me what you have done.

I beg leave to enclose to you herewith a Draft on the Bank of Australia for the sum of (£70.0) Seventy Pounds, to meet the current Expences on account of the Company; of which I request you will acknowledge the receipt.

I likewise enclose a Memorandum from Mr Ebsworth, dated the 15th Instant, relative to your a/c to the 31st July last; to which I request your attention.

By the same Steamer which conveys the Box abovementioned, you will receive a brown-paper parcel containing some letters which I request you will cause to be <u>delivered</u> as soon as convenient.

The Letter herewith sent, addressed to the Governors & Directors I request you will send <u>by the *Elizabeth*</u> in particular, as it contains a Bill of Lading of Hides shipped on that vessel.

Letter No. 947

Port Stephens
14th September 1833

To Henry Dangar Esq.
Neotsfield
Hunter's River

Sir,

I beg leave to acknowledge the receipt of your Letter of the 9th instant, announcing the Completion of the Survey and Map of the Company's Coal-Grant at Newcastle.

The Map has been retained by Mr Croasdill till a safe opportunity offers for sending it to Port Stephens.

I herewith enclose to you a Draft on the Bank of Australia for (£6.7.0) Six Pounds, Seven Shillings, being the amount of your Accounts for Expences incurred in completing the Newcastle Grant. I request you will enclose to me the Receipt for the same.

Being much in want of the Company's Theodolite for the Survey of the harbour of Port Stephens, I request you will return it, to the care of Mr Croasdill, with as little delay as possible.

Letter No. 948.

Port Stephens
18th September 1833

James Laidley Esq.
Deputy Commissary General

Sir,

With reference to my letter (No 713) addressed to you on the 5th of October 1832, I beg leave to remind you that another year has nearly elapsed without any payment being made of the Accounts therein named for Provisions furnished by the A. A. Company to the Military Detachment at Port Stephens, between the 24 May & the 24 December 1828 – all which Accounts were duly rendered to Mr Scott at Newcastle by your desire before the close of that year.

Under my Instructions from the Directors of the A. A. Company, it will shortly become my duty to put these and other outstanding Accounts into the hands of the Company's Solicitor, for the purpose of recovering the Amounts with Interest, in due course of Law.

Letter No. 949

Port Stephens N. S. Wales
19th September 1833

The Right Honorable E. G. Stanley
H. M. Principal Secretary of State for the Colonies

Sir,

On the 12th instant I did myself the Honor, as Commissioner for managing the Affairs of the A. A. Company in New South Wales, to address to you a letter on the subject of a Claim against H. M. Local Government for Coals furnished by the Company, which Claim His Excellency General Bourke had declined recognizing, for the reasons which I have explained in that Communication.

I am now, as unexpectedly as unwillingly again under the necessity of addressing you on a subject of still greater importance to the Company's Interests, as relates to their Coal Works at Newcastle.

For this purpose I beg once more to call your attention to Mr Twiss' to Mr Brickwood (the Company's Secretary in London) dated 31st July 1828, which formed the Basis of that Agreement between H. M. Government and the Company on the faith of which the latter have erected & are maintaining, Coal Works at so heavy an expence and by virtue of which they are bound to provide against any failure in the supply of Coals to the Public.

In this letter the following Condition occurs:

Thirdly: "That although the assistance required by the Company, in regard to Convict labourers, must necessarily depend upon the means which the Colonial Government may have at its disposal for affording it, yet as the Government will cease to raise the Coal which may be required for the General Purposes of the Colony, every possible facility and encouragement for this object, be afforded to the Company, so that no scarcity of this Article may take place, and the quantity raised be, as far as depends on the assistance of Convict labour, at all times, if possible, adequate to the demand."

In accordance with this stipulation, General Darling, the late Governor of the Colony, did afford every facility & encouragement, as regards Convict Labour in erecting & maintaining the Coal Works. Previous to the working of the Coals being entirely transferred to the Company, a few, extra Mechanics were lent to them from the Government Establishment at Newcastle for a certain number of Months; at the expiration of which they were duly returned to Government. Since that time the Company's Establishment of Convicts at their Colliery has continued nearly as follows; the number and other particulars here stated being bona fide the Establishment on the 31st ultimo

Blacksmith	1
Stone-Cutter	1
Bricklayer	1
Carpenter	1
Sawyers (one pair)	<u>2</u>
	6
Miners & Labourers	<u>37</u>
	43

It may be necessary to explain to you that the above small Establishment of Six Convict Mechanics, is as necessary to the effective maintenance of the Coal Works, as the Miners & Labourers are. The Blacksmith and Carpenter are incessantly occupied in keeping the various parts of the 'Pit Gear' as well as the Coal Waggons, Coal Skips, and Railway in repair; the latter being 329 yards in length. The same remark applies to the Bricklayer; the Chimney, as well as the brickwork about the Boiler, and round the Pit needing constant repair, and the Services of a Stone-Cutter, tho' not continually required are some times needed to keep the Stone foundation of the Steam Engine in sound Condition. The one pair of Sawyers is quite indispensable, as well to provide wood for the different buildings not yet completed, as to keep the Pit supplied with 'Prop-wood', for supporting the roof, above five hundred props being at the present consumption required per Month, or about 6,300 per Year, all of which have to be brought from several miles' distance.

Upon the above-mentioned Establishment, (which however as regards <u>regular Miners</u>, is at times barely sufficient to keep up the Supply of Coals) the operations of the Company's Colliery were proceeding with tolerable prospects of success and the encreasing consumption (under their improved mode of working) was beginning to reduce the actual cost of raising the Coals to the low & hitherto losing price at which they were sold, when I received a Communication from the Colonial Secretary of a very alarming nature; inasmuch as it intimates an intention, on the part of the present Local Government, to deny to the Company's Colliery for the future that moderate assistance in the labour of Convict Mechanics to which, for two years past, they have been considered entitled, and without which they must struggle afresh for the very smallest profit upon this important part of their undertaking.

On the 19th ultimo I applied in the usual Form to the proper Board, for the assignment of a Bricklayer & a Sawyer, for the Colliery, in place of two such men about to receive Tickets of Leave. At the same time I wrote a letter to the Colonial Secretary, (A, of which a copy is hereunto annexed) stating for the Governor's information the particular circumstances of my application. I also annex (B) a Copy of the Colonial Secretary's reply.

Under these circumstances, I am compelled to appeal to your decision, whether it be in accordance with the Spirit, or even with the letter, of the Stipulations above referred to, that the Company should be refused the Assignment of two Convicts for the purposes I have mentioned, in consequence of any "Regulations established" <u>since those Stipulations were entered into</u> – Regulations which have never been opposed to this specific claim of the Company until now; and which, if applied to the Company's

Colliery, will alter the whole bearing of their Agreement with H. M. Government.

It may be proper for me to acquaint you that the Salaries & Wages now paid by the Company to <u>Free Persons employed exclusively in their Colliery</u>, comprising a Manager – a Book-Keeper – an Engineer – a Brakesman and a Blacksmith, amount to £1187.18.1 per Annum which I am sure you will consider more than a reasonable Annual outlay for Free labour in an infant Establishment of this nature; whereas the principle now about to be acted upon by H. E. General Bourke would shortly encrease this outlay to the Amount of between £300 & £400 per Annum for the maintenance of six more free Mechanics.

I beg leave, Sir, most respectfully to assure you that it is impossible for the A. A. Company to continue the working of the Coal Mines at the present price of Nine Shillings per Ton to the Public, & Eight Shillings per Ton to the Government, if this new and unexpected obstruction be thrown in the way of their operations.

It may not be improper for me to add, in justice to the A. A. Company & to myself as their Agent, that while difficulties are thus opposed by the Government to the economical working of the Company's Mines, it has been, and still is, my most anxious desire to afford to the Government every possible convenience & advantage. As one proof of this, I may mention that so far from taking advantage of the <u>letter</u> of the Company's Stipulation, to deliver the Coals to the Government "<u>at the Pit's Mouth</u>", I have always delivered it on board the Vessels, by the Rail-road, constructed at several thousand Pounds expence for that purpose by which arrangement alone the Government has been enabled to do away with an expensive Establishment of Carts, working oxen, drivers & labourers, for shipping their Coals in the former slow method at the Old Wharf now nearly gone to decay. I am confident in stating that Sixpence per Ton is thus saved to the Government upon every Ton of Coals they consume, while, on the other hand, <u>Ten</u> Tons of Coals are now delivered on board the Vessel in the space of time in which a Cart could deliver <u>One</u>, should the Company's Agent be disposed to insist, (as he justly might,) on complying with the literal terms of their Agreement.

On all these grounds I do myself the Honor most earnestly, on behalf of the A. A. Company, that directions may be given for affording to their Colliery "every possible facility & encouragement", as regards Convict labour, in performance of the Stipulation entered into by H. M. Home Government on this head, and expressly, that the Company may not be deprived of that precise kind of labour which amongst Free Persons it is most difficult and expensive to obtain in N. S. Wales namely that of mechanics such as those above referred to.

Australian Agricultural Company
Established and Incorporated by Act 5 Geo IV. Cap 86. and by Royal Charter

Notice is hereby given that a further Call of One Pound per Share has been made by the Governors and Directors upon the Proprietors of Stock in this Company.

The Proprietors resident in New South Wales and Van Diemen's Land, are requested to cause the Amount upon their respective Shares to be paid on or before the 30th day of November next, into the Bank of Australia where Receipts will be given for the same.

W. E. Parry, Commissioner for managing the Affairs of the A. A. Company in New South Wales.
Port Stephens
20th September 1833

Government Gazette	
Sydney Gazette	Two insertions each
Sydney Herald	
Sydney Monitor	
Australian	

Letter No. 950

Port Stephens
20th September 1833

Messrs George Bunn & Co.
Sydney

Gentlemen,

Enclosed you will receive 21 Letters addressed to some of the Colonial Proprietors of Stock in the A. A. Company respectively which I request you will cause to be forwarded to them without delay.

With reference to any further Proceedings which the Governors & Directors may institute on this head, I request you will insert opposite to each name in the accompanying list, the manner in which you have disposed of the respective letters, and that you will return the List to me signed by yourselves for transmission to the Court of Directors.

I beg you will inform your Mr Bunn, that as I understand the Calls on his Shares will be paid by Mr Buckle in London, the Notice now sent is merely for his information.

I am &c &c &c
(Signed) **W. E. Parry Commissioner to the Company**

List of 21 (Twenty One) Proprietors of Stock in the Australian Agricultural Company to whom Circulars are addressed announcing the Fifteenth Call – One Pound per Share.

Name	Address	How disposed
The Honorable Alexander Berry Esq.	√ Sydney	
George Bunn Esq.	√ Sydney	
The Executors of the late J. T. Campbell Esq.	√ Sydney	
The Honorable Robert Campbell Esq.	√ Sydney	
Mr D. G. Forbes	√ Sydney	
Mr F. W. Forbes	√ Sydney	
T. A. Hely Esq.	√ Sydney	
Patrick Hill Esq.	Liverpool	
The Rev. Richard Hill	√ Sydney	
The Executors of the late Thomas Macvitie Esq.	√ Sydney	
The Rev. Samuel Marsden	Parramatta	
James Murdoch Esq.		
Peter Murdoch Esq.		
James Norton Esq.	√ Sydney	
The Executors of the late John Ovens Esq.	√ Sydney	
The Executors of late John Oxley Esq.	√ Sydney	
G. T. Palmer Esq.	Parramatta	
A. B. Spark Esq.	√ Sydney	
John Stephen Esq.	√ Sydney	
The Executors of the late Charles Throsby Esq.	Glenfield	
The Executors of the late Edward Wollstonecraft Esq.	√ Sydney	

Letter No. 951

Port Stephens
20th September 1833

John Henderson Esq.
Newcastle

Sir,
 Enclosed you will receive 3 (three) Letters addressed to some of the Colonial Proprietors of Stock in the A. A. Company respectively which I request you will cause to be forwarded to them without delay.
 With reference to any further Proceedings which the Governors & Directors may institute on this head, I request you will insert opposite to each name in the accompanying list, the manner in which you have disposed of the respective letters, and that you will return the List to me signed by yourselves for transmission to the Court of Directors.

List of 3 (Three) Proprietors of Stock in the Australian Agricultural Company to whom Circulars are addressed announcing the Fifteenth Call - One Pound per Share.

Name	Address	How disposed of
The Honorable E. C. Close Esq.	√ Hunters River	
John Henderson Esq.	√ Newcastle	
Robert Scott and Helenus Scott Esqres	√ Glendon Hunters River	

Letter No. 952

Port Stephens
20th September 1833

To The Honorable The Colonial Secretary

Sir,
   I do myself the Honor to acknowledge the receipt of your Letter of the 9th instant, acquainting me, by the Governor's direction, that His Excellency regrets not being able to assign to the Australian Agricultural Company's Colliery at Newcastle a Bricklayer & a Sawyer.
   As this new and unexpected obstruction to the economical working of the Coal Mines appears to me completely at variance with the Conditions (as regards Convict Labour) upon which the Company has embarked its capital, and on a strict adherence to which engagement the success of the Company's undertaking must mainly depend, I have considered it my duty to address to His Majesty's Secretary of State for the Colonies the enclosed Communication, which is left open for His Excellency's perusal, and which I have the Honor to request may be forwarded by the earliest convenient opportunity.

Letter No. 953

Port Stephens
26th September 1833

Henry Dangar Esq.

Sir,
   I beg leave to enclose to you a Copy of a Letter addressed to me by the Honorable Colonial Secretary dated 20th instant with its two Enclosures relating to the A. A. Company's Grant at Newcastle.
   And I request you will certify the correctness (or the contrary) of the two

Descriptions of the said Grant therein contained, informing me also whether the Remarks in the letter, upon the space relinquished by the Company and said by the Surveyor General to contain only 59 Acres 2 Roods and 20 Perches, instead of 67 Acres, be correct according to your last Survey.

You will oblige me by an early & if possible a final Reply to this Communication, that no further delay may be incurred in transmitting the Descriptions to England, to enable H. M. Government to cause the Grant to be passed under the Great Seal.

Letter No. 954

Port Stephens
26th September 1833

Henry Dangar Esq.

Sir,

H. M. Government having directed that the A. A. Company, be put in possession of the Two Locations which I selected for them at Liverpool Plains, & at Peel's River respectively & a Surveyor being required to complete whatever arrangements may be necessary on the part of the Company.

I request you will inform me, whether you are willing to undertake the Service, & if so, on what terms, it being understood that the arrangements alluded to, are to include _everything_ as to the measuring & marking out of the two Grants, the completion of Maps in duplicate, & any correspondence or communication which may be required with the Surveyor General, or Government Surveyors in order to complete this business.

I request you will mention whether you are willing to find the requisite men & other equipment for this service or not; & it will perhaps be better to state what your Terms are in either case.

As I am requested by the Government immediately to name some professional person on the part of the Company; & as I have deemed it my duty, to communicate with other Surveyors on this subject, in order to have the Service performed at the cheapest possible rate, I request you will favor me with an immediate reply to this communication.

Letter No. 955

Stroud
26th September 1833

Joseph Watson.

Joseph Watson,

In reply to your note of yesterday's date, I have no objection to cancel your Agreement with the A. A. Company, as you request from & after the 30th instant.

But you are at liberty to remain at your present residence until the *Lambton* goes to Newcastle, of which I will give you due notice; and you will then have a free passage with your Family as you have requested.

Letter No. 956

Port Stephens
28th September 1833

Honorable Colonial Secretary
&c &c &c

Sir,
I have the Honor to acknowledge the receipt of your letter of the 16th instant, acquainting me by direction of H. E. The Governor, that the Secretary of State has consented to the appointment of a Stipendiary Magistrate & Constabulary at Port Stephens, upon condition that the A. A. Company provide & maintain in repair certain Buildings & consent to incur certain other Expences, as proposed in my letter of the 1st of March 1832.

Assuming that the Constabulary intended to be maintained here by H. M. Government is the same in point of numbers & efficiency as the present Establishment – namely, Three Constables, at Two Shillings & Three pence per diem if Free, and at One Shilling & Nine pence per diem if Prisoners, as intimated to me by your letter of the 27th of July 1832, I beg leave respectfully to offer the following Remarks on the arrangement now proposed.

<u>I have no objection to incur on the part of the Company the Expense detailed in my letter of the 1st of March 1832;</u> but there are some points connected with those details, which, on the present occasion, appear to me to require a somewhat more explicit understanding.

1st The Police Clerk whom I proposed maintaining is to be a Prisoner, as may be inferred from the Sum of £19 per Annum for his maintenance, named in my letter of the 1st of March 1832. I mention this, because a "<u>Residence</u> for the Clerk" is stated as one of the Conditions, in your letter to which I have now the Honor of replying.

2d In order to prevent any future misunderstanding as to the particular quantity of Stationery to be used annually in the Police Office, I beg leave to propose that it be fixed at the actual Supply furnished by the Government to this Bench for the year ending 30th June 1833. To enable me to comply with this Arrangement, (should His Excellency approve it) I request to be furnished with a Statement of the quantity thus supplied.

3d For the reason stated in the last Paragraph, I would suggest the propriety of also fixing the quantity of Arms, Irons, Oil, & Cooking Utensils, to be supplied by the Company to the Police. I request, therefore, that His Excellency will be pleased to propose what he considers a fair proportion of each.

I have thought it necessary thus to enter into detail on points which may appear to be of minor importance, because, without an explicit understanding, some misapprehension & difficulty may hereafter occur.

With reference to that part of your letter which intimates the intention of the Governor to withdraw the Detachment of Military from Port Stephens, without substituting a Force of Mounted Police, as proposed in my letter of the 1st of March 1832, I beg leave respectfully to assure His Excellency that, in my opinion, such a measure cannot be adopted without incurring a very serious risk. Although the Infantry force now stationed here is certainly not so available in aid of the Police as a smaller number of Mounted Soldiers would prove, yet, I cannot contemplate a removal of <u>all</u> Military force without great alarm; because it comes within my own knowledge, from personal experience, that, notwithstanding the repeated attacks made by the Blacks upon the Company's Servants, and the several Murders which have ensued, yet there exists, on the part of these Natives, a very great dread of the Military – a feeling which is absolutely essential to the security of the Persons & Property belonging to the Company necessarily scattered over a wide extent of this Estate.

Under these circumstances, it becomes my duty unequivocally to declare it as my opinion that the carrying into effect of His Excellency's present intention would be the signal of a series of attacks upon the Company's Stations, which would give rise to the most frightful atrocities.

As His Excellency's determination is stated to be founded on the circumstance of the Company's Lands in this neighbourhood being shortly about to be diminished in extent, I beg leave to point out that this fact in no-wise obviates the necessity of an efficient Military Protection; in as much as no reduction in the population of the Company's Establishment will take place in consequence of that circumstance. On the contrary it is intended to <u>increase</u> this Establishment as rapidly as the assignment of men will permit, whilst the useless portion of Land abandoned by the Company in February 1831, was <u>never at anytime occupied by a single Individual in the Company's Service</u>.

I would therefore again suggest the propriety of a Force of Mounted Police being substituted for the Military Detachment about to be withdrawn; but, should the exigencies of the Service not allow of the number which I proposed in my letter of the 1st of March 1832, I would respectfully submit that a Non-Commissioned Officer and three Privates of the Mounted Police be stationed here, which force, it may be hoped, if properly employed, would prove sufficient for the Security of this District, while, at the same time, their Services might likewise be available for the District of Williams' River.

[Margin: *Enclosure with Colonel Dumaresq's Letter to the Major of Brigade dated 12th July 1837*]

Letter No. 957

Port Stephens
28th September 1833

Thomas Broadhurst
At Mr John Feales
Miller – Windsor

Thomas Broadhurst

In reply to your letter of the 7th instant for which I have been waiting since February last, to know where to find you, I now enclose a letter addressed by Mr Hely to the Colonial Treasurer, which will enable you, on application, to obtain from the latter Gentleman the Money belonging to you in the Savings Bank.

Letter No. 958

Port Stephens
28th September 1833

Board for Assignment of Servants

Gentlemen

In conformity with the Regulations I request that Fifty Convict Servants may be assigned to me of the following Description; vizt
50 Agricultural Labourers
50 Shepherds

I reside at Port Stephens in the County of Gloucester. I am Commissioner to the A. A. Company and hold about 458,000 Acres of Land; of which 500 Acres are cleared, and 470 Acres are in tillage.

I possess 331 Horses, 2,786 Head of Cattle and 32,000 Sheep; I now employ 68 Free, and 366 Convict Servants; about 180 have been in my service upwards of three years, and 20 upwards of one year. No assigned servants have been returned to the Government. None have absconded except such as have been apprehended by Police except two.

My Agent, Mr Bunn residing at Sydney is fully empowered to receive such Servants as may be assigned to me & to defray all Expenses incurred on their account.

An application, as above, forwarded at the same date, for
3 Carpenters
2 Blacksmith
1 Wheelwright

Letter No. 959

Port Stephens
30th September 1833

John Armstrong Esq.
Sydney

Sir,
    H. M. Home Government having acceded to my Selection of Two Locations for the A. A. Company at Liverpool Plains & Peel's River respectively each consisting of between 200,000 and 300,000 Acres or about 550,000 Acres in all,
    I request you will inform me whether you are willing to undertake the final delineation & description of the same, & if so upon what terms.
    The Lands have been entirely Surveyed, & Maps made of them by Mr Dangar, and the Country is peculiarly adapted to quick & accurate surveying.
    I request you will favor me with an early reply & I remain…

Letter No. 960

Port Stephens
30th September 1833

Messrs George Bunn & Co
Sydney

Gentlemen,
    I herewith enclose a Requisition for Stores required by the A. A. Company with which I request you will comply by return of the *Lambton*.
    I herewith return to you the Invoices of Goods per *Lambton* of the 29 August and 10th instant – Mr Ebsworth suggests that they be made out afresh, to obviate the necessity of corrections in them.

Letter No. 961

Port Stephens
5th October 1833

Messrs George Bunn & Company
Sydney

Gentlemen
    Herewith I beg leave to enclose to you Bills on the Governors and Directors of the A. A. Company, to the Order of your Mr Bunn, as undermentioned; which I request Mr Bunn will endorse, and lodge in the Bank of Australia, to my Credit as Commissioner to the Company.

No. 295	for	£100
No. 296	"	£100
No. 297	"	£150
No. 298	"	£150
No. 299	"	£200
Total Amount		£700

Letters to Manning & Raymond

I request you will forward the enclosed Letters to their respective addresses as soon as convenient after their receipt, and that you will oblige me by acknowledging the receipt of this Communication

---

Letters Nos 962-973

Port Stephens
5th October 1833

To * * * * *

Sir,
On the 22d of January of the present year, I transmitted to you an Account due to the Australian Agricultural Company, amounting to * * * *; requesting that you would pay the same as early as possible, to prevent my resorting to legal measures for the recovery of the same.
Having received no reply to my Communication, I now beg leave to acquaint you that I am under the necessity of directing the Company's Solicitor to institute the necessary legal proceedings for this purpose.

-oOo-

The foregoing Letter was addressed to each of the following Individuals.

Mr J. Brown	Letter No. 962	£5.15.0
W. H. Moore Esq., Sydney	Letter No. 963	£17.5.0
Andrew Allan Esq., Bailey Park Penrith	Letter No. 964	£17.5.0
Rev. S. Marsden, Parramatta	Letter No. 965	£39.10.0
John Mackaness Esq., Sydney	Letter No. 966	£23.11.0
T. B. Wilson Esq.	Letter No. 967	£5.10.0
James Murdoch Esq., 58 Kent St Sydney	Letter No. 968	£5.15.0
Jonathon Hassall Esq., Matavia, Campbell Town	Letter No. 969	£15.14.0
Mr John Gaggin, Sydenham, Alcorn's Inn	Letter No. 970	£8.18.0
William Howe Esq., Glenlee Campbell Town	Letter No. 971	£5.15.0
George Cox Esq., Wimbourne, Penrith	Letter No. 972	£23.0.0
	Letter No. 973 not sent	

Letter No. 974

Port Stephens
5th October 1833

To John Piper Esq., Senior
Alloway Bank, Bathurst

Sir,
 With reference to your Favor of the 28th January last, acquainting me that you had directed the Sum of (£8.18.0) Eight Pounds Eighteen Shillings to be placed to my Credit in the Bank of Australia, as Commissioner to the Australian Agricultural Company,
 I have now the Honor to inform you that this Sum has not yet been received at the Bank, and to request that you will cause it to be paid at your earliest convenience.

Letter No. 975

Port Stephens
5th October 1833

J. J. Moore Esq.
or
Cumberland Cottage, Liverpool

Sir,
 With reference to your Letter of the 9th of February last, acquainting me with your intention to pay into the Bank of Australia the Sum of (£14.8.0) Fourteen Pounds Eight Shillings due to the Australian Agricultural Company, as communicated to you in my Letter of the 22d January,
 I now beg leave to remind you that this Amount still remains unpaid; and I earnestly request you will cause the same to be paid without further delay, to prevent the necessity of my putting it into the hands of the Company's Solicitor.

Letter No. 976

Port Stephens
5th October 1833

J. J. Moore Esq.
Cumberland Cottage
Liverpool

Sir,
 With reference to your Letter of the 9th of February last, on the subject of an Account due by Sir John Wylde to the Australian Agricultural Company, amounting to (£16.10.0) Sixteen Pounds, Ten Shillings.

I once more earnestly request payment of the same, having received positive Instructions to institute legal proceedings for the recovery of the debt, if not immediately settled.

Letter No. 977

Port Stephens
5th October 1833

Edward Cox Esq.
Fern Hills
Mulgooa [sic]
Penrith

Sir,
　With reference to your Letter without date, addressed to me in reply to my Communication of the 22d of January last, I beg to remind you that the Account therein alluded to (amounting to £23 Twenty Three Pounds) still remains unpaid.
　And I once more earnestly request an early payment of the same, having received positive Instructions to institute legal Proceedings for the recovery of the debt, if not immediately settled.
　Should you produce satisfactory evidence that only <u>three</u> Mares were sent, notwithstanding your application to send <u>four</u>, I shall be ready to relinquish the Company's Claim for the fourth Mare charged in the Account transmitted to you.

Letter No. 978

Port Stephens
5th October 1833

Thomas Cowper Esq.
Clifton
Cowpastures

Sir,
　With reference to your Letter addressed to me on the 4th of February last, requesting that the Claim of the Australian Agricultural Company against you, amounting to £17.5.0 Seventeen Pounds, Five Shillings, may not be urged till the latter end of June or the beginning of July,
　I now beg leave to remind you that the above Account still remains unpaid, and that, under my Instructions from the Directors of the Company, I shall, however reluctantly, be under the necessity of placing it in the hands of their Solicitor, if not immediately settled.

Letter No. 979

Port Stephens
7th October 1833

Board of Assignment of Servants

Gentlemen,
In conformity with the Regulations I request that a Convict Servant may be assigned to me of the following Description; vizt
One Gardener
I reside at Port Stephens in the County of Gloucester. I am Commissioner to the A. A. Company and hold About 458,000 Acres of Land - about 500 Cleared - about 470 Acres in Tillage - possess 331 Horses – 2,786 Head of Cattle - about 32,000 Sheep - Employ 68 Free & 366 Convict Servants, of whom about 180 have been in my Service upwards of 3 Years & 120 upwards of 1 Year - No assigned Servants have been returned to Government & none have absconded except they who have been apprehended by the Police except Two.
My Agent, Mr Bunn residing at Sydney is fully empowered to receive such Servants as may be assigned to me & to defray all Expenses incurred on their account.

Letter No. 980

Port Stephens
8th October 1833

The Honorable The Colonial Secretary

Sir,
   I regret being under the necessity of appealing to His Excellency the Governor on the subject of the non-assignment of Prisoners to the Australian Agricultural Company; but the rapid decrease of the numbers, and the increasing wants of the Company's Establishment render such an Appeal necessary.
   From the 1st of May 1832 to the 31st July 1833, being a period of fifteen months, the Assignments published in the *Government Gazette*, amounted to (5,020) Five Thousand and Twenty; out of which number the following Assignments have been made to the Company's Establishment at Port Stephens:

Individuals above	18 years of age	13
Individuals	18 years of age	4
Boys under	18 years of age	13 of whom 3 are not above 14 years old
Total		30

Out of the above number, One Bough Carpenter and One young lad a Painter are the only Mechanics, and these of very inferior skill in their respective trades.

Within the same period, the following Prisoners have been discharged from the List of the Company's Assigned Servants:

Having become Free or obtained Tickets of Leave (of whom <u>eight</u> were retained on Salaries)	67
Died	2
Committed to Gaol for Trial	3
Absconded & not again apprehended	2
Sentenced to Iron Gangs	3
Total:	77

Thus it appears that, in this period, the number of the Company's Assigned Servants had decreased by (47) Forty Seven, and that, among those still remaining in their service, seventeen lads and boys (some of them mere children) had been substituted for the same number of men.

In the foregoing Statement, I have of course omitted the Miners who have been assigned to the Company's Colliery at Newcastle; as His Excellency is aware that these Assignments fall within the terms of a Specific Agreement between His Majesty's Government and the Australian Agricultural Company.

Whilst the number of Assigned Servants has thus decreased, it has been necessary to form a Separate Establishment at Liverpool Plains, at the same time that extensive improvements are in progress upon the Company's Estate at Port Stephens.

In accordance with the principle which, I understand, governs the Assignment of Convicts to Individual Proprietors, it may not be irrelevant to state that the Estimated Value of the Company's Property on the 30th of April last, at the present reduced prices of Stock, amounted to £103,720, exclusive of their Grants of Land; and that the annual expence of their Agricultural Establishment is £11,600; which circumstances will, I trust, appear to His Excellency to justify the appeal which I am now making.

I, therefore, respectfully request that His Excellency will be pleased to call the attention of the Board for the Assignment of Servants to the foregoing details, with a view to an early Assignment of men to the Company.

I beg leave, in concluding this Letter, to disclaim any wish to impute to the Gentlemen composing the Board an intentional disregard to the claims of the Company; but the facts now stated will, I hope, bear me out in the representation I have thought it my duty to make

Letter No. 981

Port Stephens
9th October 1833

Board for the Assignment of Servants

Gentlemen,

I request you will have the goodness to sanction & cause to be arranged the Transfer of an Assigned Servant belonging to the A. A. Company whose name is John McAndrew – per Ship *Eliza* sentence 7 years – convicted at Mayo, March 1832, to Mr James Edward Ebsworth of the Company's Establishment; also William Jones, assigned servant to Mr Ebsworth, who arrived per Ship *Captain Cook* – Sentence Life – convicted at Southwark in 1832, to the Service of the A. A. Company, in Exchange for the above, each Party being agreed.

I have the Honor to be &c &c &c
W. E. Parry. Commissioner to the Company
I agree to the above
J. E. Ebsworth

Letter No. 982

Port Stephens
9th October 1833

Honorable Colonial Secretary

Sir,

I do myself the Honor to acknowledge the receipt of your letter of the 16th ultimo acquainting me, by command of the Governor, that the Secretary of State has been pleased to order that I be put in possession, as Commissioner of the A. A. Company, of the Two Locations selected by me, & reported at the beginning of the last year, & recommending that I should name some professional person, on behalf of the Company to communicate with the Surveyor General on this subject.

In reply I beg to acquaint you for the information of His Excellency, that I have taken the necessary steps for procuring a proper person to communicate with the Surveyor General accordingly & that I will lose no time in acquainting you therewith when I have been enabled to find a person to entrust with this duty.

Letter No. 983

Port Stephens
9th October 1833

Honorable Colonial Secretary

Sir,

With reference to the arrangements now in progress for the Establishment of a Police [sic] at Port Stephens, I beg leave respectfully to draw the attention of His Excellency the Governor to a circumstance in some degree connected therewith.

It has hitherto been the practice for the Company to allow Constables, Runaways and other persons in charge of, or belonging to the Police, to have a Passage in the *Lambton* Cutter, free of Expense to the Government. Under the arrangement now in course of completion, it will of course not be in my power any longer to incur this Expense on the part of the Company without a proper remuneration; & I beg leave therefore, to propose, for His Excellency's consideration that this item of Expense be put on the same footing as in other parts of the Colony, when conveyance is furnished in private Vessels. With respect to Freight or Passage Money on account of the Government, I am willing to receive the same Amount as is paid to & from Newcastle, tho' the distance to Port Stephens is Thirty Miles greater. Should His Excellency be pleased to approve of this proposal, I request to be informed upon what authority & by what Vouchers I am required to furnish freight or passage & in what manner the Accounts are to be rendered for the same.

Letter No. 984

Port Stephens
11th October 1833

W. H. Mackenzie Esq.
Bank of Australia

Sir,

I beg leave to enclose to you a Draft endorsed to your order for (£108.14.-) One Hundred & Eight Pounds & Fourteen Shillings which I request you will be good enough to place to the Credit of my Account as Commissioner for the A. A. Company.

Letter No. 985

Port Stephens
12th October 1833

Honorable Colonial Secretary

Sir,
 The Act of Parliament relating to the Incorporation of the A. A. Company, requiring that the Calls made upon the Proprietors shall be inserted in the *London Gazette*, I lately sent a Notice of a Call to the Printer of the *Government Gazette* of this Colony, in the same manner as is practised in London. The Printer informs me that he cannot insert this Notice, and the object of the present communication is to request that you will do me the favor to allow an official notification to that effect to be conveyed to me from your office merely in order to secure the Company against the imputation of an infraction of the Act, in the course of any future legal Proceedings, which the Directors may deem it expedient to institute for the recovery of Amounts due by the Colonial Proprietors.

Letter No. 986

Port Stephens
12th October 1833

To Messrs Robert Campbell Junior & Co.
Sydney

Gentlemen
 I have the pleasure to enclose to you herewith a Draft on the Bank of Australia (No. 1898) to your Order, for the Sum of £23.15.5, being the Amount of your Invoice of Sugar purchased by the A. A. Company. I have directed Captain Corlette to call for the Receipt.
 I also request that you will furnish the Company with Three Tons more of the same Sugar, if at the same price; which the *Lambton* will receive on her arrival at Sydney, probably in the early part of next week.

Letter No. 987

Port Stephens
14th October 1833

Messrs George Bunn & Company
Sydney

Gentlemen,
 I beg leave to enclose to you herewith, a Draft on the Bank of Australia to your Order, for the Sum of £50 (No. 1897) to meet the Current Expences

on account of the A. A. Company. I request you will acknowledge the receipt of the same, by post.

I request you will do me the favor to cause the accompanying Letters to be delivered by some trustworthy person as early as may be convenient.

Letter No. 988

Port Stephens
14th October 1833

To Mr James Rainey
Sussex Street

Sir,

Mr Turnbull has put into my hands your Letter addressed to him on the 5th instant acquainting him that a Report has been raised of your having given dissatisfaction in the Casting Work you have performed for the A. A. Company.

In reply, I have great pleasure in contradicting this Statement, by assuring you that Mr Turnbull, the Company's Engineer, has at all times been satisfied with the work you have done for the Company; and, from the Report he has made to me, I shall be always glad to employ you whenever there may be work to do for the Company.

I consider it justice to you to add, that you are at liberty to make any use you please of this Communication.

P S. As the Company has a small quantity of Old Iron to sell from time to time, I request you will inform me what price you are willing to give for it per Cwt, Cash, or in part payment of Castings.

Letter No. 989

Port Stephens
19th October 1833

The Honorable The Colonial Secretary

Sir,

Captain Moffatt, the Resident Magistrate at Port Stephens, having been directed by the Governor to communicate with me on the subject of a Letter addressed to you by Mr Wynter, a Magistrate of the Territory, dated 18th of September last, and enclosing a Deposition of Henry Herring, a Convict Constable, relative to certain transactions said to have occurred between the Servants of the Australian Agricultural Company and the Native Blacks on this Estate,

I do myself the Honor to acquaint you that, in compliance with His Excellency's Commands, I have caused to be brought in from the Company's distant Stations the different Individuals in their Service, whose testimony Captain Moffatt thought requisite to obtain, relative to the serious charges against him, myself and others of the Company's Servants. I trust that the information thus collected, and now about to be transmitted to you by Captain Moffatt, will satisfactorily show that no outrage whatever has been committed upon the Blacks by any of the Company's Servants.

With respect to the charge brought more immediately against myself, of having offered a Reward for the Heads of certain Natives, it may perhaps be sufficient for me unequivocally to declare that I never, directly or indirectly, offered any such Reward; that so inhuman & disgusting a piece of barbarity never entered my head; and, that I never even heard of a Report of such a thing, as relates either to Captain Moffatt or myself, until, to my utter astonishment, I saw it stated in your letter addressed to that Officer on the 3d Instant.

On the present occasion, I consider it proper to abstain from offering any observations on the conduct of Mr Wynter in this business, further than to remark that, had this Magistrate, when passing through the Company's Estate on his way to Sydney, and receiving hospitality at their several stations, communicated to the Bench of Magistrates of this District the Reports he had heard, and which he was about to lay officially before His Majesty's Government, we should most readily have united with him in making the requisite investigation.

As Mr Wynter's first Complaint dated the 10th of August, alluded to in your Letter of the 3d instant to Captain Moffatt, is still a secret to the accused Parties, tho' of so serious a nature as to have been referred to the Attorney General, I request that His Excellency the Governor will be pleased to direct that a Copy of that Communication be forwarded to the Bench of Magistrates at Port Stephens. I also respectfully entreat that the further intelligence which Mr Wynter is invited by His Excellency to acquire on this subject, in accusation of myself or others of the Company's Servants, may likewise be communicated to us, in order to enable us to refute allegations so false & injurious as those to which I have now the Honor of replying.

Letter No. 990

Port Stephens
19th October 1833

Board for Assignment of Servants

Gentlemen,

In conformity with the Regulations I request that Two Convict Servants may be assigned to me of the following Description; vizt

Two Horse Shoers.

I reside at Port Stephens in the County of Gloucester. I am Commissioner to the A. A. Company and hold about 458,000 Acres of Land - about 500 Cleared - about 470 Acres in Tillage - possess 331 Horses

– 2,786 Head of Cattle - about 32,000 Sheep - Employ 68 Free & 366 Convict Servants, of whom about 180 have been in my Service upwards of 3 Years & 120 upwards of 1 Year - No assigned Servants have been returned to Government & none have absconded except they who have been apprehended by the Police except Two.

My Agent, Mr Bunn residing at Sydney is fully empowered to receive such Servants as may be assigned to me & to defray all Expenses incurred on their account.

Letter No. 991

Port Stephens
19th October 1833

Henry Dangar Esq.
Neotsfield – Hunter's River

Sir,

I beg leave to acknowledge the receipt of your letter of the 1st instant, and to acquaint you that, having compared your terms therein proposed with those offered by other Surveyors for performing the same service, I find that yours are considerably the highest. But, in consideration of the superior local knowledge which you possess of the Portions of Land selected for the Company, I am willing to employ you in the completion of this Service, provided you accede to the following terms.

As it is not my intention to accept any offer for performing this service at a certain Sum per diem for an indefinite period, I propose to allow you £225 for the full completion of it, which will be equivalent to your own terms of £2.10 per diem for the utmost extent of the period you mention, namely 60 working days, £50 being also allowed for the two Maps in Duplicate including all necessary correspondence & other Communications on the subject, & £25 to cover all travelling expenses incurred in this business.

The Company to equip a small party of Men upon the same footing as usual in their surveying – journies with Rations, Surveying Instruments, pack bullocks and a Horse for your own use; it being understood that you meet & take charge of the Party at Maitland on a day hereafter to be appointed.

It will, of course, be understood that the Service now under consideration shall include a complete and durable <u>marking</u> of the several boundary lines, or that you be responsible that it be properly & sufficiently done by the Government Surveyor; and also that the Field Books and other Remark Books, together with Copies of any Correspondence between the Government & yourself on the Subject be considered the property of the Company, & delivered to their Agent at the same time with the Maps.

I request you will acquaint me, by return of the Messenger who carries this, whether you are willing to accept the terms I have now proposed; & if so, that you will forward to me by him a Requisition for the several Items necessary for the equipment of the party. It will also be requisite that you should say when you could be ready to proceed on this service, to enable me to make the necessary arrangement with H. M. Government.

Letter No. 992

Port Stephens
19th October 1833

James Laidley Esq.
Deputy Commissary General – Sydney

Sir,
I have the Honor to transmit to you herewith an Account (in Triplicate) amounting to (£33.1.3) Thirty three Pounds, One Shilling & Three Pence for Supplies to the Military Detachment stationed at Port Stephens between the 1st of July and 30 September 1833 together with the Vouchers complete for the same.

I also transmit herewith an account (in Triplicate) amounting to (£3.11.9) Three Pounds Eleven Shillings & Ninepence for Supplies to Sundry Individuals on account of H. M. Government to the 30th September last with the Vouchers complete.

And I regret to be obliged again to remind you that several Accounts of the A. A. Company against H. M. Government similar to that last mentioned, & amounting to more than £50 still remain unpaid.

Letter No. 993

Port Stephens
19th October 1833

George Jenkin Esq.

Sir,
After mature consideration of the subject of your letter of the 4th instant I beg to offer the following Remarks on the proposal therein contained.

It does not appear clear whether your Proposal for a Three Years Engagement with the Company is intended to include your present Money Allowances of £41 per Annum or not. If this be your intention, I will venture to accede to it for the first Two Years (vizt at £150 per Annum in all) continuing your present Extra Rations, leaving to the Court of Directors to confirm or annul the proposal for the Three Years (vizt at £200 per Annum in all).

Should it have been your intention to propose the above terms, in addition to your present Money Allowances and Extra Rations, I have no hesitation in saying that it is quite out of my power to consent to this proposal, or to exceed the Terms which I have mentioned above.

With reference to the period of your Service in the Company's Employment, and your Conduct therein, which has been highly satisfactory & creditable, I beg to add that I do not think the Directors would approve of my engaging any new officers to perform the same duties at a Salary much above half that which I have now proposed for your acceptance.

Letter No. 994

Port Stephens
19th October 1833

William Smyth
Wheelwright – Maitland

William Smyth,
As the Waggon which you are now completing for the A. A. Company will be required the present Season for Wool I request you will make such additions to it as Mr Charles Hall may mention to you as requisite for that purpose.

Letter No. 995

Port Stephens
21st October 1833

James Raymond Esq.
Sydney

Sir,
Herewith I beg to hand you an Account for Ten Rams, which you will receive by the *Lambton* amounting to (£31.10.-) Thirty One Pounds & Ten Shillings.

I request you will pay the same into the Bank of Australia to my Credit as Commissioner to the A. A. Company, and that you will settle with Mr Corlette for the Amount of the freight in that Vessel.

Notice

Conveyance from Sydney being required for about 260 Bales of Wool belonging to the A. A. Company, Persons desirous of contracting for the same or for any part thereof are requested to address Tenders to me for that purpose, on or before the 30th day of November next.

The Wool will be ready to ship between the 1st of December & the 15th of January.

W. E. Parry, Commissioner for the A. A. Company
Port Stephens
21st October 1833

| *Sydney Gazette* *Sydney Herald* *Sydney Monitor* *Australian* | Two insertions each |

Letter No. 996

Port Stephens
21st October 1833

Dr Mitchell
General Hospital – Sydney

Sir,
    I have the Honor to enclose to you the case of the Prisoner of the Crown named in the Margin an Assigned Servant of the A. A. Company whom I request you will receive into the General Hospital. I beg, however, to draw your attention to Mr Stacy's opinion that this Man's disease is feigned, which from various circumstances, I am also inclined to believe.
    Mr George Bunn George St – Sydney, will receive him when you think proper to discharge him from Hospital.

Isaac Lyons,
Adamant, Life

Letter No. 997

Port Stephens
21st October 1833

Messrs George Bunn & Co.
Sydney

Gentlemen,
    I enclose to you a Requisition for Supplies which I request you will forward by return of the *Lambton*.
    With reference to my letter addressed to you on the 4th September, on the subject of the Damage done to the Company's Goods ex *Richard Reynolds*, I request you will inform me what steps you have taken respecting the Bale of Canvas No. 827, not yet received at Port Stephens, and which I understand from Captain Corlette, to have been seriously damaged on board that ship.

Letter No. 998

Port Stephens
21st October 1833

Honorable Colonial Secretary

Sir,
  In reply to your letter of the 20th ultimo I have the Honor to acquaint you that the Description therein contained of the Two Thousand Acres of Land intended to be granted to the A. A. Company at Newcastle has been certified by Mr Dangar to be correct; and with reference to the Portion of which the Surface Right is intended to be relinquished on the part of the Company, in consideration of receiving, in lieu thereof, certain Town Allotments, I now have the Honor to enclose a Copy of a Description thereof just received from Mr Dangar, by which it would appear that neither the Description formerly given by that Gentleman, nor that given by the Government Surveyor, turns out to be correct, the real extent being 87 Acres. Mr Dangar acquaints me that he has no doubt of Mr White's readiness to correct the former Error made in the Description of this Portion of Land.

Letter No. 999

Port Stephens
31st October 1833

Thomas Simes
Carrington

Thomas Simes
  The Australian Agricultural Company having no further occasion for your Services, I now give you notice of the same, and I will direct Three Months' Salary to be paid to you from this date, according to the terms of your Agreement with the Company.

Letter No. 1,000

Port Stephens
4th November 1833

John Armstrong Esq.
Surveyor
Hunter Street
Sydney

Sir,
  With reference to your two Communications addressed to me on the 5th and 28th ultimo respectively, I beg leave to acquaint you that it will not be in my power, on the part of the Australian Agricultural Company, to accept any

terms for the Services therein alluded to, except for some specific Sum of Money for the entire completion of the whole business.

Having, however, taken into consideration the several tenders made to me on this occasion, I am now induced to propose for your acceptance the following Conditions:

1st You are to proceed to Port Stephens to receive my Instructions, so soon as I may require you to do so; the time of which will depend in great measure on the arrangements of His Majesty's Government, and on the movements of the Government Surveyor appointed to accompany you, with whom you will previously be in communication at Sydney. Condition

2d You are to proceed from Port Stephens, via Maitland, to Liverpool Plains &c, having the entire charge of the men, horses, cattle and all other property belonging to the Company employed in this service, from the time the party leaves Port Stephens till its return there. You are to be responsible, so far as in you lies, for the preservation and economical use of all the property thus committed to your charge, and, on your return, to deliver to the Company's Commissioner a proper account of the same. Condition

3d The Service to be performed by you will consist in your accompanying the Government Surveyor in the final delineation and accurate marking of the Two Locations selected by me for the Australian Agricultural Company, as exhibited in Mr Dangar's Maps; one of these being situated or bordering upon Liverpool Plains, commencing near 'Warrah'; the other in the vicinity of Peel's River. In performing this Service, you will as the Company's Surveyor, be required to see that strict justice be done to their interests in every respect, and that the marking of all the Boundaries be performed as permanently as possible, independently of such marks as may be usual with the Government Surveyors. You are to keep an Accurate Field Book, and a Journal containing Remarks as to the quality of the land, the situation & quantity of water, the kinds and abundance of timber, in the line of the several Boundaries, and generally as to every other particular which is of interest and importance to a Grantee in such cases. Condition

4th Within * weeks after the return of the Surveying Party to Port Stephens, you will be required to deliver to the Company's Commissioner, all the <u>Field Books, Journals, Sketches, rough Maps</u> &c &c together with a neat and correct Map (in duplicate) of each Location, such as may be framed & exhibited, for the information of the Proprietors, in the Company's Office in London; and likewise a Description (in duplicate) of each Location, such as is usually considered sufficient for legal purposes in the Granting of Lands in this Colony; such Maps & Descriptions to be certified as correct by the proper Government Authorities. Condition
* Mr Armstrong to propose the number of weeks.

5th You are likewise to undertake to communicate, either personally or in writing (as the case may be) with the Colonial Secretary, the Surveyor General, the Government Surveyor, or other Officers of His Majesty's Government, as well as with the Company's Commissioner, on every occasion when it may be requisite to do so for the full completion of this Service. And, in any case of dispute or disagreement with His Majesty's Government (which, however, is by no means likely to occur) you will be required, as Surveyor to the Company, to take your full share in the final and satisfactory settlement of any such dispute or disagreement. Condition

Condition   6th For the performance of the above-mentioned services, I beg leave to offer you the following Remuneration; payment to be made within One Month after the Fourth Condition shall have been complied with.

	£ s d
Twenty Shillings per day, for ten days, from leaving Sydney till commencing the Survey	10.0.0
Besides the above, to be allowed a Passage in the *Lambton* to Port Stephens, and Flour, Meat & Lodging while there.	
Forty Shillings per day during the Survey supposing it to occupy Ten Weeks or Sixty Working Days	120.0 0
During the Survey, to be allowed a horse, together with Flour, Meat, Tea & Sugar, and such other articles of equipment as are usual on the Company's Surveying Parties, including Instruments, Stationery &c	
Twenty Shillings per day, for ten days, after the Survey is completed	10.0.0
Besides the above, to be allowed a Passage in the *Lambton* to Sydney, with Flour, Meat & Lodging, while at Port Stephens, as before.	
Duplicate Maps & Descriptions of each of the Two Locations, @ £5 for each Map with its Description	20.0.0
For all additional trouble in communicating with His Majesty's Government, or with the Company's Commissioner, as named in the Fifth Condition	15.0.0
Total	£175.0.0.

Should the foregoing terms be acceptable to you, I request you will deliver to the Colonial Secretary the enclosed letter which is left open for your perusal; if not, you will be so good as to return it to me.

I have further to request that you will let me have your answer (by post) without delay; and should you accept the terms proposed, I beg you will inform me from time to time, when the Government Surveyor will be ready to meet you at Maitland.

It may also be necessary for you to send me a List of the Instruments and Drawing Materials you will require.

Letter No. 1,001

Port Stephens
4th November 1833

Honorable Colonial Secretary

Sir,
    With reference to the concluding part of your letter addressed to me on the 16 of September, I have authorized Mr John Armstrong, Surveyor, to

communicate with the Surveyor General relative to the final delineation, marking & description of the Two Portions of Land which I have selected for the A. A. Company at Liverpool Plains and Peel's River respectively.

I request you will be pleased to acquaint Mr Armstrong, who is the Bearer of this letter when and in what manner he is to communicate with the Surveyor General.

Letter No. 1,002

Port Stephens
4th November 1833

James Laidley Esq.
Deputy Commissary General
Sydney

Sir,

I have the Honor to acknowledge the receipt of your letter of the 26th ultimo & I return herewith the several Documents duly signed, for the payment of the Two Sums specified in the margin due to the A. A. Company.

£120.8. -
£33.1.4.¼

Letter No. 1,003

Port Stephens
5th November 1833

Honorable Colonial Secretary

Sir,

I have the honor to enclose to you herewith an Account, in Triplicate, amounting to (£46.8.-) Forty six Pounds & Eight Shillings for Coals supplied by the A. A. Company to the Department of the Master Attendant between the 1st of July and 30th of September last, together with the requisite Vouchers.

£46.8.-

I request you will be pleased to obtain the sanction of H. E. The Governor to the payment of this Amount with as little delay as possible.

Letter No. 1,004

Port Stephens
5th November 1833

James Laidley Esq.
Deputy Commissary General

Sir,
I have the honor to enclose to you herewith an Account, in Triplicate, amounting to (£203.4.-) Two Hundred & Three Pounds and Four Shillings for Coals supplied by the A. A. Company to the Commissariat Department of H. M. Colonial Government between the 1st of July & 30th of September last, together with the requisite Vouchers; and I request you will have the goodness to pay the Amount into the Bank of Australia, to my Credit as Commissioner to the Company, with as little delay as possible.

Letter No. 1,005

Port Stephens
6th November 1833

Messrs George Bunn & Company
Sydney

Gentlemen
Herewith I transmit to you a Draft on the Bank of Australia for the Sum of (£50) Fifty Pounds, No. 1919, to meet the Current Expences on account of the Australian Agricultural Company.

I also enclose to you herewith Bills on the Governors and Directors, for the sum of (£500) Five Hundred Pounds, namely
No. 301 for £250
No. 302 for £250
Being drawn, as usual, to the order of Mr Bunn, I request that Gentleman will endorse them and lodge them in the Bank of Australia to my credit as Commissioner to the Company.

With reference to your Communication of the 31st ultimo, I request you will send by the *Lambton*, when she returns to Sydney, the Bale of Canvas No. 827, with the Protest and Survey held thereon for the information of the Directors.

The Company's Books being still kept open for want of your a/c to the 30th September last, I request you will favor me with it as early as convenient.

You will oblige me by acknowledging (by post) the receipt of this Communication & its Enclosures.

[Letter No. 1,005a]

Contract for Flour

Persons desirous of supplying the Servants of the Australian Agricultural Company at Warrah Liverpool Plains with Flour for Eleven Months, from the 1st February 1834 are requested to address Tenders to me, under cover, to Mr Henderson, Newcastle on or before the 1st of January next.

The following quantities of Flour to be delivered Quarterly at the Company's Station at Warrah – vizt

(350) Three Hundred and fifty Pounds of good First Flour, and

(5,000) Five Thousand pounds of Good Seconds Flour.

On the 1st February – 1st May – 1st August – and 1st November respectively.

But in the event of any slight variation in the quantity required, fourteen days notice of the same will be given to the Contractor, prior to the intended delivery.

Tenders to specify in words, the price per One Hundred Pounds, at which the Flour will be delivered at the Company's Station.

No Tender will be accepted for less than the whole Quantity required nor unless it be delivered at Warrah.

Payment will be made in Cash or by Drafts of the Company upon the Bank of Australia as soon as an Account made out & certified in such form as the Company may prescribe, shall be presented to me.

The Contractor will be required to give Security for the due performance of his Contract.

W. E. Parry Commissioner to the A. A. Company
Port Stephens
11th November 1833

Letter No. 1,006

Port Stephens
11th November 1833

Messrs George Bunn & Company
Sydney

Gentlemen

In reply to your Letter of the 31st ultimo, I beg leave to acquaint you that I accept your Tender for receiving on board the Ship *Lochiel* at Newcastle, to be conveyed to London, the Wool belonging to the Australian Agricultural Company. The wool to be received on board between the present time and the 15th January, on which latter day, or before it, the ship is to sail for England. The rate of freight to be three half pence, and five per cent primage.

I have desired Captain Corlette, who is just sailing for Newcastle, to enquire when the *Lochiel* will be ready to receive the Company's Wool, of which above 100 Bales will be ready for shipment before the close of this month. I request you will inform me (by post) on what day the *Lochiel* is bona fide intended to leave Newcastle.

I request you will have the four enclosed Letters delivered, to the Editors of the respective Newspapers.

Letter No. 1,007

**Port Stephens
11th November 1833**

**Messrs Lamb Buchanan & Co.
Sydney**

Gentlemen,

In reply to your letter of the 24th ultimo, offering to receive the Wool belonging to the A. A. Company on board the *Royal Admiral* or the Funchal, for conveyance to England,

I beg to acquaint you that I regret not being able to accept your offer, having received & accepted a lower Tender for the same.

[Letter No. 1,007a]

**Port Stephens
12th November 1833**

1 copy sent to Charles Taggart - Mr Onus' Overseer of Cattle	
1 copy sent to Nicholas Connelly - Mr Pringle's Overseer of Cattle	By Mr C. Hall in December 1833
1 copy sent to Mr William Taylor, Overseer of Sheep and Cattle	

To the name of the Stockkeeper or Agent.

The Local Government having been directed to put me into immediate possession of the land, now occupied by the Stock in your charge, which land is granted to the Australian Agricultural Company,

I request you will, with as little delay as possible, remove the Stock in your charge, the Station being required immediately for the Company's Sheep.

Letter No. 1,008

Port Stephens
2nd November 1833

Henry Dangar Esq.
Neotsfield – Hunters River

Sir,
 I have to acknowledge the receipt of your letter of the 25th ultimo, declining to accept the Terms I had proposed to you for the final delineation & marking of the Two Grants of the A. A. Company at Liverpool Plains and Peel's River, without the addition of certain other Sums contingent on circumstances therein named.
 I beg leave to acquaint you that, being unable to accede to these additional payments, I regret that it will be out of my power to avail myself of your Services on this occasion, and that I have therefore accepted the Tender of another Surveyor.

Letter No. 1,009

Port Stephens
13th November 1833

W. H. Mackenzie Esq.
Accountant
Bank of Australia

Sir,
 I herewith enclose to you Mr Croasdill's Draft on the Bank of Australia (No. 124) for the Sum of (£80) Eighty Pounds, endorsed to your Order. I request you will place it to my credit at the Bank, as Commissioner for the A. A. Company.

Letter No. 1,010

Port Stephens
13th November 1833

Messrs George Bunn & Company
Sydney

Gentlemen
 I beg leave to transmit to you herewith Fifteen [sic] Letters to Colonial Proprietors of Stock in the A. A. Company, containing the Annual Report of the Directors. I request you will cause these to be delivered, when it can conveniently be done without expence.
 I also request you will cause the other letters herewith to be delivered without delay.

For the names
[see Letter 950]

Letter No. 1,011

Port Stephens
21st November 1833

Rev. C. P. N. Wilton M. A.
Newcastle

Sir,

<small>Henry Williams, *Marquis of Huntley*. Life</small>

The Prisoner of the Crown named in the margin, an Assigned Servant of the A. A. Company is desirous of marrying Lydia Quay, *Rosslyn Castle*, 7 years, an Assigned Servant of J. E. Stacy Esq. the Company's Surgeon at this place. Being desirous of promoting Matrimony among the well-conducted Prisoners, I beg leave to inform you that Williams is now in the receipt of a Gratuity of £25 per Annum, and, if his conduct continues good, I see no reason to doubt his still enjoying this advantage till he receives the indulgence of a Ticket of Leave, to which, under the Regulations, he will be entitled in less than twelvemonths. Lydia Quay will, I believe, be free in about the same time. She is an excellent Sempstress, and could easily, by her own exertions, support a family.

Annexed is Mr Stacy's Certificate that he has no objection to Lydia Quay's marrying; and I request you will be so good as to take the necessary steps for obtaining the consent of His Excellency the Governor, under the circumstances above detailed.

I certify that I have no objection to the marriage of Lydia Quay, my Assigned Servant, as requested in the above letter from Sir Edward Parry (Signed) "J. E. Stacy".

> **ORIGINAL CORRESPONDENCE.**
>
> *To the Editors of the Sydney Herald.*
>
> GENTLEMEN,—A statement having lately appeared in the *Australian* Newspaper, which has since been copied into the *Sydney Monitor*, imputing to the servants of the Australian Agricultural Company, under my control, the commission of certain barbarities towards the Aboriginal Natives upon the Company's estate; I request you will give publicity to this my assurance that the imputation is wholly unfounded.
>
> The circumstances which have given rise to this calumny, have long since been laid before the Government, to whom the Company's servants, as well as the Bench of Magistrates at this place, confidently look for that redress and explanation which an aspersion of this nature demands.
>
> It would, therefore, be improper at present to publish the documents relating to the transactions alluded to; but it will become my duty to expose at the proper time, and in the right quarter, the propagator and abettors of this foul and injurious slander.
>
> I am, Gentlemen,
> Your obedient Servant,
> W. E. PARRY.
>
> Port Stephens,
> November 21, 1833.

Illustration 6:
Sydney Herald,
2 December 1833
(Letter No. 1,011a)

[Letter No. 1,011a]

To the Editors of the
Australian
Sydney Monitor
Sydney Gazette
& Sydney Herald

Port Stephens 21st November 1833

Gentlemen (or Sir)

A Statement having lately appeared in the *Australian* Newspaper which has since been copied into the *Sydney Monitor*, imputing to the Servants of the Australian Agricultural Company under my Control the commission of certain barbarities towards the Aboriginal Natives upon the Company's Estate, I request you will give publicity to this my assurance that the imputation is wholly unfounded.

The circumstances which have given rise to this Calumny, have long since been laid before the Government; to whom the Company's Servants, as well as the Bench of Magistrates at this place, confidently look for that redress and explanation which an aspersion of this nature demands.

It would, therefore, be improper, at present, to publish the documents relating to the transactions alluded to; but it will become my duty to expose, at the proper time & in the right quarter, the propagator and abettors of this foul and injurious slander.

Letter No. 1,012

Port Stephens
21st November 1833

The Honorable Colonial Secretary
&c &c &c

Sir,

I have the Honor to acknowledge the receipt of your Letter of the 15th instant; and I beg to acquaint you in reply that I have given directions for any Runaways from Port Macquarie which may come to Baker's Station on the Estate of the Australian Agricultural Company to be retained there, if possible, until the arrival of the Constable from Mr Wynter's.

But I beg to add that, as Runaways may often arrive at that Station when none but the Company's Hut Keeper is on the spot, I fear it will seldom be practicable to retain them till the arrival of the Constable.

Letter No 1,013

Port Stephens
21st November 1833

Honorable Colonial Secretary

Sir,
 With reference to your Letter of the 3d ultimo addressed to Captain Moffatt the Resident Magistrate relative to certain transactions said to have taken place between the Servants of the A. A. Company and the Black Natives in this District, and to the Depositions on the subject taken in consequence of that letter, since transmitted to you by Captain Moffatt,
 We request that, as the circumstances alluded to, have been misrepresented through the medium of the Colonial Newspapers, His Excellency the Governor will be pleased to adopt such proceedings as he may think best, with a view to disabuse the Public mind, with respect to the calumnies alluded to, and to relieve the Magistrates and Company's Servants from a charge of so serious & painful a nature.

We are &c &c &c
W. E. Parry J. P.
R. G. Moffatt J. P.
J. E. Ebsworth J. P.

Letter No. 1,014

Port Stephens
25th November 1833

Messrs George Bunn & Co.
Sydney

Gentlemen,
 Herewith I beg leave to transmit to you a Memorandum from Mr Ebsworth with reference to your Account Current to which I request your attention and remain

Letter No. 1,015

Port Stephens
26th November 1833

Colonial Secretary

Sir,
 I have the Honor to acknowledge the receipt of your Letter of the 23d instant calling upon me, by Command of His Excellency the Governor to

provide a Fund for the purposes of Religion & Education, as mentioned in the Secretary of State's Despatch dated the 21st of April 1830, for the benefit of that portion of the A. A. Company's Original Selection of Land to be retained by them at Port Stephens.

In reply, I do myself the Honor to remark that the Secretary of State's Despatch above alluded to, contains, in addition to the Terms to which His Excellency refers, the following very important Agreement:

"In order to enable the Company the better to make all or any of the before mentioned provisions, I have agreed to allow, that the Company shall take the Reserve already allotted for Ecclesiastical purposes at Port Stephens, or such a part of it, as shall be proportioned to the quantity of their old allotment which they may retain & a proportionate quantity of Land adjoining the second and third Locations for the same purpose, in all not exceeding the present Reserve, on a Lease for 99 years, determinable at the option of H. M. Government at the end of any 21 years of that period, upon giving two years notice to the Secretary of the Company in London. This Lease is to be executed in behalf of the Company, by their Corporate Seal" &c &c

As the Lease of these Lands has not been made to the Company this Circumstance alone might be sufficient to justify my declining to provide the funds now called for. But, I beg leave to repeat what I had the Honor of stating to the Governor at a Conference with which His Excellency favored me at Parramatta, that the Agreement under which these funds were to be provided by the Company, was totally annulled by the late change in the System of disposing of Crown Lands in this Colony. The decision to this effect on the part of H. M. Government was communicated by Lord Howick to the Directors of the A. A. Company on the 5th of March 1831, in the following terms:

"That the Commissioners for Enquiry into the Revenues and Expenditure of New South Wales had presented to the House of Commons a Report recommending an abandonment of the System of retaining any Lands in that Colony under the Description of 'Clergy & School Reserves'; and that in accordance with such recommendation, H. M. Government had determined no longer to retain such Lands, but to put them up to sale in the same manner as other Lands were to be sold, under the arrangements lately made in respect of the disposal of Lands in New South Wales.

The Agreement, therefore, which had been entered into with the A. A. Company to grant to them a Lease, for 99 years, of the Clergy & School Reserves, in consideration of their contributing certain Sums for the support of one or more Clergymen, <u>could not be fulfilled</u>. No such Lease could be granted, and on the other hand the Company could not be called on for the proposed Contribution of Money".

Letter No. 1,016

Port Stephens
27th November 1833

James Laidley Esq.
Deputy Commissary General
Sydney

Sir,
   The Honorable Colonial Secretary having informed me, by letter dated the 19th instant, that His Excellency the Governor has been pleased to approve of the same rate being paid for passage &c in the *Lambton*, on Government account, as that which is paid by contract to and from Newcastle, and that you have received Instructions to communicate with me, in order that I may be apprised of the Accounts and Vouchers which it will be necessary to render to you,
   I do myself the Honor to request that you will give me this information as soon as possible, and also that you will be good enough to inform me of the rate for freight & passage which the Government contract to pay to & from Newcastle.

Letter No. 1,017

Port Stephens
27th November 1833

Simon Dodd Esq.

Sir,
   I beg leave to acknowledge the receipt of your letter of the 13th instant & at the same time to assure you that my delaying to write to you, according to my promise, had not arisen from any neglect, but from the difficulty under which I found myself of giving you any employment. The fact is, that, as the Bricks have scarcely been commenced making, with which the Salt House is to be erected, I do not see that the Company has, <u>as yet</u> any occasion for the Services of a gentleman possessing your qualifications. Nor, indeed, shall I feel myself at liberty to engage any person permanently in the capacity you mention.
   I think it very probable however, that I may require advice, as to locality &c, whenever the erection of the Buildings &c is about to commence. Perhaps, therefore, you will be so good as to inform me on what terms you would (if unemployed) make it convenient, some few weeks hence, to meet me by previous appointment, at Newcastle, & to remain there with me for two or three days, for the purpose above-mentioned.

Letter No. 1,018

Port Stephens
28th November 1833

James Laidley Esq.
Deputy Commissary General
Sydney

Sir,
 I have the Honor to acknowledge the receipt of your Letter of the 19th instant, enclosing Cash Vouchers, for my Signature, for the Sum of £203.4.0, due to the Australian Agricultural Company for Coals.
 And I now beg leave to return the Vouchers, duly signed.

Letter No. 1,019

Port Stephens
29th November 1833

James Laidley Esq.
Deputy Commissary General, Sydney

Sir,
 In reply to your Letter of the 19th instant I beg leave to acquaint you that I deferred offering a Tender for the Supply of Provisions to the Military Detachment at Port Stephens for the ensuing year in consequence of an intimation from the Government that the Detachment was about to be withdrawn.
 But in the event of their remaining at Port Stephens, I am willing on the part of the A. A. Company to furnish the Supplies at the undermentioned prices, vizt
 Flour at (3^d) Three pence per lb
 Beef at ($2¼^d$) Two pence farthing per lb

Letter No. 1,020

Port Stephens
3rd December 1833

Mr John Smith
Newcastle

Sir,
 In reply to your letter of the 27th ultimo, I regret that it is not in my power to furnish you with a Baker & Butcher in exchange for other men, as there are not, in the Company's Service, any persons of those Trades who can be spared. Indeed, I am just about to apply for a Butcher, in the room of a man expecting a Ticket of Leave.

Letter No. 1,021

Port Stephens
5th December 1833

Colonial Secretary

Sir,

Agreeably to your request contained in your Communication of the 2d instant, I have the Honor to transmit to you herewith a Duplicate of my letter addressed to the Secretary of State on the 12th of September 1833.

Letter No. 1,022

Port Stephens
5th December 1833

S. A. Perry Esq.
Deputy Surveyor General

Sir,

In reply to your letter of the 28th ultimo, I do myself the honor to enclose to you herewith a Map of the A. A. Company's Original Selection of Land, on which the Portion now to be retained by the Company is marked out, with reference to the accompanying Extract from my Memorandum addressed to the Local Government on the 21st February 1831 and approved of by H. E. General Darling.

Letter No. 1,023

Port Stephens
6th December 1833

Henry Dangar Esq.
Neotsfield

Sir,

Should you not have sent the A. A. Company's Theodolite to Newcastle; when this reaches you, I request you will be so good as to deliver it to Mr Armstrong or his order.

Letter No. 1,024

Port Stephens
9th December 1833

John Armstrong Esq.
Surveyor

Sir,
    The Party intended to be placed under your command for the final delineation & marking of the A. A. Company's Two Locations beyond the Liverpool Range being now ready, I request you will proceed on that service, according to the terms contained in my Letter addressed to you on the 4th ultimo, to which you have acceded.

    Having pointed out to you in that communication, the duties which you are required to perform, it will be unnecessary for me to repeat what I have there said –especially as our personal communication has afforded me an opportunity of explaining to you in detail my views & wishes in the whole of this important subject.

    I now place in your hands the Several Maps & other documents in my possession (as per annexed List) which may assist you in performing this service. These documents I request you will return to me whenever the Service may have been completed.

    In the marking of those Portions of the Boundary lines which occasionally cross Liverpool Plains, there will be some difficulty in making a continuous line of marks, owing to the entire absence of Trees upon the Plain land. You will easily perceive that this circumstance renders it necessary that the marks on the Trees upon the Forest land should be the more numerous and permanent, & especially at the several points where the forest and plain unite. At these points, & at every corner or angle I request that the Letters A^{Co}A be marked on several Trees in a distinct and durable manner. The places where these marks occur, with the kind of Trees, and size & aspect of the letters should be carefully noted in every case.

    If you should find it practicable also to erect, <u>upon</u> the plain land, one or two durable posts, having the same mark, in each of the intervals between the respective portions of Forest land, it would tend materially to make the line more defined and complete.

    It is necessary for me to inform you that the whole quantity of land to which the Company is entitled in these Two Locations, is 542,080 Acres; of which the Green shaded Parallelogram near 'Warrah' amounts to 249,600 Acres. The Remainder, amounting to 292,480 Acres is intended to be taken at the Peels' River Location, in the exact form delineated & described by Mr Dangar in his Map which you copied in the Surveyor General's Office. But should it happen that the Area included between these Boundaries appear on the completion of the intended Survey by yourself & Mr Ralfe, to differ in some degree from that made by Messrs White & Dangar, I should propose that the difference be adjusted in the position of the East & West Line forming the Southern Boundary of that Location. It is of course important that the remarkable Hill called 'Durii' should still be continued as the

Southern Point of the Western Boundary Line, being a natural feature which cannot be mistaken in future.

In the course of this service, I request you will occasionally communicate to me your progress, addressing your Letters to the Care of Mr Henderson at Newcastle, and sending them by a Black to Captain Dumaresq's Estate at St Aubyns. The accompanying Letter will introduce you to Colonel Dumaresq, who, as well as William Telfer at Warrah, to whom I have likewise written, will be glad to render you every possible assistance.

List of Documents
Mr Dangar's Original Rough General Map of both Locations & intermediate Space.
Mr Dangar's Fair Map of the Country included between Peel's River & the Dividing Range, with section lines drawn.
Nineteen Sheets of Mr Dangar's Plotting of the foregoing – on a large scale.

Letter No. 1,025

Port Stephens
9th December 1833

William Telfer
Warrah

William Telfer,
Mr Armstrong being about to Survey the Company's Lands, I request you will give him every assistance in your power, receiving into your Store any articles he may wish to deposit there, and also taking charge of any provisions he may have to spare when his Survey is completed.

Mr Armstrong will require the Services of an intelligent Black, to accompany him, & to point out the best roads &c.

Letter No. 1,026

Port Stephens
9th December 1833

Henry Dangar Esq.
Neotsfield

Sir,
I have to acknowledge the receipt of your letter of the 1st instant reminding me of a probable Error in your survey of the Location selected for the A. A. Company near Peel's River arising from some irregular magnetic attraction occurring on the Range of Hills in that neighbourhood.

I beg leave to thank you for this notice, which I have communicated to the Surveyor employed by the Company to complete the Survey.

[Letter No. 1,026a]

Blacksmith wanted

Wanted immediately for the A. A. Company's Colliery at Newcastle, a Blacksmith of sober and industrious habits, capable of forging the various parts of a Steam Engine, repairing the Boilers, and performing the Smith's work of the Establishment generally.

Applications to be made, by post, to me at Port Stephens, or to Mr Henderson at Newcastle, stating the Terms. The most unexceptionable Testimonials will be required, especially as to sobriety.

W. E. Parry Commissioner for the A. A. Company
Port Stephens
9 December 1833

Sydney Gazette *Sydney Monitor* *Sydney Herald* *Australian*	Two insertions each

Letter No. 1,027

Port Stephens
9th December 1833

Board for Assignment of Servants

Gentlemen,

In conformity with the Regulations I request that one convict servant may be assigned to me of the following description:

One Blacksmith, for the Colliery Establishment of the A. A. Company at Newcastle.

I now employ 4 Free & 43 Convicts Servants at the Colliery of the Company at Newcastle.

Letter No. 1,028

Port Stephens
9th December 1833

Messrs George Bunn & Co.
Sydney

Gentlemen,

I have the pleasure to enclose to you herewith a Draft (No. 1931) on the Bank of Australia for the Sum of (£35) Thirty five Pounds, to meet the current Expenses on account of the A. A. Company.

I request you will cause the accompanying Letters to be delivered to their respective addresses as soon as convenient.

Letter No. 1,029

Port Stephens
10th December 1833

To Rev. C. P. N. Wilton M. A.
Newcastle

Sir,

I have the Honor to acknowledge the receipt of your Letter of the 5th instant, acquainting me that the Archdeacon has instructed you to visit this Settlement on Sunday the 29th instant, for the purpose of baptizing the children of some of the Residents here, in consequence, as it appears, of an application made to him to that effect; and also to "perform Divine Service, in case you should be able to obtain the use of a suitable room".

In reply I beg to acquaint you that I will take care to send horses for you to Graham's on the Friday preceding, according to your request.

The Baptism of the infants mentioned, and of any others who may be presented, can be performed at any time & place most convenient to yourself and the respective parties.

With respect to the usual Services of the Sabbath, I have no doubt that Mr Price, the Company's Chaplain, will be happy to avail himself of your assistance. I shall, therefore, communicate to him your intended visit, and leave it to yourselves to settle this matter on your arrival. I need scarcely say that any arrangement you may mutually make, will be quite agreeable to me.

Should this not meet your wishes, our usual place of worship shall be open to you between the times of our appointed Services, or the School Room at any other hour you may wish.

In regard to the Sacrament of the Lord's Supper, Sunday the 29th instant does not happen to be one of the days appointed for its administration at Carrington.

Having thus endeavoured to make such arrangements as may afford you every facility in my power, I cannot help remarking upon the want of courtesy towards myself which appears in the Archdeacon's Instructions to you on this occasion. I cannot consider it right that the Archdeacon should have ordered you to make a visit of this nature to a private Estate, of which I am the virtual Proprietor, without having first consulted me as to the arrangements requisite for this purpose, or even acquainting me with his intention. I feel especial pain in perusing that part of the Instructions which relate to your performance of Divine Service; because the Archdeacon is aware that provision is already made for the due & regular performance of Public Worship at this Settlement, and, therefore, that you cannot fulfil this part of his Instructions without a probability at least of direct interference with my arrangements.

I trust that I have ever been desirous of doing my utmost to promote the spiritual welfare of the people under my control, as well as to facilitate the visits of those Ministers of Christ, who have from time to time been permitted to come among us. But it could scarcely be deemed inconsistent with Christian Charity, if I were to protest against Instructions so arbitrary as those under which you are now about to act; the fulfilment of which without my consent amounts to little, if any thing, less than a trespass.

I beg leave to offer you my acknowledgments for your kindness in communicating to me the proposed arrangement, of which I should otherwise have been ignorant, and I have the Honor to remain, Sir…

Letter No. 1,030

Port Stephens
12th December 1833

Rev. Samuel Marsden
Parramatta

Sir,

The Sum of £26.10.11 having been paid into the Bank of Australia by 'S. Marsden' on the 4th of October, to the credit of the A. A. Company,

I request you will do me the favor to inform me whether this payment was made by you, and if so, on what account; to enable me to make the proper Entry of the same in the Company's Books.

Letter No. 1,031

Port Stephens
13th December 1833

Messrs George Bunn & Company
Sydney

Gentlemen,

I beg leave to transmit to you herewith Two parcels, containing Letters & Newspapers, which you will oblige me by having delivered to their respective addresses.

Mr Ebsworth requests I will ask you for a reply to that part of his Memorandum requiring particulars of the Items upon which you have charged commission for payments.

I request you will be so good as to inform me when a Ship is next expected to sail for England.

You will also be pleased to forward by the first Steamer after the receipt of this letter, One Ton of Fine Flour for the Port Stephens Establishment, addressed to Mr William Croasdill at Newcastle. Twenty 2 Bushel Bags are sent by this opportunity to contain the same.

Letter No. 1,032

Port Stephens
16th December 1833

John Kendrick

In reply to your letter of the 29th ultimo, I have to inform you that the Australian Agricultural Company can sell you a poney [sic] or horse, from the price of £8 upwards, deliverable at Mr Graham's Farm; and that I am willing to receive good Wheat in exchange, delivered at Mr Platt's Mill, if we can agree about the price.

Letter No. 1,033

Port Stephens
16th December 1833

W. H. Mackenzie Esq.
Accountant
Bank of Australia

Sir,
Herewith I beg to enclose to you a Draft No. 1933 on the Bank of Australia for the Sum of (£27.6.-) Twenty Seven Pounds & Six Shillings endorsed to your order, which I request you will place to the Credit of Lieutenant Colonel Dumaresq's Account.

Letter No. 1,034

Port Stephens
16th December 1833

James Raymond Esq.

Sir,
I request you will be so good as to forward to my address Four Copies of the N. S. Wales Directory as soon as it is published on account of the A. A. Company.

Letter No. 1,035

Stroud
Port Stephens
16th December 1833

Bench of Magistrates District of Williams River

Gentlemen,
Understanding that a question has arisen, as to the utility of establishing a Pound in the neighbourhood of the Williams River, I beg leave to acquaint you that such a measure would greatly promote the interests of the A. A. Company, who are suffering very much from Trespasses on that portion of their Estate which lies in that direction.

It is indeed, of so much importance to the Company that a convenient Pound should be established that I should have been glad to erect one upon their Estate, but that I have no authority to alienate a portion of land for that purpose.

Letter No. 1,036

Port Stephens
16th December 1833

William Croasdill Esq.
Newcastle

Sir,
In reply to your Letter of the 9th current, I now enclose to you two Drafts on the Bank of Australia namely,
No. 1934 – to the Order of James Steel – for £30.0.0
No. 1935 – to the Order of James Steel – for £10.8.0
the former being on Account of Steel's Salary for the quarter about to end the 31st December, according to his request; and the latter, the Balance of Wages due to the late Michael Steel.

With respect to the request made by Steel that the Company should bear a part of the expences attendant on the decease of his Son, I beg you will inform him, that, altho' I sincerely sympathize with him and his family in this afflictive dispensation, and should be happy personally to render him any assistance, it is quite out of my power to comply with his request, as his Agreement was drawn up expressly with a view to avoid any contingent expence to the Company, in addition to the allowances specified therein.

[Letter No. 1,036a]

<u>Notice</u>

Notice is hereby given, especially to those Persons who have lately been cutting Timber, and depasturing their Cattle, on that part of the Australian Agricultural Company's Estate which is adjacent to the late 'Clergy and School Estate' near Williams' River, that I have authorized an Agent to impound all Cattle thus trespassing, and to prevent the removal of any Timber from the Company's Estate.

Port Stephens
17th December 1833
W. E. Parry, Commissioner for the A. A. Company

Sydney Gazette	
Sydney Monitor	Two insertions each
Sydney Herald	
Australian	

Letter No. 1,037

Port Stephens
18th December 1833

W. H. Mackenzie Esq.
Accountant. Bank of Australia

Sir,
   Herewith I beg leave to enclose to you Mr W. Croasdill's Draft (No. 126) on the Bank of Australia, endorsed to your order for the Sum of (£111.9.-) One Hundred & Eleven Pounds & Nine Shillings, which I request you will place to the credit of the A. A. Company.

Letter No. 1,038

Port Stephens
18th December 1833

Adam Howitt
Blacksmith – Sydney

Adam Howitt,
   In reply to your letter of the 13th instant, offering your services as Blacksmith at the Colliery of the A. A. Company at Newcastle, I regret that it will not be in my power to accept your offer.

Letter No. 1,039

Port Stephens
19th December 1833

George Mackenzie Esq. J. P.
Williams River

Sir,
 In reply to your letter of this day's date I beg leave to acquaint you that I have no objection to your drays passing thro' the Estate of the A. A. Company to your Sheep Stations on the upper branches of the River Gloucester, for the reasons mentioned in your Communication

---

Letter No. 1,040

Port Stephens
24th December 1833

Rev. C. P. N. Wilton M. A.
&c &c &c

Sir,
 I beg leave to acknowledge the receipt of your letter of the 15th instant, in which you decline taking a part in the performance of Divine Service at Carrington on Sunday next, in conjunction with Mr Price the Company's Chaplain, but express your wish to make use of the Company's School Room for that purpose.
 On further consideration of the mischievous disunion likely to arise, in a Small Community like this, from your fulfilment of that part of your Instructions, while at the same time the appointed Minister is conducting Public Worship in a neighbouring Building, I am of opinion that the cause of Religion will be better served & the mischief in part avoided by Mr Price taking the Sabbath duties at Stroud on that day. Under this impression, I have requested Mr Price to do so; and you are therefore, at liberty to perform Divine Service in the usual place of Worship at Carrington. I have directed Mr White in my absence, to attend to your wishes, and to give you every accommodation you may require.
 In thus sacrificing to a sense of Christian duty all personal feeling occasioned by the discourtesy practised towards myself, I request that you will be so good as to intimate to the Authorities under whom you act, that I cannot in future permit any arrangement to be made for the performance of Divine Service on this Estate, without my previous consent.

Letter No. 1,041

Port Stephens
30th December 1833

James Norton Esq. Solicitor
Sydney

Sir,
In the Month of May 1830, the Sum of £49.13 (Forty nine Pounds & Thirteen Shillings) was lodged in the hands of the Sheriff, pending the decision of a Claim made by Mr G. M. Slade on Mr James Edward Ebsworth, as Acting Principal Agent of the A. A. Company.

The Question has since been decided by the Supreme Court in favor of the Company, but the Cash not having been refunded, I request you will be so good as to communicate on the subject with Mr Kieth, who was employed by Mr Ebsworth on that occasion, & cause the Amount due to the Company to be placed to my Credit in the Bank of Australia as Commissioner to the Company.

Letter No. 1,042

Port Stephens
30th December 1833

Honorable Colonial Secretary

Sir,
I do myself the honor to acknowledge the receipt of your letter of the 6th instant conveying to me, by direction of H. E. The Governor, the Attorney General's Opinion that the Scabby Sheep Act does not extend to the lands of the A. A. Company at 'Warrah' Liverpool Plains.

As the operation of this Act is perhaps of more importance to the Company's interests on those lands than any other, Sheep being their principal Stock now depastured there, & the number of Scabby Sheep of other Proprietors, constantly increasing in that neighbourhood, I beg you will convey to H. E. my respectful request that he will be pleased to adopt measures for extending the operation of the Act to the Lands in question as soon as may be conveniently practicable – or, if it be not in the Governor's power to do so till the Meeting of the Legislative Council, that he will then be pleased to propose such alteration in the Act as may answer the desired purpose.

Letter No. 1,043

Port Stephens
30th December 1833

Honorable Colonial Secretary

Sir,
    I do myself the honor to acknowledge the receipt of your letter of the 2nd instant on the subject of the arrangements proposed to be made for a Police Establishment at Port Stephens.
    In reply I beg leave to acquaint you that I am ready to provide the intended Free Police Clerk with Lodging, tho' it will of necessity be an unfurnished one.
    With respect to Rations for the Clerk, I would observe that in the original proposal which I made to the Government the cost of a Prisoner to perform the duties of that office was estimated thus - £9 per Annum for his Rations &c & the remaining £10 per Annum paid in money as a Gratuity to encourage good behaviour. I beg leave, therefore, to express my readiness to contribute, on the part of the Company (and in addition to the lodging) the same amount per Annum for the support of the Free Clerk, either in Money or Provisions, or in any other way which His Excellency may desire.
    I request you will convey to the Governor my respectful acknowledgments for H. E's consideration in not removing for the present the Detachment of Infantry now stationed at Port Stephens.
    As soon as I am favored with the List of Stationery, Arms, Ammunition, Handcuffs &c which His Excellency considers necessary for a year, & which are to be furnished by the Company, I will make every requisite arrangement for providing the same.

Letter No. 1,044

Port Stephens
30th December 1833

Honorable Colonial Secretary

Sir,
    With reference to the arrangement which H. E. The Governor has been pleased to approve relative to the payment for the Passage & Freight in the A. A. Company's Cutter *Lambton* on account of Government I beg leave to acquaint you that I have received from the Deputy Commissary General the information he was desired to give on this subject, <u>so far as relates to the Departments under his Control.</u>
    But, as Mr Laidley informs me that, "the Passages of Free Persons or Convicts belonging to the Surveyor General's Department, or other Colonial Establishments, are not defrayed by the Commissariat", I request you will be pleased to let me know, by way of completing my information on this subject, upon what form of Requisition I am to furnish Passages & Freight

to persons of this description; what is the Contract price for the same; how often & to whom the Account is to be rendered, & accompanied by what Vouchers. I presume that the Resident Magistrate will be the Person to make the Requisition.

Letter No. 1,045

Port Stephens
30th December 1833

James Laidley Esq.
Deputy Commissary General

Sir,
    I have the Honor to acknowledge the receipt of your letter of the 6th instant enclosing Forms for Vouchers for the providing of Passage & Freight in the A. A. Company's Cutter *Lambton* to persons in your Department.
    I request that, in order to complete my information on this subject, you will inform me whether it will be convenient to you for the Company to render their Accounts for the same <u>Monthly</u>, as I understand to be the custom with other Contractors, and also whether any particular <u>form</u> of Account be required.

Letter No. 1,046

Port Stephens
30th December 1833

Honorable Colonial Secretary
&c &c &c

Sir,
    I have the Honor to acknowledge the receipt of your Two Circulars (Nos 33/53 & 33/54) of the 25th ultimo which, however, I did not receive till the 17th instant which will account for my not replying to them sooner.
    I now beg leave to enclose a Tabular * Return of the Quantity of Land in Cultivation & an Estimate of the Produce thereof on the Estate of the A. A. Company.

* see <u>below</u>

-oOo-

On the Estate of the Australian Agricultural Company; with an Estimate of the Produce for Season 1833-4.

TABLE 2 1833-34

Acres	CROP							
	Wheat	Barley	Oats	Pease	Maize	Tobacco	Turnips	Artificial Grasses
	Acres	Acres	Acres	Acres	Acres	Acres	Acres	Acres
No 1 Farm								32
Booral	100	4	2		26	10	6	20
Stroud	130	20			20			80
Gloster					87			
Total	230	24	2		133	10	6	132

PRODUCE								
Wheat	Barley	Oats	Pease	Maize	Tobacco	Turnips	Artificial Grasses	Land In Fallow
Bushels	Bushels	Bushels	Bushels	Bushels	Tons	Tons	30 Tons Of Hay-the Remainder Used For Green Food And Grazing	Acres
3,000	80	40		650	5	60		
2,600	600			500				
				2,500				
5,600	680	40		3,650	5	60		

N.B. There are no Mines or Quarries on the Company's Estate, nor any Manufactories, Mills, or other Machinery or Works but such as are intended for private use.

The numbers in Red Ink are a very rough Estimate, a part of the Maize being just sown and the Tobacco not cut.

Port Stephens 30th December 1833
W. E. Parry Commissioner to the Australian Agricultural Company

---

Letter No. 1,047

Port Stephens
30th December 1833

John Kendrick
Hunter's River

John Kendrick,

In reply to your letter of the 17th instant, it will not be in my power to pay more than 5/- per Bushel for Wheat.

If you consent to this price, you can deliver Thirty two Bushels of good marketable quality, 60 lbs to the Bushel, to Mr Platt on account of the A. A. Company; & if he will send to Mr Croasdill at Newcastle a certificate of its delivery, (which he will do on your shewing him this letter) I will order a Pony, value £8, to be sent to Mr Graham's Farm for you.

Letter No. 1,048

Port Stephens
30th December 1833

Board for Assignment of Servants

Gentlemen,

In conformity with the Regulations, I request that two convict servants may be assigned to me of the following description:

One Miller & One Butcher

I reside at Port Stephens in the County of Gloucester. I am Commissioner for the A. A. Company and hold about 458,000 Acres of Land – about 600 Acres cleared & about 500 Acres in Tillage. I possess 345 Horses – 2,780 Head of Cattle, & 40,486 Sheep – I now employ 65 Free & Ticket of Leave – and 383 Convict Servants, of whom 188 have been in my service upwards of Three Years & 165 upwards of 1 year – no assigned servants have been returned by me to Government within the last Two Years & Two others have absconded from my service during that period without having been apprehended & returned.

letters 1834

Letter No. 1,049

Port Stephens
2nd January 1834

John McDonald Esq.
Pitt Town

Sir,
I have the Honor to acknowledge the receipt of your letter of the 16th ultimo offering to supply the Establishment of the A. A. Company at Warrah, Liverpool Plains with Flour, for Eleven Months from the 1st of February next, & in reply I beg leave to acquaint you that it will not be in my power to accept your Tender for the same.

Letter No. 1,050

Port Stephens
2nd January 1834

H. C. Sempill Esq.
Segenhoe – Hunter's River

Sir,
I have the Honor to acknowledge the receipt of your Letter of the 23d ultimo offering &c (see No. 1,049 to J. McDonald Esq.).

Letter No. 1,051

Port Stephens
2nd January 1834

Messrs George Bunn & Co.
Sydney

Gentlemen,
I herewith enclose to you Three Sets of Bills (Nos 304, 305 & 306) on the Governors & Directors of the A. A. Company, amounting in all to £500. I request Mr Bunn will be so good as to endorse the same & lodge them in the Bank of Australia to my credit as Commissioner for the Company.

I beg to draw your attention to the two enclosed Memoranda written by Mr Ebsworth & dated the 18th & 28th ultimo, relative to your Account & that of Mr Bunn with the Company.

I request you will send without fail by the *Lambton* some Castings sent for to Sydney several weeks ago, as the Company's Mill only waits for them to commence grinding – and also that you will comply with the Enclosed Requisition for Stores.

Letter No. 1,052

Port Stephens
6th January 1834

Colonial Secretary

Sir,
I have the Honor to acknowledge the receipt of your Circular of the 12th ultimo (No. 1833/57) and I beg leave to enclose herewith my Replies to the queries contained therein.

Letter No. 1,053

Port Stephens
8th January 1834

Mr John Ryan
Maitland

Sir,
I have the Honor to acknowledge the receipt of your letter of the 28th ultimo offering to supply the Establishment of the A. A. Company at Warrah, Liverpool Plains with Flour, for Eleven Months from the 1st of February next, & in reply I beg leave to acquaint you that it will not be in my power to accept your Tender for the same.

Letter No. 1,054

Port Stephens
8th January 1834

Mr William Bowen
Maitland

Sir,
I have the honor to acknowledge the receipt of your letter of the 28th ultimo offering to supply the Establishment of the A. A. Company at Warrah, Liverpool Plains with Flour, for Eleven Months from the 1st of February

next, & in reply I beg leave to acquaint you that it will not be in my power to accept your Tender for the same.

Letter No. 1,055

Port Stephens
8th January 1834

J. Eales Esq.
Hunter's River

Sir,
I have the honor to acknowledge the receipt of your letter of the 30th ultimo offering to supply the Establishment of the A. A. Company at Warrah, Liverpool Plains with Flour, for Eleven Months from the 1st of February next, & in reply I beg leave to acquaint you that it will not be in my power to accept your Tender for the same.

Letter No. 1,056

Port Stephens
8th January 1834

E. G. Cory Esq.
Gostwyck Farm – Patterson's River

Sir,
I have the Honor to acknowledge receipt of your Letter of 30th ultimo offering to supply the Establishment of the A. A. Company at Warrah, Liverpool Plains with Flour, for Eleven Months from the 1st of February next, & in reply I beg leave to acquaint you that it will not be in my power to accept your Tender for the same.

Letter No. 1,057

Port Stephens
8th January 1834

W. H. Mackenzie Esq.
Secretary and Cashier, Bank of Australia

Sir,
With reference to all former Instructions furnished to the Bank of Australia, relative to the receipt of Instalments payable on Shares in the

Joint Stock of the Australian Agricultural Company, by Proprietors resident in New South Wales and Van Diemen's Land.

I request that no further Sum be received by the Bank of Australia, on that account, from any Proprietor named in the several Lists transmitted to the Bank, with the exception of James Norton Esq., John Henderson Esq. and Messrs D. G. and T. W. Forbes respectively.

Letter No. 1,058

Port Stephens
8th January 1834

Simon Dodd Esq.
&c &c &c

Sir Edward Parry presents his compliments to Mr Dodd and, with reference to the Communication he had the pleasure of receiving from him, begs to propose that Mr Dodd should meet him at Newcastle on Tuesday the 21st instant – which, if convenient to Mr Dodd may be done by his embarking in the Steamer which leaves Sydney on Monday evening the 20th.

P. S. Sir E. Parry will be obliged by Mr Dodd's reply <u>next</u> Monday's post.

Letter No. 1,059

Port Stephens
10th January 1834

Messrs George Bunn & Company
Sydney

Gentlemen,

I beg to acquaint you that Mr Henderson informs me he has never received the 18 Bars of Iron mentioned in your Invoice of 10th September 1833, weighing 4 cwt 2 qrs 16 lbs nor did he receive any Invoice of the same. I request you will be so good as to make inquiry respecting it, as it does not appear to have been delivered from the Steamer, which was probably the conveyance by which you sent it.

Herewith you will receive a parcel addressed to Mr Norton, with some other Letters &c, which I request you will cause to be delivered as soon as convenient; some of them being of considerable importance.

A separate letter sent by post.

-oOo-

W. E. Parry. Commissioner for the A. A. Company.

    Sir Edward Parry presents his Compliments to Messrs Bunn & Company, and requests they will enquire for a Parcel sent by Steamer this day to their address.

Port Stephens
11th January 1834

Letter No. 1,060

                                                                Port Stephens
                                                              11th January 1834

Rev. S. Marsden
Parramatta

Sir,
    In reply to your letter of the 2d current I have the honor, in compliance with your request to forward your Account with the A. A. Company for the Services of their Horses.

[Letter No. 1,060a]

<u>Copy</u>

                                                                  Port Stephens
                                                              14th January 1834

Board for Assignment of Servants

Gentlemen,
    Being desirous of transferring to the A. A. Company the Two Prisoners first named in the margin (now in my Service) for the Prisoner last named, with the consent of Sir Edward Parry, I request you will be pleased to obtain H. E. the Governor's sanction for the same.

I have the Honor to be
William Cromarty

Approved
W. E. Parry Commissioner for the A. A. Company

Margin:
Thomas Matom, *Champion*, 14 Years and
James Stacey, *Asia*, 14 Years

Joshua Meares, *Baring*, Life

Letter No. 1,061

Port Stephens
15th January 1834

Captain Moffatt J. P.
&c &c &c

Sir,

I beg leave to acquaint you that, pursuant to Instructions from the Directors of the A. A. Company & in accordance with a Contract entered into with H. M. Local Government, it will not be in my power in future to convey any Goods or Passengers in the *Lambton* Cutter, free of Expense.

Passage & Freight from Port Stephens on account of H. M. Government, will be furnished on your Requisition to the Commander of the *Lambton*, according to the enclosed Forms transmitted to me by the Deputy Commissary General for this purpose. As, however, that Officer informs me that the Passages of Free Persons or Convicts belonging to the Surveyor General's Department or other Colonial Establishments are not defrayed by the Commissariat, I have applied to the Colonial Secretary to be informed in what manner & upon what form of Requisition passages are to be furnished in such cases. The Colonial Secretary's Reply shall be duly communicated to you.

With respect to Passages for Individuals on private account, the Commander of the *Lambton* is instructed to receive such persons, only by the usual order from the Company's Commissioner, or, in his absence, the Officer left in charge of their Establishment.

Goods on private account will be received on board as usual to be paid for; on delivery, at the rate charged to the Company's Servants.

Letter No. 1,062

Port Stephens
16th January 1834

Captain Moffatt J. P.
&c &c &c

Sir,

On referring to my letter addressed to you yesterday, you will, I think perceive that you have misunderstood that part which relates to Passages and Freight in the *Lambton* on account of H. M. Government. The Printed Forms were not sent, as you suppose, merely for your perusal, but as the Documents <u>appointed by the Government</u> to be used by you when Conveyance is required on their account.

I, therefore, beg leave herewith to return them (12 in number, of which one is filled up by Mr Laidley as an example) in order to prevent inconvenience to the Public Service, when any such cases occur.

Letter No. 1,063

Port Stephens
16th January 1834

J. H. Grose Esq.
Sydney

Sir,
Colonel Dumaresq & myself are desirous of making an arrangement with you, if it can be done at a moderate expence, for the conveyance of his Family & Baggage from Maitland to Port Stephens, and of my Family & Baggage from Port Stephens to Sydney, in the *Sophia Jane* about the 12th of March next.

I propose being in Sydney next week & shall feel obliged by your letting me have a line at the Pulteney Hotel, not later than the 22d instant acquainting me where I can see you, as I have also another proposal to make to you on the part of the A. A. Company.

Letter No. 1,064

Port Stephens
18th January 1834

W. H. Mackenzie Esq.
Bank of Australia
Sydney

Sir,
I enclose to you herewith 3 Sets of Bills (Nos 304, 305 & 306) upon the Governors & Directors of the A. A. Company for the Sum of (£500) Five Hundred Pounds, which, when disposed of, I request you will place to my credit at the Bank of Australia, as Commissioner for the Company.

Letter No. 1,065

Port Stephens
20th January 1834

Captain Moffatt J. P.

Sir,
I was availing myself of the first leisure moments I could command, to give consideration to the subject of your angry letter of the 15th instant when I received your no less intemperate communication of the 18th.

I am too much accustomed to your usual practice of acting under the influence of passion, even in cases which demand the coolest judgment, to be surprized at any communication of this nature from you. In the present instance, I regret principally on your own account, that you have indulged in your habitual vehemence; because it will at least delay, and may possibly altogether prevent, an adjustment of the claim you have preferred.

Had you made this representation in a reasonable temper, or in becoming terms, I should probably have been disposed at once to deviate so far from my Instructions, as to concede the point in question, as regards yourself & family individually; because on a re-perusal of the letters to which you allude, I think it does appear that, on the strength of those documents, you have some claim, tho' by no means in the shape of a "Contract" to the privilege of "free conveyance in the *Lambton* of Stores for your own private use".

As it is, I intend referring the question to the judgment of Colonial Dumaresq; & should that gentleman be of opinion that, notwithstanding any conduct of yours towards me, I am bound to maintain unconditionally the understanding alluded to, I shall, without hesitation, be guided by his opinion. You will, in that case, owe to our sense of justice & candour, what you would certainly have failed to extort by any passionate remonstrance, much less by any intemperate threats.

In the mean time & during the short period which I have now to remain at Port Stephens, you will not, I trust, deem it unreasonable in me to request that you will abstain from such rude remarks, and such unfounded aspersions, as your letters before me contain. It can not be necessary for you again to remind me that you consider such conduct an appropriate return for one unceasing effort of mine, during nearly three years to provide you with every comfort and to promote by every means in my power, your very best interests.

Letter No. 1,066

Port Stephens
20th January 1834

Rev. C. P. N. Wilton M. A.

Sir,

Captain Moffatt has asserted that I "have presumed to forbid a Minister of the Church of England coming again on the Company's Estate to administer to the Spiritual wants of himself and family".

As I have never had any communication either verbal or written with Captain Moffatt on this subject, I conclude that this unfounded assertion must have arisen from some misapprehension of what may have dropped from you in conversation. I shall be very much obliged by your informing me whether anything you said could possibly have conveyed to Captain Moffatt an idea, which, as it stands above in his own words, conveys, as your are aware an impression utterly at variance with the real truth.

Illustration 8:
(Letter No. 1065)

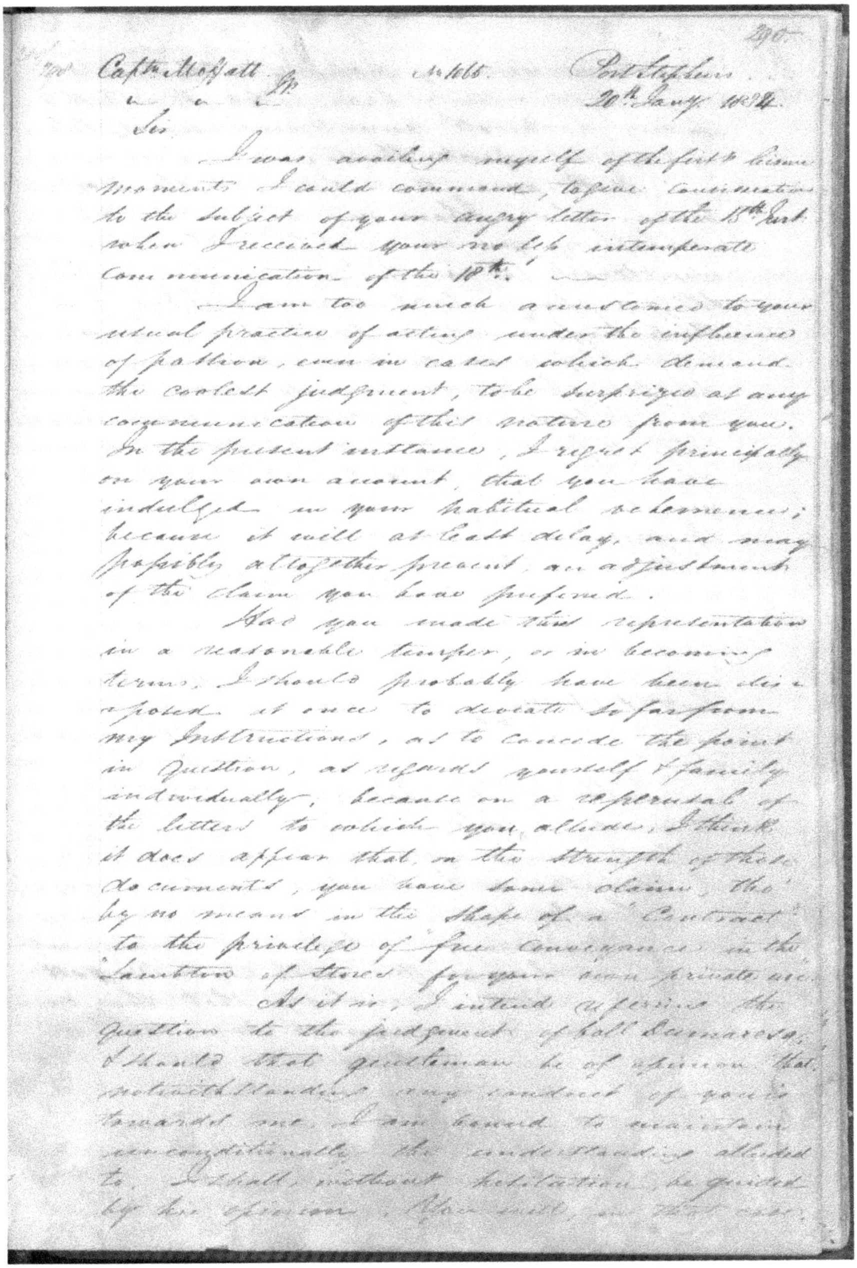

Capt Moffatt   No 1065   Port Stephens
                                               20th Jany 1834.
Sir,
   I was availing myself of the first leisure moments I could command, to give consideration to the subject of your angry letter of the 15th Inst when I received your no less intemperate communication of the 18th.

   I am too much accustomed to your usual practice of acting under the influence of passion, even in cases which demand the coolest judgment, to be surprized at any communication of this nature from you. In the present instance, I regret principally on your own account, that you have indulged in your habitual vehemence; because it will at least delay, and may possibly altogether prevent, an adjustment of the claim you have preferred.

   Had you made this representation in a reasonable temper, or in becoming terms, I should probably have been disposed at once to deviate so far from my Instructions, as to concede the point in question, as regards yourself & family individually, because on a re-perusal of the letters to which you allude, I think it does appear that, on the strength of those documents, you have some claim, tho' by no means in the shape of a "Contract" to the privilege of free conveyance, in the Sanction of Stores for your own private use.

   As it is, I intend referring the question to the judgment of Capt Dumaresq, & should that gentleman be of opinion that, notwithstanding any conduct of yours towards me, I am bound to maintain unconditionally the understanding alluded to, I shall, without hesitation, be guided by his opinion. You will, in that case,

Letter No. 1,067

Port Stephens
25th January 1834

To James Laidley Esq.
Deputy Commissary General, Sydney

Sir,
    In the absence of Sir Edward Parry, I have the honor to transmit to you herewith, an account (in Triplicate) amounting to (£32.16.8) Thirty two Pounds Sixteen Shillings and Eight pence for Supplies to the Military Detachment stationed at Port Stephens between the 1st of October and 31st December 1833 together with the Vouchers complete for the same.
    I also transmit herewith an account (in Triplicate) amounting to (£3.7.4) Three Pounds Seven Shillings and four pence for Supplies to Sundry Individuals on account of H. M. Government to the 31st December last, with the Vouchers complete.

J. Edward Ebsworth

Letter No. 1,068

Port Stephens
30th January 1834

Board for Assignment of Servants

Joshua Hemerton, Lloyd, Life

Gentlemen,
    The man named in the Margin having come to Port Stephens, without any Notice of his Assignment to the A. A. Company or to any Individual at this place, I request you will do me the favor to inform me to whom he belongs. I have rationed & employed him till I receive your reply.

Letter No. 1,069

Newcastle
22nd January 1834

John Henderson Esq.

Sir,
    In reply to your letter enclosing Mr White's Communication of the 6th instant addressed to you, I request you will acquaint Mr White that, I fixed the Company's Coal Works entirely out of the proposed Town of Newcastle, for the very purpose of avoiding any difficulty on this head, altho' by the original Stipulation I could have taken a considerable portion of the Town

itself, including the old Government Works & a large Slip of the Town water frontage. I cannot, therefore, consent to give up Twenty five Yards of the best water frontage (the water being there the deepest) to meet any new proposal for the enlargement of the Town by another Street in addition to the original Plan as it stood when I made my Selection.

Letter No. 1,070

Port Stephens
30th January 1834

Honorable Colonial Secretary

Sir,
    I have the Honor to enclose to you herewith an Account in Triplicate, amounting to (£16.16.-) Sixteen Pounds & Sixteen Shillings supplied by the A. A. Company to the Department of the Master Attendants between the 1st of October and the 31st of December 1833, together with the requisite Vouchers.
    I request you will be pleased to obtain the sanction of H. E. the Governor to the payment of this amount with as little delay as possible.

Letter No. 1,071

Port Stephens
30th January 1834

James Laidley Esq.
Deputy Commissary General – Sydney

Sir,
    I have the Honor to enclose to you herewith an Account in duplicate amounting to (£48) Forty Eight Pounds for Coals supplied by the A. A. Company to the Commissariat Department for H. M. Government of Van Diemen's Land and shipped on board the *Isabella* at Newcastle, together with the receipt of W. Kinghorne the Master, for the same; and I request you will have the goodness to pay the Amount into the Bank of Australia, to my credit as Commissioner to the Company, with as little delay as possible.

Letter No. 1,072

Port Stephens
30th January 1834

James Laidley Esq.

Sir,
    I have the Honor to enclose to you herewith an Account in duplicate amounting to (£59.12.-) Fifty nine Pounds & Twelve Shillings for Coals supplied by the A. A. Company to the Commissariat Department of H. M. Colonial Government between the 1st of October & 31st of December 1833, together with the requisite Vouchers; and I request you will have the goodness to pay the Amount into the Bank of Australia, to my credit as Commissioner to the Company, with as little delay as possible.

Letter No. 1,073

Port Stephens
3rd February 1834

James Bowman Esq.
Inspector General of Hospitals
Sydney

Isaac Lyons,
Adamant, Life

Sir,
    The Prisoner named in the margin, an Assigned Servant of the A. A. Company lately returned from the General Hospital at Sydney still refuses to work, on the plea of blindness, tho' there is more reason than ever to believe that it is entirely feigned.
    I should esteem it an obligation if you would allow Dr Mitchell to favor me with his opinion of this man's case, to enable me to determine what is to be done with him.

Letter No. 1,074

Port Stephens
3rd February 1834

Board for Assignment of Servants – Sydney

Gentlemen,
    Observing in the Government Gazette of the 15th ultimo that a Farrier has lately been assigned to the A. A. Company and no person of that Trade having been forwarded to Port Stephens, I request you will do me the favor to inform me of the Farrier's name, to enable me to make the requisite enquiry, the Company being much in need of his Services.

Letter No. 1,075

Port Stephens
3rd February 1834

J. E. Manning Esq.
Registrar, Supreme Court
Sydney

Sir,
   I do myself the Honor to enclose to you herewith the following Proceeds of Property &c &c belonging to James Henderson, (deceased) late in the Service of the A. A. Company).

   My draft on the Bank of Australia for £12.12.2½ – being the Amount of articles disposed of at Port Stephens by your desire, as per enclosed account & vouchers from the Purchasers.
   The Company's Draft on the Bank of Australia (No. 1769) for £2.17.- being the Balance of Henderson's wages to the 1st June 1833, the day of his decease.
   Two Certificates from Captain Moffatt J. P. for the apprehension of Runaways by James Henderson, entitling him to 10/- & 20/- respectively £1.10. –

   I request you will return to me the enclosed Receipts signed by yourself and I have the Honor to remain

Letter No. 1,076

Port Stephens
4th February 1834

Simon Dodd Esq.
At Mr Cracknell's 'Cat & Mutton'
Erskine Street – Sydney

Sir,
   Enclosed you will receive a Draft on the Bank of Australia No. 2017 for (£15) Fifteen Pounds, & I request you will be good enough to return the accompanying Receipt, duly signed.

Letter No. 1,077

Port Stephens
5th February 1834

James Laidley Esq.

Sir,
I have the Honor to acknowledge the receipt of your letter of the 31st ultimo enclosing Cash Vouchers for my signature for the Sum of (£32.16.8) Thirty two Pounds, Sixteen Shillings & Eight pence due to the A. A. Company for Supplies to the Military Detachment at Port Stephens and I now beg leave to return the same duly signed & request you will be good enough to cause the amount to be placed to my Credit, as Commissioner for the Company, at the Bank of Australia.

Letter No. 1,078

Port Stephens
5th February 1834

W. H. Mackenzie Esq.
Bank of Australia

Sir,
I herewith enclose to you Mr Croasdill's Draft on the Bank of Australia (No. 130) for the Sum of (£162.18.) One Hundred & Sixty two Pounds & Eighteen Shillings endorsed to your order. I request you will place it to my Credit at the Bank, as Commissioner for the A. A. Company.

Letter No. 1,079

Port Stephens
5th February 1834

G. Jenkin Esq.

Sir,
In reply to your letter of the 31st ultimo received yesterday, I beg to acquaint you that it was not my intention, in signing your new Agreement to make any <u>Money</u> allowances beyond what is actually specified therein; but I did intend that you should be allowed a Servant at the Company's expense & an order ought to have been given to that effect.

This omission has now been rectified, which will, I trust, accord with your wishes.

Letter No. 1,080

Port Stephens
11th February 1834

To Captain R. G. Moffatt J. P.
Resident Magistrate

Sir,
In acknowledging the receipt of your Letter of yesterday's date, I beg leave to thank you for the suggestion of a reduction in the weekly allowance of Oil for the Police at Carrington; and I have given directions to the Storekeeper accordingly.

Letter No. 1,081

Port Stephens
12th February 1834

W. H. Mackenzie Esq.
Secretary & Cashier
Bank of Australia

Sir,
I beg leave to enclose to you herewith Mr Manning's Promissory Note for the Sum of (£100) One Hundred Pounds, payable at the Bank of Australia 27th February / 2d March 1834, and endorsed to your Order. I request you will place the Amount to my Credit in the Bank, as Commissioner for the Australian Agricultural Company.

Letter No. 1082

Port Stephens
14th February 1834

Captain R. G. Moffatt J. P.
Resident Magistrate

Sir,
With reference to my letter addressed to you on the 20th ultimo I have the Honor to acquaint you that, in pursuance of the intention therein expressed, I have referred to Colonel Dumaresq the question alluded to; and, in accordance with the decision which we have jointly arrived at, I beg leave to enclose to you herewith a Set of Forms to be used whenever you may require "free conveyance in the *Lambton* of Stores for your own private use".

But as this permission will be at variance with the Regulations recently established, & is conceded only in virtue of an understanding applicable to yourself individually, Colonel Dumaresq & myself wish it to be distinctly understood that no such exception will be continued in favor of your Successor.

Letter No. 1,083

Port Stephens
14th February 1834

William Street
Stroud

William Street

Having consulted with Colonel Dumaresq on the subject of a fresh Agreement with you at the Expiration of your present Term, as proposed in your Letter of the 5th instant,

I have to acquaint you that your Services will not be required by the Company.

Letter No. 1,084

Port Stephens
15th February 1834

James Laidley Esq.
Deputy Commissary General
Sydney

Sir,

I have the honor to acknowledge the receipt of your letter of the 7th instant.

The information respecting the mode of payment of the Account due to the A. A. Company for the Coals supplied for His Majesty's Government of V. Diemen's Land has been duly noted.

I enclose the Cash Vouchers with my Signature attached to the receipt, & I request you will be good enough to cause the amount (£59.12.-) to be paid into the Bank of Australia to my Credit.

Letter No. 1,085

Port Stephens
15th February 1834

Captain R. G. Moffatt J. P.
Resident Magistrate

Sir,
  With reference to the Government Circular No. 1834/7 I have the Honor to forward to you the accompanying Application for Six Boys on account of the A. A. Company, in conformity with the Terms therein specified.

Letter No. 1,086

Port Stephens
19th February 1834

Mr Foss
Pitt Street, Sydney

Sir,
  With reference to your enquiry respecting Ponies to be purchased for a Carriage, I beg to acquaint you that I intend sending up to Sydney next month, two or three Pairs of Ponies for sale, some of which I hope will be found to suit your purpose.

Letter No 1,087

Port Stephens
19th February 1834

To Mr Paul
Auctioneer
Sydney

Sir,
  I intend sending to Sydney the latter end of next month, a number of superior young horses and ponies, fit for saddle or harness, which I request you will, at the proper time, advertize for Sale by Auction. Should the Sydney races occur very early in April, perhaps the horses had better be sold on the day between the races. There is also an Imported Entire Welch Poney. I request you will <u>not</u> name them as belonging to the Company or to me.

Letter No. 1,088

Port Stephens
24th February 1834

Principal Superintendent of Convicts

William Edwards, *Surry*, Life

Sir,
    Being about to leave the Colony, I do myself the Honor to request that you will obtain the Sanction of H. E. The Governor for the Transfer of the Ticket of Leave of the Prisoner of the Crown named in the Margin, (now in my private Service) from Port Stephens to Maitland.

Letter No. 1,089

Port Stephens
24th February 1834

Board for the Assignment of Servants

William Brown, *Waterloo*, Life

Gentlemen,
    Being about to leave the Colony, I do myself the honor to request that you will obtain the Sanction of H. E. The Governor to the Transfer of the Prisoner of the Crown named in the margin, now in my private service to that of the A. A. Company, he being at present employed as Schoolmaster on their Estate.

Letter No. 1,090

Port Stephens
24th February 1834

W. H. Mackenzie, Esq.
Bank of Australia

Sir,
    I beg leave to acquaint you that after the 14th proximo it is intended that Lieutenant Colonel Henry Dumaresq shall assume the management of the Affairs of the A. A. Company in N. S. Wales as their Commissioner; and that after that date, all Bills Drafts or other Documents on behalf of the Company will bear the Signature of Lieutenant Colonel Dumaresq, which is hereunto annexed for your information and guidance.

I am &c &c &c
(Signed) W. E. Parry Commissioner for the A. A. Company
Signature of Lieutenant Colonel Dumaresq
(Signed) <u>H. Dumaresq</u>

Letter No. 1,091

Port Stephens
24th February 1834

Captain Moffatt J. P.
Resident Magistrate

Sir Edward Parry presents his Compliments to Captain Moffatt and begs to acquaint him that the circumstances alluded to in his communication had no reference whatever to the Police. They were as follows:

Sir Edward Parry having been informed that it had been stated by Captain Moffatt to Mr Henry Hall, Mr Stubbs and other gentlemen that, a short time back, Mr Price had been seen in a state of intoxication, and that the authority of Constable Powers was that on which Captain Moffatt founded this Statement, Sir Edward Parry proceeded, in company with Colonel Dumaresq and Mr Price, to enquire into the origin of this Report.

On questioning Powers, he unequivocally declared that he had never communicated to Captain Moffatt, or to any other person, any thing which could, by inference, or otherwise, have conveyed such an impression. He stated that he had this day for the first time, learnt from Staunton, the Police Clerk, that Mr Price had been seen in the state above alluded to. Sir Edward Parry called Staunton, whom he saw standing at the Police Office, with a view to ascertain from him the manner in which this Report had reached him. Staunton stated that Captain Moffatt was his informant.

Sir Edward Parry further learnt from Messrs Darch and White that Captain Moffatt had likewise conveyed to them an impression of the same nature; with this addition as related by Mr White that Mr Price had run some risk of being taken to the Watch House by Powers.

Sir Edward Parry trusts that the foregoing information may afford to Captain Moffatt the means he desires of removing from the mind of Colonel Dumaresq "any erroneous impression" he may have received from these Enquiries, in like manner as they afforded to Mr Price an opportunity of vindicating his character from this groundless aspersion.

Letter No. 1,092

Port Stephens
27th February 1834

Captain Moffatt J. P.
&c &c &c

Sir Edward Parry presents his Compliments to Captain Moffatt, and, in reply to his Communication of yesterday's date, begs to acquaint him that Messrs Price and Darch decline being present at any explanation on the subject in question, except in the presence of all the persons concerned, and especially in the presence of Colonel Dumaresq.

This was forwarded to Captain Moffatt at about 4½ pm

Sir Edward Parry, tho' desirous of affording Captain Moffatt any opportunity he may desire, of explaining the circumstances alluded to, cannot but concur in the propriety of this determination; being apprehensive that, in a business which is likely to assume so serious an aspect, any verbal Communication might be liable to future misapprehension, unless each individual concerned were present.

Sir Edward Parry, therefore, begs to propose that the gentlemen and other parties concerned be assembled for this purpose, immediately on Colonel Dumaresq's return to Port Stephens, of which due notice will be given to Captain Moffatt, if agreeable to him. Sir Edward Parry has no objection to be present, if the circumstances of his departure will permit, should Captain Moffatt desire it.

Letter No. 1,093

Port Stephens
27th February 1834

Thomas Hyndes Esq.
Sydney

Sir,

In reply to your letter of the 10th instant for which I beg to offer you my best acknowledgments, I have now to inform you that, having made particular enquiry at Newcastle, as to the practicability of adopting your suggestion of selling the Coals by the Chaldron instead of the Ton, I regret to find that it will not be in my power to adopt it without very considerable inconvenience and expense, all the Waggons 'Skips' &c &c having been made to Tons or parts of Tons, in compliance with the custom established at the Government Works many years before the Company's Colliery was established there.

I very much regret, however, that the Purchasers of Coal should be put to any inconvenience such as you describe. I have communicated your proposal to Colonel Dumaresq my successor, and shall be happy to communicate further with you on the subject, on my arrival in Sydney, should you desire it.

Letter No. 1,094

Tahlee
28th February 1834

Captain Moffatt J. P.

Sir Edward Parry presents his Compliments to Captain Moffatt & begs to acquaint him that, almost at the moment of his departure for Booral, he has been much astonished at hearing from Mr White a circumstance, which he requests Captain Moffatt will call upon Mr White to relate to him.

Sir Edward cannot, in justice to Captain Moffatt, delay a moment in communicating this to him, tho' he has no time to explain further.

Letter No. 1,095

Port Stephens
27th February 1834

Messrs Castle & Dawson
Foundry, Sydney

Gentlemen,
In reply to your letter of the 15th current I beg to acquaint you that I have directed Mr Henderson to send you One Ton of Coke on Trial, the price of which is Two guineas. Should it answer your purpose the Company can now supply it at the rate of about Two Tons per week, and it can be encreased to any extent should the demand make it worth while to do so.

[Letter No. 1,095a]

Notice

Sir Edward Parry, being about to leave N. S. Wales requests that all demands against him – either as Commissioner to the A. A. Company or on his private Account may be presented to him for adjustment at the Pulteney Hotel, Sydney, before the 15th day of April next.

Port Stephens
4th March 1834

Letter No. 1,096

Port Stephens
4th March 1834

Edward Cox Esq.
Mulgoa – Penrith

Sir,
With reference to your letter of the 21st of December last, acquainting me that you had given directions to Mr Mackenzie to lodge the Sum of £17.5.- in the Bank of Australia to the Credit of the A. A. Company.

I beg leave to acquaint you that this direction has not yet been complied with and I request you will be so good as to repeat your Instructions.

Letter No. 1,097

Port Stephens
4th March 1834

John Stokes
Carrington

John Stokes,

In reply to your letter of the 1st current requesting the Cancelment of your Agreement with the A. A. Company after next Month, & requesting to be allowed three Months Salary in consideration of its Cancelment according to the Terms of your Agreement,

I have to acquaint you that I have no objection to your Agreement being cancelled on the 30th of next Month, and that I will direct three months wages to be paid, as stipulated therein.

Letter No. 1,098

Port Stephens
5th March 1834

W. H. Mackenzie Esq.
Bank of Australia

Sir,

I beg leave to forward to you herewith Bills in the Governor & Directors of the A. A. Company. (Nos 308 @ 312 inclusive) for the Sum of £650, the first four of which amounting to £500 I request you will place to my Credit as Commissioner for the A. A. Company, & the last Bill (No. 312) for £150, to the Credit of my Private Account at the Bank of Australia.

I shall be obliged by your acknowledging per post, the receipt of this Communication.

P. S. I also enclose a Draft No. 131 drawn by Mr Croasdill for £15.13.- which please to place to the credit of the A. A. Company at the Bank of Australia.

Letter No. 1,099

Port Stephens
6th March 1834

Captain Moffatt J. P.

Sir Edward Parry presents his compliments to Captain Moffatt & begs to acknowledge the receipt of his communication of yesterday, which he will lay before the Parties at the intended Meeting on Colonel Dumaresq's arrival.

Should no unforeseen occurrence arise to prevent it, Colonel Dumaresq will arrive here on the Evening of the 14th instant, & as Sir Edward Parry must leave Port Stephens in the Steamer at daylight on the following morning the Meeting must be held in that interval. Sir Edward Parry will give Captain Moffatt the earliest Notice of the hour.

With reference to an expression which Captain Moffatt on the authority of a Convict or Convicts whom he has not named, assumes that Sir Edward Parry used, Sir Edward Parry has only to remark that he did not use it. This explanation might have been given before but for Captain Moffatt's own desire, which he seems to have overlooked, that it should be offered at the intended Meeting.

Letter No. 1,100

Port Stephens
6th March 1834

Captain Moffatt
H. M. 17th Regiment

Sir,

In reply to your letter of this day's date, I have the honor to acquaint you that I have directed Mr White to issue extra to the Military Detachment such quantity of Flour as they may consider to have been damaged in the two former issues; and I request you will send a Memorandum of your own deficiency to Mr White who is directed to make it up in the next issue.

I am sorry that an accident of this kind should have occurred, but I cannot find out how it happened.

Letter No. 1,101

Port Stephens
8th March 1834

W. Ogilvie Esq.
Merton – Hunters River

Sir,
    Observing by your Notice in the Government Gazette of the 26th ultimo, that you have impounded Two Working Bullocks branded G M, I beg to inform you that they are the property of the A. A. Company, and request you will be good enough to inform me of the Amount of the Expenses, that they may be paid.
    I shall be much obliged by your allowing the Two Bullocks to remain at Merton till we have an opportunity of sending for them.

Letter No. 1,102

Port Stephens
9th March 1834

Captain Moffatt J. P.

    Sir Edward Parry presents his compliments to Captain Moffatt and, with reference to his note of this morning, will take care to furnish him with the legal information he requires, on his return to Carrington.

Letter No. 1,103

Port Stephens
10th March 1834

Captain Moffatt J. P.

    Sir Edward Parry presents his Compliments to Captain Moffatt & is much obliged to him for allowing him to peruse the documents now returned; & he now sends also Mr Norton's replies to the queries which Captain Moffatt wished to have unanswered [sic].

Letter No. 1,104

Tahlee
11th March 1834

Captain Moffatt J. P.

    Sir Edward Parry presents his compliments to Captain Moffatt & feels obliged by his note of this morning, in answer to which it does not occur to him that any Copies of the Police Proceedings can be of any Service on the approaching Trials, except those relating to Mr Barton's Assigned Servant, Foster, as Mr Barton is bringing an action for the alleged illegal detention of this man in the Company's Employment.

Should anything else occur to Sir Edward Parry he will communicate it to Captain Moffatt as requested in his note of this morning.

Letter No.1,105

Port Stephens
13th March 1834

Captain Moffatt J. P

Sir Edward Parry presents his Compliments to Captain Moffatt, and is of opinion that the Act in question cannot at present be safely dispensed with.

Should Captain Moffatt be of the same opinion Sir Edward will be glad to sign a joint letter to that effect.

Letter No. 1,106

Port Stephens
14th March 1834

Principal Superintendent of Convicts
Sydney

Sir,
With reference to my letter addressed to you on the 24th ultimo, relative to the changing of the Ticket of Leave of the Prisoner of the Crown named in the Margin, I request you will be pleased to obtain the sanction of His Excellency the Governor to its being changed to Peel's River, Mr Charles Hall, the Superintendent of the A. A. Company's Flocks who is about to reside there having agreed to engage Edwards as his Servant, provided H. E's sanction be obtained.

Margin: William Edwards, *Surry*, Life

Letter No. 1,107

Port Stephens
14th March 1834

Lieutenant Colonel Henry Dumaresq

Sir,
It having been arranged between us, in pursuance of the Instructions received from the Court of Directors of the A. A. Company that you assume

the control of the Company's Affairs, as their Commissioner after this date,

I have now the Honor to hand you herewith a Letter of Attorney from the Court of Directors empowering you to act in that capacity upon which document I have made the endorsement required by the last clause thereof.

I likewise hand you herewith certain Provisional Letters of Attorney and other documents sealed up, which will become available in case of your death, or inability to manage the Company's Affairs in this Colony.

INDEX

Abbreviations
A. A. Co.:   Australian Agricultural Company
I. S.:   Indentured Servant

Note: References are to letter numbers not page numbers.

A. A. Co.: Annual Accounts of, 936; Annual Report of, 1010; and letter of attorney empowering Lieutenant Colonel Henry Dumaresq to act as Commissioner of, 1107; Quarterly Accounts of, 936; value of property of at 3 April 1833, 980; *see also* stock in A. A. Co.
A. A. Co. Governor, London, *see* Smith, John:
A. A. Co. Stud, 706a, 898, 940d
Aborigines: allegations of outrages against by Sir Edward Parry and others in employ of A. A. Co., 989, 1011a, 1013; alleged offer of reward for heads of, 989; engagement of as guide for John Armstrong during survey, 1025; and murder of James Henderson, 906; number of, within limits of A. A. Co.'s original grant, 715; threat from at Port Stephens, 956
accidents, 764a
accommodation: for A. A. Co. servants in Newcastle, 639
accounts payable by A. A. Co., 845; for copies of *Sydney Monitor*, 900; Henry Dangar, 947; G. A. Oliver, 822; Carl Rantzsch, 749; Robert Campbell & Co, 986
accounts payable to A. A. Co.: Andrew Allan, 791, 964; Beacon Light at Newcastle, 725, 726, 727; J. Brown, 783, 962; Colonial Department, 836, 914; Colonial Government, 669, 761, 773, 810, 858, 908, 942, 949, 992, 1067; Commissariat, Newcastle, 737; Commissariat Department, 669, 670, 724, 725, 726, 743, 836, 837, 846, 871, 872, 891, 915, 920, 927, 930, 1002, 1018, 1071, 1072; Thomas Cowper, 790, 831, 978; Edward Cox, 785, 977, 1096; George Cox, 803, 972; Department of the Master Attendant, 811a, 871, 919, 1003, 1070; executors of late John Oxley, 801; executors of late John Thomas Campbell, 796; Chief Justice Forbes, 771; John Gaggin, 970; W. John Gaggin, 800; Government of Van Diemen's Land, 1071, 1084; Jonathon Hassall, 798, 969; William Howe, 802, 971; Henry Howey, 792; Thomas Hyndes, 781; A. C. Innes, 770; John Mackaness, 794, 966; George Mackenzie, 888; Rev. Samuel Marsden, 793, 965, 1030, 1060; Military Detachment at Port Stephens, 672, 673, 712, 713, 724, 754, 773, 846, 858, 908, 930, 948, 992, 1067, 1077; J. J. Moore, 788, 975; W. H. Moore, 786, 963; James Murdoch, 797, 968; Hugh Noble, 779; G. A. Oliver, 822; A. P. Onslow, 782; George T. Palmer, 789, 874; John Paul, 848; John Piper, senior, 799, 974; James Raymond, 995; separate, for supply of coal to Colonial Department and to Commissariat Department, 669, 725, 727; Benjamin Singleton, 889; William Smyth, 759; Samuel Terry, 780; Thomas Walker, 784, 811; William Wetherman, 917; T. B. Wilson, 967; Sir John Wylde, 787, 976

'Act for preventing the extension of the infectious disease commonly called the Scab in Sheep or Lambs' (3 William IV No. 5, 1832) see Scab Act
Adamant: convicts on, 996, 1073
advertisements; *see under The Australian; Sydney Gazette; Sydney Herald; Sydney Monitor*
Agamemnon: convicts on, 705
agreements re employment *see under* employment by A. A. Co.
agricultural labourers: application for assignment of, 650, 958
Alderley, Port Stephens see A. A. Co. Stud
Allan, Andrew (Bailey Park, Penrith): and account for stud service, 791; and payment of account, 964
Allen, Edmund (convict): assignment of to A. A. Co., 703, 717
Alloway Bank, Bathurst *see* Piper, John, senior
Annual Accounts of A. A. Co., 936
Annual Report, 1010
Archdeacon: and lack of consultation with A. A. Co. re visit to Port Stephens by Rev. C. P. N. Wilton to conduct baptisms and divine service, 1029
Armstrong, John (Company Surveyor): and accurate marking of land grants at Liverpool Plains and Peel's River, including boundaries, 1024; assistance for with survey of A. A. Co. land, 1024, 1025; and conditions for undertaking final delineation and accurate marking of land grants at Liverpool Plains and Peel's River, including boundaries, and remuneration for this work, 1000; and delineation and accurate marking of land grants at Liverpool Plains and Peel's River, including boundaries, 1001; and delineation and description of land at Liverpool Plains and Peel's River, 959; delivery of A. A. Co. theodolite by Henry

Note: References are to letter numbers not page numbers.

Dangar to, 1023; and examination of original grant, 649 (para. 6)
Arundel: price of shipment of wool on, 746, 747; shipment of wool on, 735
Ash Island *see* Scott, W.
Asia: convicts on, 663, 695, 703, 1060a
Aspinall, Nicholas: and sale of barilla, 665
assigned convicts: accidents to, 764a; and alleged illegal detention in A. A. Co. employment of assigned convict, 1104; application for, 650, 681, 750, 764a, 924, 979, 990, 1027, 1048; exchange of, 659, 666, 706, 981, 1060a, 1089; forwarding of, 663; inquiries re, 703, 717, 1068, 1074; medical treatment for, 675, 716, 738, 769, 824, 855, 933, 996; and procedure re certificates of freedom, 907; in published list, 663, 687, 882, 1074; receipt of, 695; refusal to supply, 949; return of, 904; *see also* agricultural labourers; bakers; blacksmiths; bricklayers; butchers; carpenters; farriers; gardeners; horseshoers; mechanics; millers; sawyers; stone-cutters; wheelwrights
Assistant Surveyor General, *see* Perry, Samuel Augustus
Attorney General: opinion of re case of apprehension of runaways, 751; opinion of re extent to which laws of the Colony of NSW apply on A. A. Co. land at Liverpool Plains, 902a
auction: of A. A. Co. surplus goods, 825
The Australian: advertisements: for blacksmith, 1026a; horse sale, 679a; horse sale, head stock keeper and shearers, 699b; merino ram sale, 682a; sale of vessel, 679b; share call, 687a, 732 [sic] a, 949a; for shearers, 940c; stud service, 706a, 940d; tenders for supply of flour to 'Warrah,' Liverpool Plains, 738a; tenders for supply of sugar for prisoners rations, 754a; tenders for transport of wool, 995a; denial of statement in *The Australian* re alleged outrages against Aborigines by servants of A. A. Co., 1011a; notices: payment for coal, 642a; prohibition of cutting of timber and depasturing of cattle on A. A. Co. land near Williams River, 1036a; order for, 880
bags bearing the mark of A. A. Co.: and information about persons in possession of, 869
Bailey Park, Penrith *see* Allan, Andrew
Baker, John (former Company gardener, I. S.): and residence on A. A. Co. Estate, 658
bakers: request for exchange of other assigned convicts for, 1020
Ball, Robert: and request for employment, 655
ballast: dumping of in port of Newcastle, 902; wool ships and, 901
bank deposit: payment for coal by, 642a
Bank of Australia: and authority for paying outstanding drafts upon Committee of Management of A. A. Co., 739; financial transactions with, 657, 674, 687, 698, 700, 701, 707, 712, 724, 726, 749, 756, 812, 828, 839, 850, 857, 866, 867, 873, 878, 912, 921, 984, 987, 1005, 1009, 1028, 1033, 1037, 1064, 1076, 1078, 1098; and instructions to re instalments payable on shares to stockholders, 1057; and notification of appointment of Lieutenant Colonel Henry Dumaresq as Commissioner of A. A. Co., 1090; and payment for coal by bank deposit, 642a; repayment of loan by A. W. Scott through, 731; and stoppage of payment of stolen draft, 736
Bannister, William (convict): transfer of assignment of, 659
baptisms, 1029
barilla: sale of, 664, 665
Baring: convicts on, 1060a
Barker, Thomas: and shipment of flour, 926
Barnes, William (Sheep Overseer, I. S.): and reward for apprehension of runaways, 690, 691, 714; submission by of affidavit in respect of outstanding claim to bench of magistrates, 708
Barrow, John (Secretary of the Admiralty): and transmission of information about scientific discovery of James King Lord Goderich, 916
Barton, William (former Company Accountant): security of property of in house to be vacated by J. E. Ebsworth, 862, 865; and alleged illegal detention in A. A. Co. employment of his assigned servant, Foster, 1104
Bathurst *see* Piper, John, senior
Beacon Light at Newcastle: accounts for supply of coal for, 725, 726, 727
Beal, Charles (carpenter, I.S.): and request for information on saleability of timber on A. A. Co. Estate, 809
Becket, James (ticket of leave): and request for employment, 697
Beckett, Thomas (convict): and apprehension of runaways, 690, 714, 751
Beckitt, Thomas *see* Beckett, Thomas
Beecher, Richard (convict): transfer of assignment of, 666
beef: tender for supply of and other rations to servants of A. A. Co., 864a; tender for supplying at Newcastle, 884; tender (with price) for supply of to Military Detachment at Port Stephens, 742
Bench of Magistrates, District of Williams River: and establishment of pound, 1035
Bengal Infantry *see* Charlton, Lieutenant
Benton, Thomas (convict): assignment of to A. A. Co., 663
Berry, Samuel (convict): death of, 941
Berry, William (convict): transfer of to A. A. Co., 680
Berryman, Charles (convict): death of, 879

Note: References are to letter numbers not page numbers.

blacksmiths: advertisement for, 1026a; application for assignment of, 750, 958, 1027; request for employment as, 1038
blankets: issue of to Aborigines, 715
Blaxland, John: and his being agent for Mr Walker, 827
blood horses: stud service, 940d
boat builder *see* Stokes, John
Board for the Assignment of Servants: application for assignment: butcher, 1048; miller, 1048; and assignment of: agricultural labourers, 650, 958; blacksmiths, 750, 958, 1027; bricklayers, 750, 924, 949; carpenters, 681, 958; gardeners, 979; horseshoers, 750, 990; sawyers, 924, 949; shepherds, 650, 958; wheelwrights, 764a, 958; and convicts in published list of assigned convicts relating to A. A. Co., 663, 687, 882; and exchange of assigned convicts with: A. A. Co., 1089; James Edward Ebsworth, 981; William Ogilvie, 666; Sir Edward Parry, 706, 1060a; J. E. Stacey, 659; and information: re assigned convict, 1068; re assigned convict farrier, 1074; and non-assignment of convicts to A. A. Co., 980; and receipt of assigned convicts, 695
Bourke, Major General Richard (Governor of NSW): and authorisation of possession of two tracts of land selected by A. A. Co. (Liverpool Plains and Peel's River), 943; and extent to which laws of the Colony of NSW apply on A. A. Co. land at Liverpool Plains, 902a; and Governor's rejection of exchange of land by A. A. Co., 649; and payment of accounts for supply of coal to Colonial government, 942, 949; and petition of Alexander Macdonald for ticket of leave, 732a; and petition of convict to be reunited with family, 689a, 699a; and price of coal supplied to Colonial Government and issue of computation of prime cost, 942; and public use of A. A. Co. property, 667; rejection of recommendation of re taking land near Peel's River as one parcel, 841; and supply of convict labour to Coal works at Newcastle, 949
Bowen, William (Maitland): and tender for supply of flour to 'Warrah,' Liverpool Plains, 1054
Bowman, Dr James (Inspector General of Hospitals, Sydney): and committal of convict to Lunatic Asylum, 679; request for opinion of Dr Mitchell in case of blindness of convict, 1073
Bowman, James *see also* Macarthur, James, James Bowman and H. H. McArthur
Boyne: convicts on, 675
boys: application for six, 1085
bran: order of, 702
bricklayer, *see* Tulk, Thomas
bricklayers: application for assignment of, 750; assignment of to A. A. Co. coal mines at Newcastle, 923, 924, 949, 952
bricklayer and mason, I. S. *see* Cowell, William
Bridges, Thomas (convict): request of to receive small sums of money, 826; and money in Savings Bank, 957 and ticket of leave, 923
Broadhurst Thomas (ticket of leave):
Brooks JP, Mr.: and dumping of ballast in port of Newcastle, 902
Brown, J.: and account for stud service, 783; and payment of account, 962
Brown, William (convict): change of assignment of, 706, 1089
Bryant, John (convict): change of assignment of, 706
bullocks: impounding of by William Ogilvie, 1101
Bunn, George (merchant and Company's agent in Sydney): and missing iron and steel, 850; and care of assigned convicts on discharge from General Hospital, Sydney, 675, 716, 738, 769, 824, 855, 933, 996; and convicts assigned to A. A. Co., 650, 663, 681, 695, 696, 703, 717, 958, 979 and 990; and convicts assigned to A. A. Co. in published list, 687; and crown or mortice wheel, 707; and damaged cans of oil, 805, 812; and deficiencies in invoice of goods, 749; and delivery of goods, 850; and delivery of packets and letters, 740; and distribution of letters, 864; and financial matters, 657, 674, 687, 696, 700, 707, 729, 749, 756, 812, 828, 839, 850, 857; and grinding of wheat to flour, 674; and letters to proprietors of stock in A. A. Co. in respect of call of shares, 688, 733; and letting of unfurnished cottages, 864b; and men discharged from General Hospital, Sydney, 694; and missing iron and steel, 805, 812; and non-delivery of iron and steel, 752; parcel for, 741; and payment of Thomas Emmett, 812; and payment of hospital fees, 752; and receipt of iron and steel and deficiencies therein, 756; and recovery of cost of damaged cans of oil on the *Governor Halkett*, 749; and requisition for drugs, spirits and castings, 752; and requisition of kennels, 729; and requisitions, 857; and return of kangaroos skins, 752; and sales of hides, 700; and shipment of castings, 674; and shipment of wool, 729, 747; and stock in A. A. Co., 934; and tenders for supply of sugar for prisoners rations, 754a; and transport of coal to Sydney, 700; and transport of flour and other goods, 707; and voucher for freight of cask of oil, 857; *see also* George Bunn & Co
Burnett, Mrs William: application re payment of living expenses, 748
Burnett, William (former Company Superintendent of Agriculture): agreement with re payment of passage to England and

Note: References are to letter numbers not page numbers.

living expenses, 748
Burrell: convicts on, 666, 941
butchers: application for assignment of, 1048; request for exchange of other assigned convicts for, 1020
call of shares, 687a, 688, 689, 732 [sic] a, 733, 734, 874a, 875a, 876, 949a, 950, 951; non-publication of advertisement re in *Government Gazette*, 985; *see also* stock in A. A. Co.
Camden: convicts on, 882
Campbell, John Thomas, late *see* executors of late John Thomas Campbell
Campbell, Robert, Jr, & Co *see* R. Campbell Jr & Co
Campbell Town (Campbelltown) *see* Cowper, Thomas; Hassall, Jonathon; Howe, William
Canton, China *see* Thomas Dent & Co
canvas: bale of not received, 997, 1005
Captain Cook: convicts on, 642, 981
carpenters: application for assignment of, 681, 958
Carrington: reduction in allowance of oil for the Police at, 1080 *see* Howitt, Adam; May, W.; Stokes, John; Stubbs, Richard
carts *see* public carts
cash: proposal to Messrs Hughes and Hosking to take coal for, 774
casting: quality of by James Rainey, 988
castings: requisition for, 752; shipment of, 674, 1051
Castle & Dawson: and delivery to of coke on trial, and price thereof, 1095
Castle Forbes *see* Larnach, John
Caswell RN retired, Lieutenant William, (Tanilba): and security of property of William Barton in house to be vacated by J. E. Ebsworth, 862; and inventory thereof, 865
cattle: claimed by Jeremiah Warlters, 732; impounding of trespassing on A. A. Co. land near Williams River, 1036a; removal of from A. A. Co. property at 'Warrah,' at Liverpool Plains, 806a
certificates of freedom: procedure re in case of assigned servants who have become free, 907
Chambers, Charles H.: and documents re claim of Carl Rantzsch and others against Mr Dutton, 755
Champion: convicts on, 879, 1060a
Charlton, Lieutenant: and purchase of stallions, 896
cheese: sale of, 911
Chief Justice, Sydney: and financial matters, 698
City of Edinboro': and transshipment of wool from the *Lambton* to, 747
Clergy and School Reserve: lease of and provision of fund for religion and education by A. A. Co., 1015; survey and mapping of, 649 (para. 12)

Cleveland (horses): sale of, 679a, 699b; stud service, 940d
Clifton, Campbell Town *see* Cowper, Thomas
Clifton, Cowpastures *see* Cowper, Thomas
Clyde: convicts on, 706
coal: account for supply of for Beacon Light at Newcastle, 725, 726, 727; account for supply of to Colonial Department, 914; account for supply of to Colonial Department and to Commissariat Department, 836; account for supply of to Colonial Government, 810, 942, 949; account for supply of to Colonial Government and to Commissariat Department, 669; account for supply of to Commissariat Department, 669, 670, 724, 726, 836, 837, 846, 871, 915, 920, 930, 1004, 1018, 1071, 1072; account for supply of to Government of Van Diemen's Land, 1071, 1084; accounts for supply of to Department of the Master Attendant, 811a, 871, 919, 1003; measurement of quantities of, 671; payment for by bank deposit, 642a; payment for not on credit, 651; price of supplied to Colonial Government, 895, 914, 915, 942, 949; prime cost of, 942; problems with payment of accounts for supply of to Commissariat Department, 725; and proposal by Thomas Hyndes of sale of by chaldron instead of by ton, 1093; proposal to Messrs Hughes and Hosking to take for cash, 774; receipt for payment of account for supply of to Master Attendants' Department, 811a; supply of to Colonial Government 'at the pit's mouth' and 'on board vessel,' 949; for supply of to Commissariat Department, 837; transport of to Sydney, 700; *see also* coke
coal grant at Newcastle, 764; application for, 721; description of, 953; finalisation of, 887; request for decision on, 764, 841; surveying of by Henry Dangar, 840, 844, 947, 953
coal mines *see* Coal Works, Newcastle
Coal Works, Newcastle: accommodation for A. A. Co. servants, 639; and assignment of blacksmith, 1027; assignment of bricklayer and sawyer to, 923, 924, 949, 952; and assignment of convicts, 980; convict labour for, 949, 952; convict mechanics at, 949; cost of, 942; economic working of, 949, 952; maintenance of, 949; and proposed Town of Newcastle, 1069; request for employment as blacksmith at, 1038
Cockayne, James (convict): medical treatment of, 855, 933
Cohen, Philip Joseph (Maitland): and Hunter River Jockey Club, 890; and subscription to Maitland Jockey Club, 910
coke: and delivery of to Castle & Dawson, 1095; price of, 1095
collieries *see* Coal Works, Newcastle
Colonial Department: account for supply

Note: References are to letter numbers not page numbers.

of coal to, 836; separate accounts for supply of coal to and to Commissariat Department, 669, 725

Colonial Government: account for supplies to, 773, 858, 908, 992, 1067; account for supply of coal to, 942, 949; accounts for supply of coal to, 669; non-payment of accounts by, 761; payment of account for coal supplied to, 810; rates for freight and passage to be paid by, 1016, 1044, 1061; rejection of grant of Liverpool Plains and Peel's River land by, 835; and use of A. A. Co. property by, 667; use of police establishment of A. A. Co. by, 667; see also Colonial Department; Colonial Secretary, Sydney; Commissariat Department; Deputy Commissary General; Governor of New South Wales

Colonial Secretary, Sydney see McLeay, Alexander

Colonial Treasury: and payment of coal for Beacon Light at Newcastle, 725; see also Riddell, Campbell Drummond

Commissariat, Newcastle: accounts for supplies to, 737

Commissariat Department: account for supply of coal to, 872, 920; accounts for supply of coal to, 669, 670, 724, 726, 836, 837, 846, 871, 915, 920, 930, 1004, 1018, 1071, 1072; non-payment of accounts by, 743; payment of account for supply of coal, 927; payment of accounts, 1002; problems with payment of accounts for supply of coal to, 725; separate accounts for supply of coal to and to Colonial Department, 669, 725; and supply of meat and flour to Military Detachment at Port Stephens, 672; tender for supplies to by A. A. Co., 742

Commissariat Office see Commissariat Department

Commissioner: succession to Sir Edward Parry as, 925; see also Parry, Sir Edward

Committee of Management of A. A. Co. (late): and authority for paying outstanding drafts upon, 739; and payment of draft upon, 749

Committee of the Maitland Jockey Club: and arrangements for races, 898

Company Accountant, see Barton, William; Ebsworth, James Edward

Company Agent, see Dawson, Robert.

Company Assistant General Superintendent, see Nisbet, Dr Alexander

Company Assistant Superintendent of Flocks see Jenkin, George

Company Bookkeeper at Newcastle, see Croasdill, William

Company Chief Clerk, see Ebsworth, Thomas Lindsay

Company Coal Establishment Manager, see Henderson, John

Company Colliery Engineer, see Steel, James

Company Commissioner, see Parry, Sir Edward

Company Farm Overseer, see Tozer, Thomas Norris

Company Gardener, see Baker, John, I.S.

Company London Office Clerk, see Ebsworth, Henry Thomas

Company Store Keeper, see Wetherman, William; White James Charles

Company Superintendent of Agriculture, see Burnett, William

Company Superintendent of Flocks, see Dutton, William Hampden; Hall, Charles

Company Superintendent of Stud, see Hall, Henry

Company Surgeon and Botanist, see Stacy, Dr James Edward

Company Surveyor see Armstrong, John; Dangar, Henry

Company Wool Classer, see Swayne, John

Connelly, Taylor Nicholas: and removal of stock from A. A. Co. property, 1007a

Constable, William (convict): and change of ticket of leave, 860; withdrawal by of monies kept in his name, 856

constables see constables in A. A. Co.'s establishment; Government Constables

constables in A. A. Co.'s establishment: public use of, 667; see also convict constables; free constables; scourger; ticket of leave constable

convict constables: discharge of one, 677; salaries and allowances of, 644

convict labour: supply of to Coal works at Newcastle, 949, 952

convicts: absconding of, 662; assigned (see assigned convicts); committal of to Lunatic Asylum, 661, 679; death of, 879; marriage of, 1011; money kept in names of, 826, 849, 856; petition of to be reunited with family, 689a; quit rent and, 704; transfer of from A. A. Co., 642; transfer of to A. A. Co., 642, 680; see also convict constables; convict labour; ticket of leave; ticket of leave constables

Coombes, James: and ticket of leave application, 645

Coombs, William (convict): medical treatment for, 824

Cooper, Thomas (convict): transfer of to Edward W. Lord, 642

Corlette, Captain James (of the *Lambton*), 651, 664, 665; and advertisement for shearers, 699b, 931a; and forwarding of box for Governors and Directors of A. A. Co., 946; and goods damaged on *Richard Reynolds*, 997; packets for, 740; and receipt of damaged goods, 936; and sale of hides and other items, 700; and sale of new vessel, 679b; and transshipment of wool from the *Lambton* to the *Arundel*, 700; and transshipment of wool from the *Lambton* to the *City of Edinboro'* or the *Arundel*, 747; and transport of coal to Sydney, 700; and transport of flour, 760; and transport of wool on the *Lochiel*, 1006

Note: References are to letter numbers not page numbers.

Cory, Edward Gostwyck (Patterson's River): and tender for supply of flour to 'Warrah,' Liverpool Plains, 1056
cottages see unfurnished cottages to let
Countess of Harcourt: convicts on, 904
court house (A. A. Co.'s): public use of, 667
Court of Directors: communication of Henry Dangar with, 830; request of J. E. Stacy to, 829
Cowell, William (bricklayer and mason, I. S.): and exchange of men, 775, and request for information on limestone discovered near Stroud for making of lime, 808
Cowpastures see Cowper, Thomas
Cowper, Thomas (Clifton, Cowpastures/Campbell Town): and payment of account, 831, 878; and stud service, 790
Cox, Edward (Fern Hills, Mulgoa): and payment of account, 977, 1096; and stud service, 785
Cox, George (Wimbourne, Penrith): and payment of account, 972; and stud service, 803
Cox, James (Maitland): and transfer of convict to A. A. Co., 680
Craig-darroch see Mackenzie, George
Craigievar: shipment of wool on, 729
credit: payment for coal on, 651
Croasdill, William (Company Bookkeeper at Newcastle): draft drawn by, 878, 1009, 1037; and map of coal grant at Newcastle and Company theodolite, 947; and drafts for salary of James Steel and balance of wages for late Michael Steel, 1036; and order of flour, 1031; see also Baker, John
crown or mortice wheel, 707
Cumberland Cottage, Liverpool see Moore, J. J.; Wylde, Sir John
Dangar, Henry (Company Surveyor), 648; and A. A. Co. theodolite, 1023; and communication to Court of Directors, 830; and description of land grant at Newcastle, 998; and duties to be performed before quitting Port Stephens and financial settlement, 840; and error in survey of land near Peel's River, 1026; and examination of Liverpool Plains and Peel's River, 649 (paras 17–23); and letter from Henry T. Ebsworth, 932; and maps of land at Liverpool Plains and Peel's River, 1024; and payment for survey and map of coal grant at Newcastle, 947; and price of rams, 939; proposal of meeting with Mr White in Newcastle, 637; and request for opinion on alternative locations re land grant in view of rejection of Liverpool Plains and Peel's River by Colonial Government, 834; and return of A. A. Co. theodolite, 947; and road through property of L. Myles, 853; and survey and map of coal grant at Newcastle, 947; survey and mapping of Clergy and School Reserve, 649 (para. 12); survey and mapping of land between Peel's River and Dividing Range, 764; and survey of Coal Grant at Newcastle, 953; and survey of land north of Manning River, 10–11), 649 (paras 7; and surveying and mapping land at Liverpool Plains and Peel's River, 959; surveying and mapping of country adjacent to Newcastle for application for coal grant, 721; and surveying and mapping of land at Liverpool Plains and Peel's River, 954; and surveying of coal grant at Newcastle, and gratuity, 844; termination of services of, 835, 841; and terms for surveying and mapping work, 991, 1008

Dangar, William: and price of rams, 939
Darch, Henry (Sir Edward Parry's secretary): and alleged drunkenness of Mr Price, 1092; and report of alleged drunkenness of Mr Price, 1091
Darling, General Ralph (Governor of NSW): and exchange of land grants, 649 (para. 5); and supply of convict labour to Coal Works at Newcastle, 949
Davidson, James (convict): medical treatment for, 769
Davis, John (convict): transfer of assignment of, 666
Dawson, Robert. (former Company Agent): and loan to A. W. Scott, 731
death: of convicts, 879, 941
debt: settlement of by W. Scott, 745
Dent, Thomas, & Co see Thomas Dent & Co
Department of the Master Attendant: accounts for supplies to, 1070; accounts for supply of coal to, 871, 919, 1003; receipt for payment of account for supply of coal to, 811a
Deputy Commissary General see Laidley, James
Devitt, Michael (convict): petition of to be reunited with family, 689a
Dimotte, Daniel (convict): committal of to Lunatic Asylum, 661, 679, 820
discovery: scientific, by James King, 916
divine service, 1029, 1040
Dodd, Simon: and draft on Bank of Australia, 1076; and meeting with Sir Edward Parry, 1058; and request for employment, 1017
Dormer, Ellen: hospital expenses for, 905
drugs: requisition for, 752
drunkenness: of Mr Price, alleged, 1091, 1092
drunkenness and disorderly conduct, 814
Dumaresq, Lieutenant Colonel Henry (St Helier's): and alleged drunkenness of Mr Price, 1092; and arrangements for transport on the *Sophia Jane* of family and baggage of, 1063; and arrangements for travel to Port Stephens, 925; and assistance to John Armstrong with survey, 1024; draft on Bank of Australia to credit of, 921; and draft to credit of, 1033; and free conveyance on the *Lambton* of stores for private use of Captain R. G.

Note: References are to letter numbers not page numbers.

Moffatt, 1065, 1082; and letter of attorney empowering him to act as Commissioner of A. A. Co., 1107; and meeting with after arrival, 1099; non-renewal of agreement of employment of William Street, 1083; and report of alleged drunkenness of Mr Price, 1091; and succession to Sir Edward Parry as Commissioner, 925; and tender for supply of flour to 'Warrah,' Liverpool Plains, 768

Dutton, William Hampden (former Company Superintendent of Flocks): and documents re claim of Carl Rantzsch and others against, 755

Eales, John: and tender for supply of flour to 'Warrah,' Liverpool Plains, 1055

Ebsworth, Henry Thomas (Clerk in the Company's London Office): letter to Henry Dangar, 932

Ebsworth, James Edward (Company Accountant): decision of Supreme Court in favour of A. A. Co. in case of claim by G. M. Slade on, for the Company, 1041; exchange of assigned convicts with, 981; removal of, 862; and reward for William Barnes for apprehension of runaways, 690, 691, 714; security of property of William Barton in house to be vacated by, 862; security property of William Barton in house occupied by, 865; and submission by William Barnes of affidavit in respect of outstanding claim to bench of magistrates, 708; in support of petition of convict to be reunited with family, 689a, 699a

Ebsworth, Thomas Lindsay (Company Chief Clerk): memorandum from re sketch of account, 674

Editors, *The Australian*: denial of statement in *The Australian* re alleged outrages against Aborigines by servants of A. A. Co., 1011a; and order for copies of, 880

Editors, *Sydney Gazette*: denial of statement in *The Australian* re alleged outrages against Aborigines by servants of A. A. Co., 1011a

Editors, *Sydney Herald*: denial of statement in *The Australian* re alleged outrages against Aborigines by servants of A. A. Co., 1011a

Editors, *Sydney Monitor*: and A. A. Co. account, 900; denial of statement in *The Australian* re alleged outrages against Aborigines by servants of A. A. Co., 1011a; order for copies of, 640

Edwards, William (convict): alteration of ticket of leave of, 1106; alterations of ticket of leave of, 1088; change of assignment of, 706

Eliza: convicts on, 675, 981

Elizabeth: bill of lading for hides carried by, 946; transport of tea, 883

Ellen: transport of flour on, 676, 753; and transport of flour on, 699; transport of wheat on, 652

Emmett, Thomas (convict): erroneous payment of, 812

employment by A. A. Co.: and allowance on quitting for Thomas N.Tozer, 863; cancellation of agreement with: John Stokes re, 1097; Joseph Watson re, 1097; continuation of agreement with: H. Hall re, 806, 821; Henry Hall re, 776; James Steel re, 777, 817; John Swayne re, 778, 819; of former convicts, 705; non-renewal of agreement with William Street re, 1083; proposed cancellation of agreement re by Thomas N. Tozer, 859; request for, 655, 682, 693, 697, 720, 854, 1017, 1038; terms for three-year engagement of George Jenkin, 993; terms of new agreement of with George Jenkin, 1079; *see also* shortage of men; termination of services

Enquiry into the Revenues and Expenditure of New South Wales: and abandonment of retention by Government of Clergy and School Reserves, 1015

exchange of land grants – claim for two parcels: at Liverpool Plains and on Peel's River: appointment of professional person to communicate with Surveyor General re land grants at Liverpool Plains and Peel's River, 982; arguments against acceptance of Governor's recommendation of alternative single parcel near Peel's River, 841; authorisation for, 943; consent to by British government, 5, 26, 29, 31, 33), 649 (paras 4; grievances of A. A. Co. against Surveyor General in relation to, 842; proposal re land between Peel's River and Dividing Range, 764; rebuttal of arguments against, 649 (paras 27–59); rebuttal of Surveyor General's arguments in favour of alternative single parcel near Peel's River, 841 (A–L); request for advice re alternatives in view of rejection of Liverpool Plains and Peel's River land by Colonial Government, 835; request for reconsideration of rejection of by Governor Bourke, 649; written authority from Governor Bourke for temporary occupation of land at Liverpool Plains, 902a

executors of late John Oxley: and stud service, 801

executors of late John Thomas Campbell: and stud service, 796

families: difficulties in supporting, 654, 658; petition of convicts to be reunited with, 689a, 699a

farriers: inquiries re assigned convict, 1074

Feales, John (miller, Windsor): and money in Savings Bank for Thomas Broadhurst, 957

Fern Hills, Mulgoa , Penrith *see* Cox, Edward

Field, John (convict constable): and reward for apprehension of runaways, 690; transfer of from A. A. Co. service to Government service, 677

Note: References are to letter numbers not page numbers.

Field, Robert (convict): and compliance with regulations of ticket of leave of, 730
financial matters, 657, 674, 687, 698, 700, 701, 707, 729, 749, 756, 812, 828, 839, 850, 873, 894, 905, 912, 946, 961, 987, 1005, 1014, 1051; settlement of debt to A. A. Co. by W. Scott, 745; *see also* accounts
Florentia: convicts on, 643, 705
flour: and issue of extra to Military Detachment at Port Stephens as replacement for damaged flour, 1100; order for, 753, 1031; order for for surveying party, 648; order for from Hughes & Hosking, 760; quality of, 702; shipment of, 926; supply of to Military Detachment at Port Stephens, 672; tender for supply of and other rations, 864a; tender for supply of at Newcastle, 886; tender for supply of to Liverpool Plains, 723; tender (with price) for supply of to Military Detachment at Port Stephens, 742, 1019; tenders for supply of to 'Warrah,' Liverpool Plains, 738a, 765, 766, 767, 768, 1005a, 1049, 1050, 1053, 1054, 1055, 1056; transport of on the *Ellen*, 699; transport of on the *Lambton*, 707; wheat to be ground into, 651, 674, 753
Forbes, Chief Justice: and account, 771
Foreman, Lukin (convict): petition of to be reunited with family, 699a
Foss, Mr: and purchase of ponies, 1086
Foster (convict): and alleged illegal detention in A. A. Co. employment of, 1104
4 horse power high pressure portable beam engine with fly wheel, etc., 897a
4 horse power high pressure steam engine: sale of, 908a, 909, 913, 935
Fox's Tooth Keys, 657
free constables: salaries and allowances of, 644; transfer of one to Government service, 677
free store: continuation of by Richard Stubbs, 814, 816, 823
Freith, Thomas (convict): death of, 879
French merino rams: price of, 939
Funchal: transport of wool, 1007
fund for religion and education: provision of by A. A. Co. and lease of Clergy and School Reserves at Port Stephens, 1015
Gaggin, W. John: and payment of account, 970; and stud service, 800
gardeners: request for assignment of convicts, 979
General Hospital, Sydney: admission of assigned convicts to, 675, 716, 738, 769, 824, 933, 996; care of A. A. Co.'s men discharged from prior to return to work, 694
George Bunn & Co: and bale of canvas not received, 997, 1005; and ballast of wool ships, 901; and deficient articles, 905; and delivery of letters and newspapers, 1031; and financial matters, 867, 873, 894, 905, 912, 936, 946, 961, 987, 1005, 1014, 1028, 1031, 1051; and forwarding of box for Governors and Directors of A. A. Co. and letters, 946; and goods damaged on *Richard Reynolds*, 997; and goods destroyed by sea water, 936; and hospital expenses for Ellen Dormer, 905; and information on sailings for England, 1031; and letters for James Norton, 1059; and letters to proprietors of stock in A. A. Co. in respect of Annual Report, 1010; and letters to proprietors of stock in A. A. Co. in respect of call of shares, 875, 875a, 950; and miners, 905; and non-receipt by John Henderson, Newcastle, of bars of iron, 1059; parcel sent to, 1059a; and payment for order of tea, 899; and payment from J. E. manning for freight and iron, 935; and promissory notes of W. Manning, 936; and Quarterly and Annual Accounts of A. A. Co., 936; and requisitions, 867, 894, 909, 936, 960, 997, 1051; and requisitions of flour, 1031; and sale of 4 horse power high pressure steam engine, 908a, 909, 913; and salt and vinegar, 894; and shipment of castings, 1051; and tender for transport of wool on the Lochiel to London, 1006; *see also* Bunn, George
Georgiana: convicts on, 659
glass-making: 893
Glenlee, Campbell Town *see* Howe, William
Goderich, Viscount (Secretary of State for the Colonies): and authorisation of possession of two tracts of land selected by A. A. Co. (Liverpool Plains and Peel's River), 943; forwarding of letter to, 944; and price of coal supplied to Colonial Government, issue of computation of prime cost, and payment of accounts, 942; and request documents on A. A. Co. claim for exchange land grants be passed on to for resolution, 841, 842; and transmission of information about scientific discovery of James King to, 916
Goodwin, James (convict): and alteration to ticket of leave, 929; request of to receive small sums of money, 826, payment of monies to credit of, 849
Goodwin, William (convict): assignment of to A. A. Co., 663, 695
Gostwyck Farm, Patterson's River *see* Cory, E. G.
Goulburn *see* Howey, Henry
Government Constables: payment of supplies for, 722
Government Gazette: advertisement re share call, 949a; non-publication of advertisement re share call, 985
Government Surveyor, *see* White, George Boyle (Government Surveyor):
Governor Halkett: damaged cans of oil on, 749, 805
Governor of New South Wales *see* Bourke,

Note: References are to letter numbers not page numbers.

Major General Richard; Darling, General Ralph
grazing rights at Liverpool Plains, 649 (paras 35–38), 684, 685, 686
Grose, Joseph Hickey (steamship owner).: and arrangements for transport on the Sophia Jane of families and baggage of, respectively, Lieutenant Colonel Henry Dumaresq and Sir Edward Parry, 1063
Guilford: convicts on, 826, 849, 929
Hadell, Gottfried (former Overseer of Shepherds, I. S.): draft in favour of, 739
Hall, Charles (Company Superintendent of Flocks): and alteration of ticket of leave of William Edwards, 1106; and construction of wagon by William Smyth, [994]; and examination of land to west of Clergy and School reserve, 649 (para. 13); and examination of original grant, 649 (para. 6); and price of rams given to Henry Dangar, 939; and removal of stock from A. A. Co. property, 1007a; and sale of merino rams, 682a
Hall, Henry (Company Superintendent of Stud): and apprehension of runaways, 751; and arrangement with Maitland Jockey Club for races; and continuation of employment agreement, 776, 806; and report of alleged drunkenness of Mr Price, 1091; and salary and continuation of employment agreement, 821; and sale of Cleveland horse, 679a, 699b
Hames, George (convict): assignment of to A. A. Co., 663, 695
Hamlyn, Richard Julian: and request for employment, 693
Hancock, Charles (convict): alteration to ticket of leave of, 638
Hancock, Charles (ticket of leave constable): transfer of from A. A. Co. service to Government service, 677
Hassall, Jonathon (Campbelltown): and payment of account, 969; and stud service, 798
head stock keeper: advertisement for, 699b
Hely, Peter (convict): medical treatment for, 675
Hely, Frederick Augustus and money in Savings Bank for Thomas Broadhurst, 957; and payment of monies to credit of James Goodwin, 849
Hemerton, Joshua (convict): assignment of, 1068
Henderson, James (convict): disposal of property of after his murder, 906; and proceeds of sale of property of, balance of his wages and reward for apprehension of runaways, 1075
Henderson, John (Manager of Company Coal Establishment): and A. A. Co.'s Coal Works and proposed Town of Newcastle, 1069; and letters to proprietors of stock in A. A. Co. in respect of call of shares, 689, 734, 876, 951; and non-receipt of bars of iron, 1059; parcel for, 741; and payment for rams, 888; and payment of account to John Reid, 938; and repair of public carts at Newcastle, 758; and tenders for supply of flour, sugar and salt at Newcastle, 886; and tenders for supply of flour to 'Warrah,' Liverpool Plains, 738a, 1005a
Hercules: convicts on, 661, 679, 820
Herring, Henry (convict-constable): allegations by Wynter and against Sir Edward Parry and others in employ of A. A. Co. in relation to Aborigines, 989
Hewitson, William (convict): return of to employment of A. A. Co., 705
hides: bill of lading for, 946; sale of, 700
Hooghley: convicts on, 645
horse races *see* races
horses: purchase of stallions, 896; sale of, 1032, 1087; stud service, 701a, 706a, 783, 784, 785, 786, 787, 788, 789, 790, 791, 792, 793, 794, 796, 797, 798, 799, 800, 801, 802, 803, 811, 832, 940d, 977, 1060; *see also* Cleveland (horses); ponies
horseshoers: request for assignment of, 750, 990
Hosking *see* Hughes & Hosking
hospital expenses, 905
hospital fees: payment of, 752
Howe, William (Campbelltown): and payment of account, 971; and stud service, 802
Howey, Henry: claim of on A. A. Co. re stud service, 832; and stud service, 792
Howitt, Adam (blacksmith, I. S.): and quitting service of A. A. Co., 653; and request for employment as blacksmith at A. A. Co. colliery at Newcastle, 1038; and support of his family, 654
Hughes, John Terry: and sale of goods from India to by Mrs Poole, 851
Hughes & Hosking: and order for flour, 760; and taking coals for cash, 774
Hunter River Jockey Club: patron of and subscription to, 890
Hunter's River *see* Dangar, Henry; Dumaresq, Lieutenant Colonel Henry; Eales, J.; Ogilvie, William; Oliver, G. A.
Hunter's River Sweepstakes: nominations to Committee of, 833
Hyndes, Thomas: and payment of account for stores by, 781; and proposal to sell coal by chaldron instead of ton, 1093
Hyson Skin (tea): order for, 899; supply of, 883
impounding: of A. A. Co. bullocks by William Ogilvie, 1101; of cattle depastured on A. A. Co. land near Williams River, 1036a
infectious diseases: prosecution for infringement of law re, 847; *see also* Scab Act
Innes, Archibald Clunes: and account for supplies to, 770

Note: References are to letter numbers not page numbers.

Inspector General of Hospitals, Sydney, *see* Bowman, Dr James
insolent or improper language: of A. A. Co. servants, 853
invoices: for wheat, 652
iron and steel: bought by J. E. Manning, 850; non-delivery of, 752, 756, 805, 850; non-receipt of bars of iron by John Henderson, Newcastle, 1059; price for old iron, 988; *see also* casting; castings
Irrawang *see* King, James
Isabella: transport coal to Government of Van Diemen's Land, 1071
Jelf, Robert (convict): and application for ticket of leave for Sydney, 897
Jenkin, George (Company Assistant Superintendent of Flocks): and terms for three-year engagement with A. A. Co., 993; and terms of new agreement for employment with A. A. Co., 1079
John: convicts on, 705
John's Mill, Williams River *see* Singleton, B.; Yeoman, George
Jones, Richard: and order for tea, 899; and supply of tea, 883
Jones, Robert: and return of convict to Government, 904
Jones, Thomas (Paterson's River): and Cleveland colt, 701a
Jones, William (convict): exchange of assignment of, 981
kangaroo skins: return of, 752
Kendrick, John: and order for wheat and price of wheat, and pony, 1047; and sale of pony/horse to, 1032
kennels: requisition of, 729
King, James (Irrawang): and specimens of cut glass, sand for glass-making, and vine-cuttings, 893; and transmission of information about his scientific discovery to Lord Goderich, 916
Kinghorne, W.: and transport coal to Government of Van Diemen's Land on the *Isabella*, 1071
Kinross, Hunter's River *see* Oliver, G. A.
Kent St, Sydney, *see* Murdoch, James
King St, *see* Warlters, Jeremiah
Laidley, James (Deputy Commissary General): and account for supplies to Colonial Government, 773, 858, 908, 992, 1067; and account for supplies to Military Detachment at Port Stephens, 673, 773, 846, 858, 908, 930, 992, 1067, 1077; and account for supply of coal, 1018; and account for supply of coal and other provisions and deductions made thereto, 724; and account for supply of coal for Beacon Light at Newcastle, 726; and account for supply of coal to Colonial Government, 669, 670; and account for supply of coal to Commissariat Department, 726, 837, 846, 872, 915, 920, 930, 1004, 1072; and account for supply of coal to Commissariat Department to be shipped on the *Isabella* to Government of Van Diemen's Land, 1071; and account for supply of coal to Government of Van Diemen's Land, 1084; and account for supply of meat and flour to Military Detachment at Port Stephens, 672; and accounts to be paid, 891; and delay in payment of account for supplies to military Detachment at Port Stephens, 948; and financial matters, 701; and forms of vouchers for freight and passage for which Government contracts to pay, and periodicity of payment, 1045; and information of rates for freight and passage which Government contracts to pay, 1016, 1044; and measurement of quantities of coal, 671; and non-payment of accounts by Commissariat Office, 743; and payment for freight and passage on the *Lambton*, 1061; and payment of account for coal, 927; and payments for supplies, 712; and payments for supplies and deductions made thereto, 713; and receipt for payment of accounts, 1002; and repair of public carts at Newcastle, 758; and tender for supplies to Commissariat Office (including rum, bread and mutton) and Military Detachment at Port Stephens (beef and flour), 742; and tender for supplies to Military Detachment at Port Stephens (beef and flour), 1019
Lake Macquarie *see* Warner, Mr
Lamb Buchanan & Co: and tender for transport of wool, 1007
Lambton: deficiency in vinegar transported on, 894; discontinuation of free freight and passage on for Colonial Government business, 1061; examination of bottom of, 729; free conveyance on of stores for private use of Captain R. G. Moffatt, 1065, 1082; free passage on for Government police, 983; free passage on for Joseph Watson and family, 955; and goods destroyed by sea water, 936; passage on for Joseph Watson, 940 (a); transshipment of goods from the *Prince Regent*, 850; transshipment of wool from to the *City of Edinboro'* or the *Arundel*, 747; transport of barilla, 664, 665; transport of castings, 674, 1051; transport of cheese, 911; transport of coal, 651, 700; transport of flour, 702, 707, 760, 926; transport of stores, 857, 960; transport of sugar, 813, 838; transport of surplus goods for auction, 825; transport of wheat, 674; *see also* Corlette, Captain James
land grant to A. A. Co.: exchange of portion of (see exchange of land grants); original (see original land grant)
land in cultivation: return, 853a
language *see* insolent or improper language
Larnack [Larnach], John (Castle Forbes): and information about persons in possession of

Note: References are to letter numbers not page numbers.

bags bearing the mark of A. A. Co., 869; and tender to supply flour to 'Warrah,' Liverpool Plains, 766

legal opinion: of Attorney General re case of apprehension of runaways, 751; request for on claim of Henry Howey on A. A. Co. re services of one of Company's horses, 832; request for on refusal to pay living expenses to Mrs William Burnett, 748

Leman, Samuel (convict): withdrawal by of monies kept in his name, 856

letter of attorney: empowering Lieutenant Colonel Henry Dumaresq to act as Commissioner of A. A. Co., 1107

Leyton: convicts on, 855, 933

licence for public houses: free, application for by Richard Stubbs, 641; held by Richard Stubbs, 692, 814, 815

licence of occupation: for lands near Newcastle to be granted to A. A. Co., 922

lime: making of from limestone discovered near Stroud, 808

limestone: discovered near Stroud and making of lime, 808

Lindinger, T. *see* Meyer, T. A.

Linsky, John (convict): absconding of, 662

Liverpool *see* Moore, J. J.; Wylde, Sir John

Liverpool Plains: alternative locations for land grant in view of rejection by Colonial Government of land at Peel's River and, 834; application of law of Colony of NSW at, 902a; appointment of professional person to communicate with re land grants at Peel's River and, 982; and assignment of convicts, 980; authorisation for land grant at, 943; consent to by British government to exchange of land grants at Peel's River and, 5, 26, 29, 31, 33), 649 (paras 4; delineation and accurate marking of land grants at Peel's River and, 1000, 1001; and delineation and description of land at, 959; examination land at Peel's River and, 649 (paras 17–23); examination of, 649 (paras 17–23); grazing rights at, 649 (paras 35–38), 684, 685, 686; information on in Surveyor General's Office, 649 (paras 14–17); offer of supplies for by James Scott, 918; rejection by Colonial Government of grant of land at Peel's River and, 835; surveying and mapping of land at, 954, 959; tenders for supply of flour to, 723; written authority from Governor Bourke for temporary occupation of land at, 902a; *see also* exchange of land grants; 'Warrah,' Liverpool Plains

Lloyd: convicts on, 1068

loan: repayment of by A. W. Scott, 731

Lochiel: transport of wool to London, 1006

Lord, Edward W.: and exchange of convict workers, 642

Lord, Simeon: and price offered for sheep skins, 744

Lunar: and deficient articles, 905

Lunatic Asylum: committal of convict to, 661, 679, 820

Lyons, Isaac (convict): medical treatment of, 996; request for opinion of Dr Mitchell in case of blindness of, 1073

McArthur, Hannibal Hawkins *see* Macarthur, James, James Bowman and H. H. McArthur

Macarthur, James: and claim by William Wetherman, 711

Macarthur, James, James Bowman and H. H. McArthur: and request for legal opinion on claim of Henry Howey on A. A. Co. re services of one of Company's horses, 832

Macarthy, Florence (convict): medical treatment for, 675

Macauley, Alexander *see* Becket, James

Macdonald, Alexander (convict): petition of for ticket of leave, 732a

McDonald, John (Pitt Town): and tender for supply of flour to 'Warrah,' Liverpool Plains, 1049

McGarvie, Patrick (former convict): alleged runaway, 757

McIntyre, Peter: letter to [unreadable], 772

Mackaness, John: and payment of account, 966; and stud service, 794

Mackenzie, George (Craig-dorroch): and payment of account for rams, 888; and permission for his drays to pass through A. A. Co. land, 1039

Mackenzie, W. H.: and draft on Bank of Australia, and matters relating to share call, 878; and draft on Bank of Australia to credit of Lieutenant Colonel Henry Dumaresq, 1033; and instructions to Bank of Australia re installments payable on shares to stockholders, 1057; and notification of Bank of Australia of appointment of Lieutenant Colonel Henry Dumaresq as Commissioner of A. A. Co., 1090; and promissory note of W. Manning, 1081; and transactions with Bank of Australia, 866, 984, 1009, 1037, 1064, 1078, 1098

Mackie, John: and sale of barilla, 664

McLeay, Alexander (Colonial Secretary): and account, 845; and account for supplies to Department of the Master Attendant, 1070; and account for supply of coal to Colonial Department, 836; and account for supply of coal to Colonial Government, 669, 725; and account for supply of coal to Commissariat Department, 836, 871; and account for supply of coal to Department of the Master Attendant, 871, 919, 1003; and accounts for supply of meat and flour to Military Detachment at Port Stephens, 672; and allegations against servants of A. A. Co. in relation to Aborigines, 1013; and allegations by Wynter and Henry Herring against Sir Edward Parry and others in employ of

Note: References are to letter numbers not page numbers.

A. A. Co. in relation to Aborigines, 989; and alteration of ticket of leave of Charles Hancock, 638; and application for coal grant in country adjacent to Newcastle, including map, 721; and application for free licence for public house, 641; and application for ticket of leave to work for A. A. Co. by James Coombes, 645; and appointment of professional person to communicate with Surveyor General re land grants at Liverpool Plains and Peel's River, 982; and appointment of stipendiary magistrate and constabulary at Port Stephens, 956; and arguments for rejection of Governor's recommendation re taking land near Peel's River as one parcel and rebutting views of Surveyor General, and requesting documents on issue be passed on to Secretary of State for the Colonies for resolution, 841; and assignment of bricklayer and sawyer to A. A. Co. coal mines at Newcastle, 923, 952; and Attorney General's opinion and examination of Thomas Beckett, John Swayne and Henry Hall re apprehension of runaways, 751; and authorisation of possession of two tracts of land selected by A. A. Co. (Liverpool Plains and Peel's River), 943; and claim for reward for apprehension of runaways by William Barnes, 714; and committal of convict to Lunatic Asylum, 661, 820; and compliance with regulations of tickets of leave of Robert Field and other convicts, 730; and delineation and accurate marking of boundaries of land grants at Liverpool Plains and Peel's River, 1001; and description of land grant at Newcastle, 998; and dumping of ballast at port of Newcastle, 902; and duplicate of letter to Secretary of State, 1021; and establishment of police at Port Stephens, 983; and establishment of police at Port Stephens and A. A. Co. contribution thereto, 1043; and extension of Scab Act, 1042; and extent to which laws of the Colony of NSW apply on A. A. Co. land at Liverpool Plains, 902a; and finalisation of coal grant at Newcastle, 887; and forwarding of letter to Secretary of State for the Colonies, 944; and free passage on the *Lambton*, 983; and information of rates for freight and passage which departments of Government apart from departments under Deputy Commissary General contract to pay, 1044; and issue of computation of prime cost of coal supplied to Colonial Government, 942; and legality of Sir Edward Parry and J. Edward Ebsworth sitting on bench in case of Richard Stubbs, 692; and licence of occupation for lands near Newcastle to be granted to A. A. Co., 922; and list of ticket of leave men at Port Stephens, 762; and non-assignment of convicts to A. A. Co., 980; and non-payment of accounts, 761; and non-publication of share calls in *Government Gazette*, 985; and payment for freight and passage on the *Lambton*, 1061; and payment of account for coal by Deputy Commissary General, 927; and payment of account for coal supplied to Colonial Government, 810, 942; and petition, 903; and price of coal supplied to Colonial Government, 895, 942; and price of coal supplied to Colonial Government, and account for arrears, 914; and problems with payment of accounts for supply of coal to Commissariat Department, 725; and proposal in relation to grant of land between Peel's River and Dividing Range, and re coal grant at Newcastle, 764; and proposal to replace Military Detachment at Port Stephens with force of mounted police, 956; and prosecution of infringements of law re infectious diseases, 847; and provision by A. A. Co. of fund for religion and education and lease of Clergy and School Reserves at Port Stephens, 1015; and public use of A. A. Co. property, 667; and receipt of circular, 1052; and receipt of petition, 945; and redemption of quit rent in respect of convict labour, 704; and rejection of criticism of attitude towards Surveyor General, 842; and removal of Military Detachment at Port Stephens, 956; and request for documents on grievances against Surveyor General be passed on to Secretary of State for the Colonies for resolution, 842; and request for extension of Scab Act to 'Warrah,' Liverpool Plains, 1042; and request of ticket of leave men receiving small sums of money, 826; and restatement of grievances against Surveyor General, 842; and retaining of runaways that may come on to A. A. Co. land, 1012; and retention of Military Detachment at Port Stephens, 1043; and return of number, etc. of Aborigines in district and issue of blankets to Aborigines, 715; and reward for information about dumping of ballast at port of Newcastle, 902; and survey of anchorages of Swan River, 668; and survey of lands near Newcastle to be granted to A. A. Co., 922; and tabular return of the quantity of land in cultivation and the produce thereof on Estate of A. A. Co., 1046; and temporary occupation of land near 'Warrah,' 683, 847; and transfer of convicts, 642; and warrant for lands near Newcastle to be granted to A. A. Co., 922

Macpherson, Mr: and miners, 905

McQuaid: and exchange of men with William Cowell, 775

Macvitie, Thomas (Managing Director, Bank of Australia): and authority for paying outstanding drafts upon Committee of

Note: References are to letter numbers not page numbers.

Management of A. A. Co., 739; letter for, 740; and stoppage of payment of stolen draft, 736

magistracy: and control of police, 710; *see also* Ebsworth, J. Edward; Moffatt, Captain; Parry, Sir Edward; Resident Magistrates, Port Stephens; Stipendiary Magistrate, Port Stephens

Maitland *see* Bowen, William; Cohen, P. J.; Cox, James, Ryan, John; Smyth, William; Yeoman, George

Maitland Jockey Club: and arrangements for races, 898; subscription to, 910

Malabar: convicts on, 638

Mangles: convicts on, 662

Manlius: convicts on, 659, 897

Mann, John (convict): assignment of to A. A. Co., 882

Manning, James Edye (Registrar of the Supreme Court): and proceeds of sale of property of late James Henderson, balance of his wages and reward for apprehension of runaways, 1075; and property of late James Henderson, 906

Manning, J. E., senior: and accounts for sale of steam engine and models to, and for freight and iron, 935; and sale of 4 horse power high pressure steam engine, 913; promissory notes of, 936, 1081

Manning & Raymond: letters to, 961

mapping: of Clergy and School Reserve, 649 (para. 12); of coal grant at Newcastle, 947; of country adjacent to Newcastle for application for coal grant, 721; of land at Liverpool Plains and Peel's River, 954; of land between Peel's River and Dividing Range, 764; tenders for, 991, 1000, 1008; terms for undertaking, 991

maps: of land at Liverpool Plains and Peel's River, 1024

Mariner: convicts on, 689a

Marquis of Hastings: convicts on, 856

Marquis of Huntl(e)y: convicts on, 856, 879, 1011

marriage: of two convicts, 1011

Marsden, Rev. Samuel: and payment of account, 965, 1030; and stud service, 793, 1060

Master Attendant's Department *see* Department of the Master Attendant

Matavia, Campbell Town *see* Hassall, Jonathon

Matom, Thomas (convict): transfer of assignment of, 1060a

Matthewson, John (convict): medical treatment for, 738

May, William (shepherd and ploughman, I. S.): and cancellation of agreement with, 660

McAndrew, John (convict): exchange of assignment of, 981

Meares, Joshua (convict): transfer of assignment of, 1060a

meat: supply of to Military Detachment at Port Stephens, 672

mechanics: shortage of, 639, 980; and work at Coal Works at Newcastle, 639, 949

medical treatment: for assigned convicts, 675, 716, 738, 769

Melville: convicts on, 642

Merchant, *see* Spark, Alexander Brodie

merchant and Company's agent in Sydney, *see* Bunn, George

Merchant, Richard (shepherd, I. S.): affidavit of re apprehension of runaways by William Barnes, 714; and apprehension of runaways, 690

merino rams: advertisement re sale of, 682a

Merton, Hunter's River *see* Ogilvie, William

Meyer, T. A.: and request for employment, 854

Military Detachment at Port Stephens: account for supplies to, 930; accounts for supplies to, 673, 712, 713, 724, 754, 773, 846, 858, 908, 992, 1067, 1077; and delay in payment of account for supplies to, 948; and issue of extra flour to as replacement for damaged flour, 1100; removal of current, 931; replacement of, 956; retention of, 1043; supply of meat and flour to, 672; tender for supplies to by A. A. Co., 742, 1019; withdrawal of, 1019

miller, Windsor, *see* Feales, John

millers: application for assignment of convicts, 1048

Mills, John (convict): claim of to ticket of leave, 718, 719

miners, 905, 949; assignment of, 980

Minerva: convicts on, 680

Minstrel: convicts on, 769

Mitchell, Dr James: and admission of assigned convict to General Hospital, Sydney, 716, 738, 769, 824, 855, 933, 996; request for opinion of in case of blindness of convict, 1073; and treatment of assigned convicts, 675

Mitchell, F.: and payment for coal, 651

Mitchell, Major Thomas Livingstone (Surveyor General): appointment of professional person to communicate with re land grants at Liverpool Plains and Peel's River, 982; and Coal Grant at Newcastle, 953; and delineation and accurate marking of land grants at Liverpool Plains and Peel's River, including boundaries, 1001; and description of land grant at Newcastle, 998; grievances of A. A. Co. against, 842; prejudice of against A. A. Co., 56, 59), 649 (paras 55, 842; rebuttal of arguments of against exchange of land grants, 649 (paras 35–59); rebuttal of arguments of in favour of alternative single parcel near Peel's River, 841 (A–L); and surveying of range on south-western side of Peel River, 637

Moffatt, Captain Robert Gerald (17th Regiment, Resident Magistrate): and allegations against servants of A. A. Co. in relation to Aborigines, 1013; and allegations by Wynter and Henry Herring against Sir

Note: References are to letter numbers not page numbers.

Edward Parry and others in employ of A. A. Co. in relation to Aborigines, 989; and alleged drunkenness of Mr Price, 1092; and alleged prohibition of Rev. C. P. N. Wilton's coming on to A. A. Co. Estate, 1066; and application for six boys, 1085; and arrival of Lieutenant Colonel Henry Dumaresq, 1099; and circumstance to be related to Mr White, 1094; and closing of public house on A. A. Co. Estate, 814, 815; and competency to hold court in Stroud in respect of charges against a constable, 710; and copies of police proceedings re alleged illegal detention in A. A. Co. employment of Foster, assigned servant of Mr Barton, 1104; and discontinuation of free freight and passage on the *Lambton* on account of Colonial Government, 1061; and employment of A. A. Co. court house, constables, clerk and other property for public purposes, 667; and examination of Thomas Beckett, John Swayne and Henry Hall re apprehension of runaways, 751; and forms to be used re freight and passage on the *Lambton* on account of Colonial Government, 1062; and free conveyance on the *Lambton* of stores for his private use, 1065, 1082; and issue of extra flour to Military Detachment at Port Stephens to replace damaged flour, 1100; and keys of records of Police Office, 709; and Minutes of an Enquiry to be lodged among Police records, 732 [sic]; and muster of ticket of leave men and list of such men, 763; and number and allowances and duties of A. A. Co.'s police establishment, 644; and payment of Resident Magistrate by A. A. Co., 646; and provision of legal information to, 1102, 1103; and reduction in allowance of oil for the Police at Carrington, 1080; and reimbursement for payment of supplies to Government Constable, 722; relations of with Sir Edward Parry, 710, 1065; and removal of current Military Detachment at Port Stephens, 931; and report of alleged drunkenness of Mr Price, 1091; and request for payment of account for supplies to Military Detachment at Port Stephens, 754; requesting opinion of re safety of dispensing with a particular Act, 1105; and retention of constables in Police Department, 678; and reward for William Barnes for apprehension of runaways, 690, 691, 714; and some expression allegedly used by Sir Edward Parry, 1099; and submission by William Barnes of affidavit in respect of outstanding claim for reward to bench of magistrates, 708; in support of petition of convict to be reunited with family, 689a, 699a; and ticket of leave for John Mills, 718, 719; and transfer of constables from A. A. Co. service to Government service, 677

money kept in names of convicts: to his credit, 849; request of to receive, 826; withdrawal of, 856

Moore, Joshua John (Liverpool): and account of Sir John Wylde, 976; and payment of account, 975; and stud service, 788

Moore, W. H.: and payment of account, 963; and stud service, 786

mounted police: proposal to replace Military Detachment at Port Stephens with force of, 956

Mudie, James: and tender for supply of flour to Liverpool Plains, 723

Mulgoa, Penrith *see* Cox, Edward

murder: of James Henderson by Aborigines, 906

Murdoch, James (Kent St, Sydney): and payment of account, 968; and stud service, 797

Murphy, Anthony (former convict): return of to employment of A. A. Co., 705

Murray, Sir George (Secretary of State for the Colonies): 649 (para. 5)

mutton: tender for supply of and other rations, 864a

Myall River and Lakes: Aborigines in neighbourhood of, 715

Myles, Lawrence (William's River): and request for permission to use road through property of, 868; and road through property of and insolent or improper language of A. A. Co. servants, 853

Neotsfield, Hunter's River *see* Dangar, Henry; Dangar, William

New South Wales Directory: order for copies of, 1034

Newcastle: accommodation for Company employees in, 639; accounts for supplies to Commissariat, 737; accounts for supply of coal for Beacon Light at, 725, 726, 727; application for coal grant in country adjacent to, 721; assignment of bricklayer and sawyer to coal mines at, 923, 924; coal grant at, 764; and description of land grant at, 998; dumping of ballast in port of, 902; finalisation of coal grant at, 887; glass-making at, 893; lands near to be granted to A. A. Co., 922; licence of occupation for lands near to be granted to A. A. Co., 922; prices tendered for supplying beef at, 884; proposal of meeting between Henry Dangar and party and Mr White in, 637; proposed Town of and A. A. Co.'s Coal Works, 1069; repair of public carts at, 758; survey of lands near to be granted to A. A. Co., 922; surveying and mapping of country adjacent to for application for coal grant, 721; surveying of coal grant at, 840, 844; tender for supply of beef at, 884; tender for supply of flour at, 886; tender for supply of provisions at, 885; tender for supply of salt at, 886; tender for supply of sugar at, 886; *see also* Baker,

Note: References are to letter numbers not page numbers.

John; Brooks, Mr; coal grant; Croasdill, W.; Henderson, John; Reid, John; Scott, A. W.; Smith, John; Steel, James; Wilton, Rev. C. P. N.

Newman, William: theft of bank draft in favour of, 736

Nicholson, John: and payment of account for supply of coal for Beacon Light at Newcastle, 727

Nicholson, Mr: and accounts for supply of coal to Colonial Government, 669

Nisbet, Dr Alexander (Company Assistant General Superintendent): and examination of land to west of Clergy and School reserve, 649 (para. 13); and examination of Liverpool Plains and Peel's River, 649 (paras 17–23); and nominations to Committee of Hunter's River Sweepstakes, 833

Noble, Hugh: and payment of account for stores by, 779

Norton, James (solicitor): and letters for, 1059; and recovery of monies owed to A. A. Co. by C. M. Slade, 1041; reply of to queries by Captain R. G. Moffatt, 1103; and request for legal opinion on refusal to pay living expenses to Mrs William Burnett, 748

Nowlan, William (Patrick's Plains): and removal of stock from A. A. Co. land near 'Warrah,' 686

Ocean: convicts on, 730

Ogilvie, William (Merton, Hunter's River): exchange of assigned convicts with, 666; impounding of A. A. Co. bullocks by, 1101

oil: damaged cans of on *Governor Halkett*, 749, 805; reduction in allowance of for the Police at Carrington, 1080; voucher for freight of cask of, 812

Oliver, George Adam (Kinross, Hunter's River): and account against A. A. Co. for services rendered and account from A. A. Co. for articles from store, and requisitions for expenses, 822; and parcels for John Henderson and George Bunn, 741

Onslow, Arthur Pooley: and payment of account for stores by, 782

Onus, Mr: and removal of stock from A. A. Co. property, 1007a

original land grant: portion of abandoned by A. A. Co., 956; unfitness of, 6–9), 649 (paras 3; *see also* Port Stephens

outfit money, 888

Overseer of Sheep, I.S., *see* Telfer, William

Overseer of Shepherds, I. S., *see* Hadell, Gottfried; Rantzsch, Carl I.S.

Oxley, John, late *see* executors of late John Oxley

Palmer, George Thomas (Parramatta): and payment of account, 874; and stud service, 789

Parnell, Thomas (Richmond): and removal of stock from A. A. Co. land near 'Warrah,' 684

Parramatta *see* Macarthur, James; Macauley, Alexander; Marsden, Rev. S.; Palmer, George T.

Parramatta Fair: sale of horse at, 679a

Parry, Sir Edward (Company Commissioner): and arrangements for transport on the *Sophia Jane* of family and baggage of, 1063; Darch, Henry (Sir Edward Parry's secretary), and examination of Liverpool Plains and Peel's River, 649 (paras 21–23); and examination of original grant, 8–9), 649 (para. 6; exchange of assigned convicts with, 706, 1060a; and meeting with Simon Dodd, 1058; notice re settlement of accounts with, 1095a; and provision of legal information to Captain R. G. Moffatt, 1102, 1103; relations of with Captain R. G. Moffatt, 710, 1065; and reward for William Barnes for apprehension of runaways, 690, 691; some expression allegedly used by, 1099; and submission by William Barnes of affidavit in respect of outstanding claim to bench of magistrates, 708; in support of petition of convict to be reunited with family, 689a, 699a

passage money, 748, 888

Patrick's Plains *see* Larnack, John; Nowlan, William

Patterson's River *see* Cory, E. G.; Jones, Thomas

Paty: and accounts for supplies to, 737

Paul, John: and receipt of payment for provision of sundry goods to, 848; and sale of cheese, 911

Paul, John, senior: and auction of A. A. Co. surplus goods, 825

Paul, Mr: and sale at auction of horses and ponies, 1087

Peck, Thomas (convict): alteration of ticket of leave of, 728

Peel's River: alternative locations for land grant in view of rejection by Colonial Government of land at Liverpool Plains and, 834; appointment of professional person to communicate with re land grants at Liverpool Plains and, 982; arguments for rejection of Governor's recommendation re taking land near as one parcel, 841; authorisation for land grant at, 943; consent to by British government to exchange of land grants at Liverpool Plains and, 5, 26, 29, 31, 33), 649 (paras 4; delineation and accurate marking of land grants at Liverpool Plains and, 1000, 1001, 1024; and delineation and description of land at, 959; examination of, 649 (paras 17–23); examination of Liverpool Plains and, 649 (paras 17–23); proposal in relation to grant of land between Dividing Range and, 764;

Note: References are to letter numbers not page numbers.

rebuttal of arguments by Surveyor-General in favour of alternative single parcel near, 841 (A–L); rejection by Colonial Government of grant of land at Liverpool Plains and, 835; surveying and mapping of land at, 954, 959; surveying and mapping of land between Dividing Range and, 721, 764; surveying of range on south-western side of, 637; *see also* exchange of land grants

Penrith *see* Allan, Andrew; Cox, Edward; Cox, George

Perry, Samuel Augustus (Assistant Surveyor General): and map of original selection of land with retained section marked, 1022

petitions of convicts to be reunited with their families, 689a, 699a

Phillip, Thomas Emmett (convict): transfer of assignment of, 659

Phillips, William (convict): and request by Robert Jones to return to Government, 904

Phoenix: convicts on, 757

Piper, John, senior (Alloway Bank, Penrith): and payment of account, 974; and stud service, 799

pit's mouth: supply of coal to Colonial Government at and 'on board vessel,' 949

Pitt Town *see* McDonald, John

police: A. A. Co.'s role in maintaining, 956; establishment of at Port Stephens, 956, 983, 1043; magistracy and control of, 710; reduction in allowance of oil for at Carrington, 1080; wages of at Port Stephens, 956; *see also* constables in A. A. Co.'s establishment; Government Constables; mounted police; Police Department (of A. A. Co.); police in Government service; Police Office

police clerk: salaries and allowances of, 644, 956, 1043

Police Department (of A. A. Co.): discharge of constables from, 677; duties of, 644; public use of, 667; retention of constables in, 678; salaries and allowances of, 644, 956; *see also* convict constables; free constables; police clerk; scourger

police establishment of A. A. Co. *see* Police Department (of A. A. Co.)

police in Government service: salaries of constables, 677; transfer of constables from A. A. Co. service to, 677, 678

Police Office: keys to records of, 709

Police records: Minutes of an Enquiry to be lodged among, 732 [sic]

ponies: for John Kendrick, 1047; purchase of, 1086; sale of, 1032, 1047

Poole, Mrs: offer of sale of goods from India by to John Terry Hughes, 851; offer of sale of goods from India by to R. Stubbs, 852, 861

Port Stephens: advertisement for shearers at, 699b; appointment of Stipendiary magistrate and Constabulary at, 956; establishment of police at, 956, 983, 1043; number of Aborigines within limits of A. A. Co.'s original grant at, 715; portion of land abandoned by A. A. Co. at, 956; provision by A. A. Co. of fund for religion and education and lease of Clergy and School Reserves at, 1015; threat from Aborigines at, 956 *see also* Caswell, Lieutenant, retired; Ebsworth, J. Edward; Military Detachment at Port Stephens; Moffatt, Captain; original land grant; Resident Magistrate, Port Stephens

pound: establishment of in District of Williams River, 1035; *see also* impounding

Powers, Constable: and report of alleged drunkenness of Mr Price, 1091

Price, Charles: A. A. Co. chaplain, 1029, 1040; alleged drunkenness of, 1092; and report of alleged drunkenness of, 1091

prices: of coal supplied to Colonial Government, 895, 914, 915, 942, 949; of coke, 1095; of French merino and Saxon rams, 939; offered by Simeon Lord for sheep skins, 744; of pony/horse, 1032; of shipment of wool on the *Arundel*, 746, 747; for supply of beef and flour to Military Detachment at Port Stephens, 742, 1019; tendered for supplying beef at Newcastle, 884; of wheat, 1047

prime cost: of coal supplied to Colonial Government, 942

Prince Regent: transshipment of goods from to the *Lambton*, 850

Principal Superintendent of Convicts: alteration of ticket of leave, 1106; and alteration of ticket of leave, 728, 860, 929, 1088; and application for ticket of leave, 897; and convict absconding, 662; and death of Samuel Berryman, 941; and deaths of convicts, 879; and procedure re certificates of freedom in case of assigned servants who have become free, 907; and report on alleged runaway, 757; and return of convict after punishment, 643; and return of convicts whose sentences have been served to employment of A. A. Co., 705; and withdrawal by convicts of monies kept in their names, 856

Pringle, Mr: and removal of stock from A. A. Co. property, 1007a

prisoners constables *see* convict constable

property of A. A. Co.: public use of, 667

public carts: repair of, 758

public houses on A. A. Co. Estate at Stroud: application by Richard Stubbs for free licence for, 641; closing of, 814, 815, 816; licence for held by Richard Stubbs, 692

Puddefoot, Mr: and payment of Thomas Emmett, 812

Quarterly Accounts of A. A. Co., 936

Quay, Lydia (convict): and marriage to Henry Williams, 1011

quit rent in respect of convict labour, 704

Note: References are to letter numbers not page numbers.

quitting service of A. A. Co.: Howitt, Adam, 653
R. Campbell Jr & Co: and deficiency in supply of sugar, 813; and supply of sugar, 838; and tender for supply of sugar, 804; *see also* Robert Campbell Jr & Co
races: Maitland Jockey Club and, 898; *see also* Hunter River Jockey Club
Rainey, James (Sussex St): and quality of casting work, and price for old iron, 988
rams: payment for by George Mackenzie, 888; price of, French merino and Saxon, 939; purchase of by James Raymond, 995
Rantzsch, Carl (former overseer of shepherds, I. S.): documents re claim of against Mr Dutton, 755; payment of bills to, 749
rates for freight and passage: to be paid by Colonial Government, 1016, 1044, 1061
Raymond, James: and account for purchase of rams, 995; and order for copies of New South Wales Directory, 1034
recommendations: of application by Richard Stubbs for free licence for public house, 641
records of Police Office: keys to, 709; Minutes of an Enquiry to be lodged among, 732 [sic]
Reeves, Joshua: of the *Ellen*, 652
Registrar of the Supreme Court, *See* Manning, James Edye
Reid, John (Newcastle): and payment of account to, 938; tender for supply of provisions at Newcastle, 885
Renown: non-delivery of iron and steel from, 752, 805, 812, 850
rent: payable for premises occupied by Richard Stubbs, 843, 940 (b)
Resident Magistrates, Port Stephens: payment of by A. A. Co., 646; salaries and allowances of, 644; *see also* Ebsworth, J. Edward; Moffatt, Captain R. G.
retail business on A. A. Co. Estate, 851, 852, 861; *see also* Stubbs, Richard
return of the quantity of land in cultivation and the produce thereof on Estate of A. A. Co., tabular, 1046
reward: alleged offer of for heads of Aborigines, 989; for apprehension of runaways by James Henderson, 1075; for information about dumping of ballast in port of Newcastle, 902; for William Barnes for apprehension of runaways, 690, 691, 708
Richard Reynolds: and goods damaged on, 997; and goods destroyed by sea water, 936
Richmond *see* Parnell, Thomas; Thorley, Philip
Riddell, Campbell Drummond (Colonial Treasurer): receipt for payment of account for coal supplied to Master Attendants' Department, 811a

roads: on A. A. Co. land at Liverpool Plains and Peel's River, 943; through property of L. Myles, 853, 868
Robert Campbell Jr & Co: payment for sugar by A. A. Co. and further order, 986; *see also* R. Campbell Jr & Co
Rosslyn Castle: convicts on, 1011
Royal Admiral: transport of wool, 1007
runaways: alleged, 757; case of apprehension of, 690, 691, 708, 714, 751; retaining of any that may come on to A. A. Co. land, 1012; and reward for apprehension of by James Henderson, 1075
Ryan, Constable: and payment of supplies for, 722
Ryan, John (Maitland): and tender for supply of flour to 'Warrah,' Liverpool Plains, 1053
salaries and allowances: claim for extra allowance by William Wetherman, 870; of convict constables, 644, 956; of free constables, 644, 956; of free labour at Coal Works at Newcastle, 949; of free or ticket of leave constable (Stroud), 644; of H. Hall, 821; of James Steel and balance of wages for late Michael Steel, 1036; of police clerk, 644, 956, 1043; of Resident Magistrate, 644; of scourger, 644; of James Steel, 817; of John Swayne, 818
sale: of 4 horse power high pressure steam engine, 908a, 913, 935; of barilla, 665; of cheese, 911; of Cleveland horses, 679a, 699a; of goods from India, 851, 852, 861; of hides, 700; of merino rams, 682a; of ponies/horses, 1032, 1087; of spirits, 692, 814, 861; of vessel, 679b
salt: purchase of, 894; tender for supply of at Newcastle, 886
salt house: construction of, 1017
sand: for glass-making, 893
Saunders: and exchange of men with William Cowell, 775
Savings Bank: money in for Thomas Broadhurst, 957
sawyer: assignment of to A. A. Co. coal mines at Newcastle, 952
sawyer, I. S., see Watson, Joseph
sawyers: assignment of to A. A. Co. coal mines at Newcastle, 923, 924, 949
Saxon rams: price of, 939
scab: prosecution for infringement of law re, 847, 902a
Scab Act: application of on A. A. Co. land at Liverpool Plains, 902a; prosecution for infringement of, 847; request for extension of to 'Warrah,' Liverpool Plains, 1042; *see also* infectious diseases
Scabby Sheep Act *see* Scab Act
school master at Carrington, *see* Simes, Thomas
Scott, Alexander Walker (Newcastle): and nominations to Committee of the Hunter's River Sweepstakes, 833; and repayment of

Note: References are to letter numbers not page numbers.

loan, 731; and tender for supply of flour, sugar and salt at Newcastle, 886
Scott, Helenus: and information about persons in possession of bags bearing the mark of A. A. Co., 869
Scott, James (Stonehenge): offer of supplies for A. A. Co. Establishment at Liverpool Plains by, 918
Scott. William (Ash Island): and settlement of debt to A. A. Co., 745
scourger: salaries and allowances of, 644
Secretary of State: and consent to exchange of land grants, 649 (para. 4)
Secretary of State for the Colonies *see* Lord Goderich; Sir George Murray; Hon. E. C. Stanley
Segenhoe *see* Sempill, H. C.
Sempill, Hamilton Collins (Segenhoe): and 4 horse power high pressure portable beam engine with fly wheel, etc., 897a; and supply of tobacco, 656; and tender for supply of flour to 'Warrah,' Liverpool Plains, 765, 1050
services of A. A. Co. stallions *see under* horses
Sesostris: convicts on, 824
settlers: grazing rights of at Liverpool Plains, 649 (paras 35–38), 684, 685, 686
17th Regiment, Resident Magistrate, *see* Moffatt, Captain Robert Gerald
shares: call of, 687a, 688, 689, 732 [sic] a, 733, 734, 874a, 875a, 876, 949a, 950, 951; instructions to Bank of Australia re installments payable on to stockholders, 1057; non-publication of advertisement re call in *Government Gazette*, 985; *see also* stock in A. A. Co.
Sharpe, William: and request for employment, 720
shearers: advertisement for, 699b, 931a, 940c; application for assignment of convicts, 958
sheep: removal of from A. A. Co. property at 'Warrah,' at Liverpool Plains, 806a; *see also* merino rams; rams
Sheep Overseer, I. S, *see* Barnes, William
sheep skins: price for offered by Simeon Lord, 744
shepherd, I. S., *see* Merchant, Richard
shepherd and ploughman, I. S., *see* May, William
shepherds: request for assignment of convicts, 650
shortage of men, 687, 703, 704, 705, 717
Simes, Thomas (school master at Carrington): termination of services of and termination payment, 999
Singleton, Benjamin (John's Mill, William's River): and account for payment, 889; and grinding of wheat into flour, 652; order for flour, 676; and order of flour, 648
Slade, George Milner (former free storekeeper at Port Stephens): and recovery of monies owed to A. A. Co. by, 1041

slop clothing: William Wetherman and deficiency in, 928
Smith, Cornelius,: and request for employment, 682
Smith, J. G.: and purchase of stallions by Lieutenant Charlton, 896
Smith, John: and exchange of assigned convicts (baker and butcher), 1020; and tender for supplying beef at Newcastle, 884; and tender to supply flour to 'Warrah,' Liverpool Plains, 767
Smith, John (Governor of A. A. Co., London): and price of coal supplied to Colonial Government, issue of computation of prime cost, and payment of accounts, 942
Smyth, William (Maitland, former wheelwright, I. S.): and construction of wagon, [994]; and payment of account, 759
Snodgrass, Honourable Lieutenant Colonel: and removal of current Military Detachment at Port Stephens, 931
Sophia Jane: arrangements for transport the of families and baggage of, respectively, Lieutenant Colonel Henry Dumaresq and Sir Edward Parry on, 1063
Spark, Alexander Brodie (merchant): and drafts to credit of A. A. Co. and Lieutenant Colonel Dumaresq, 921; and nominations to Committee of the Hunter's River Sweepstakes, 833; and price of shipment of wool on the *Arundel*, 746; and shipment of wool on the *Arundel*, 735; and subscription to Maitland Jockey Club, 910
spirits: illegal sale of on A. A. Co. property, 861; requisition for, 752; sale of by Richard Stubbs on A. A. Co. property, 692, 814
St Helier's, Hunter's River *see* Dumaresq, Lieutenant Colonel
Stacey, James (convict): transfer of assignment of, 1060a
Stacy, Dr James Edward (Company Surgeon and Botanist): and committal of convict to Lunatic Asylum, 661; exchange of assigned convicts with, 659; and payment of Thomas Emmett, 812;and support for request to Court of Directors, 829
Stanley, Right Honorable Edward G (Secretary of State for War and Colonies): and dispute with Colonial Government re price of coal supplied to Colonial Government, issue of computation of prime cost, and payment of accounts, 942; and dispute with Colonial Government re supply of convicts for Coal Works at Newcastle, use of convict mechanics, and payment of accounts, 949
stationery: provision of, with other items, by A. A. Co. to police at Port Stephens, 956, 1043
Staunton (police clerk): and report of alleged drunkenness of Mr Price, 1091
steam engine *see* 4 horse power high pressure steam engine

Note: References are to letter numbers not page numbers.

steamship owner, *see* Grose, Joseph Hickey (
Steel, James (Company Colliery Engineer): and continuation of employment agreement, 777; drafts for salary of and balance of wages for late Michael Steel, 1036; and salary and continuation of employment agreement, 817
Steel, Michael (late): balance of wages for, 1036
Stipendiary Magistrate, Port Stephens: appointment of, 956
stock: removal of from A. A. Co. property, 1007a; removal of from A. A. Co. property at 'Warrah,' at Liverpool Plains, 684, 685, 686; *see also* cattle; sheep
stock in A. A. Co.: of George Bunn, 692; holding of by Sir Edward Parry and J. Edward Ebsworth and legality of their sitting on bench in case of Richard Stubbs, 692; instructions to Bank of Australia re instalments payable on shares to holders of, 1057; letters to proprietors of re call of shares, 688, 689, 733, 734, 875, 875a, 876, 950, 951; *see also* shares
stock keeper *see* head stock keeper
Stokes, John (boat builder, I.S): cancellation of agreement of employment, and termination pay, 1097
stone-cutters, 949
Stonehenge *see* Scott, James
store *see* free store
storekeeper at Port Stephens, *see* Slade, George Milner; Stubbs, Richard
Street, William (harness maker, I. S.): non-renewal of agreement of employment with, 1083
Stroud: public house at: application by Richard Stubbs for free licence for, 641; closing of, 814, 815, 816; licence for held by Richard Stubbs, 692; *see also* Hall, Henry; Stubbs, Richard; Tozer, Thomas N.
Stubbs, Richard (free store keeper at Port Stephens): application for free licence for one of his two public houses on A. A. Co. Estate, 641; application for licence for public house, 641; and closing of public house, continuation of free store and debts to by A. A. Co. servants, 823; and closing of public house and continuation of free store, 814, 816; and lowering of rent for premises occupied by, 940 (b); packet for, 740; and rent payable for premises occupied by, 843; and report of alleged drunkenness of Mr Price, 1091; and retail business being carried on by others on A. A. Co. Estate, 861; and sale of goods from India to by Mrs Poole, 852; and sale of spirits to A. A. Co. servants, 692
Stud *see* A. A. Co. Stud
stud service *see under* horses
sugar: deficiency in supply of by R. Campbell Jr & Co, 813, 838; payment to Robert Campbell Jr & Co for and further order, 986; tender for supply of, 804, 864a; tender for supply of at Newcastle, 886; tenders for supply of for prisoners' rations, 754a
Superintendent of Company's Flocks *see* Hall, Charles
Supreme Court: decision of in favour of A. A. Co. in case of claim by G. M. Slade on James Edward Ebsworth, for the Company, 1041; and proceeds of sale of property of late James Henderson, balance of his wages and reward for apprehension of runaways, 1075
Surrey: convicts on, 663
Surry: convicts on, 706, 718, 1088
surveying: of Clergy and School Reserve, 649 (para.12); of coal grant at Newcastle, 840, 844, 947, 953; of land at Liverpool Plains and Peel's River, 954; of land between Peel's River and Dividing Range, 764; and land grants, 841 (L); of land near Peel's River and error in, 1026; of land north of Manning River, 10–11, 14), 649 (paras 7; of lands near Newcastle to be granted to A. A. Co., 922; of range on south-western side of Peel's River, 637; tenders for, 991, 1000, 1008; terms for undertaking, 991; of Williams River Estate, 840
Surveyor-General *see* Mitchell, Major Thomas Livingstone
Surveyor General's Office: information on Liverpool Plains in, 649 (paras 14–17)
Sussex St, *see* Rainey, James
Swayne, John (Company Wool Classer): and apprehension of runaways, 690, 714, 751; and continuation of employment agreement, 778; and increase in salary and duties, 807; and salary and continuation of employment agreement, 819
Sydenham Alcorn's Inn *see* Gaggin, W. John
Sydney Gazette: advertisements: for blacksmith, 1026a; for head stock keeper, 699b; horse sale, 679a; merino ram sale, 682a; sale of vessel, 679b; share call, 687a, 732 [sic] a, 874a, 949a; for shearers, 699b, 940c; stud service, 701a, 706a, 940d; tenders for supply of flour to 'Warrah,' Liverpool Plains, 738a; tenders for supply of rations (beef or mutton, flour, sugar, tea), 864a; tenders for supply of sugar for prisoners rations, 754a; tenders for transport of wool, 995a; unfurnished cottages to let, 864b; denial of statement in *The Australian* re alleged outrages against Aborigines by servants of A. A. Co., 1011a; and nominations to Committee of Hunter's River Sweepstakes, 833; notices: payment for coal, 642a; prohibition of cutting of timber and depasturing of cattle on A. A. Co. land near Williams River, 1036a
Sydney Herald: advertisements: for blacksmith, 1026a; for head stock keeper,

Note: References are to letter numbers not page numbers.

699b; horse sale, 679a, 699b; merino ram sale, 682a; sale of vessel, 679b; share call, 687a, 732 [sic] a, 874a, 949a; for shearers, 699b, 940c; stud service, 706a, 940d; tenders for supply of flour to 'Warrah,' Liverpool Plains, 738a; tenders for supply of rations (beef or mutton, flour, sugar, tea), 864a; tenders for supply of sugar for prisoners rations, 754a; tenders for transport of wool, 995a; unfurnished cottages to let, 864b; denial of statement in *The Australian* re alleged outrages against Aborigines by servants of A. A. Co., 1011a; notices: payment for coal, 642a; prohibition of cutting of timber and depasturing of cattle on A. A. Co. land near Williams River, 1036a

Sydney Monitor: advertisements: for blacksmith, 1026a; for head stock keeper, 699b; horse sale, 679a, 699b; merino ram sale, 682a; sale of vessel, 679b; share call, 687a, 732 [sic] a, 874a, 949a; for shearers, 699b, 940c; stud service, 701a, 706a, 940d; tenders for supply of flour to 'Warrah,' Liverpool Plains, 738a; tenders for supply of rations (beef or mutton, flour, sugar, tea), 864a; tenders for supply of sugar for prisoners rations, 754a; tenders for transport of wool, 995a; unfurnished cottages to let, 864b; copies of ordered, 640; denial of statement in *The Australian* re alleged outrages against Aborigines by servants of A. A. Co., 1011a; notices: payment for coal in, 642a; prohibition of cutting of timber and depasturing of cattle on A. A. Co. land near Williams River, 1036a

Taggart, Charles: and removal of stock from A. A. Co. property, 1007a

Tanilba, Port Stephens *see* Caswell, Lieutenant William

Taylor, William: and removal of stock from A. A. Co. property, 1007a

tea: order for, 899; supply of, 883; tender for supply of and other rations to servants of A. A. Co., 864a; *see also* Hyson Skin (tea)

teeth: extraction of, 657 (*see also* Fox's Tooth Keys)

Telfer, William (overseer of sheep, I.S.): and assistance to John Armstrong with survey, 1024, 1025

Telligherry: apprehension of runaways at, 690; *see also* Swayne, John

temporary occupation: of land near 'Warrah,' Liverpool Plains, 683, 684, 685, 686, 841, 902a

tenders: for supply of beef and flour to Military Detachment at Port Stephens, 742, 1019; for supply of flour, sugar and salt at Newcastle, 886; for supply of flour to Liverpool Plains, 723; for supply of flour to 'Warrah,' Liverpool Plains, 738a, 765, 766, 767, 768, 1005a, 1049, 1050, 1053, 1054, 1055, 1056; for supply of provisions at Newcastle, 885; for supply of provisions that must include rum, bread and mutton to Commissariat Office, 742; for supply of rations (beef or mutton, flour, sugar, tea), 864a; for supply of sugar, 804; for supply of sugar for prisoners rations, 754a; for surveying and mapping work, 991, 1000, 1008; for transport of wool, 995a, 1006, 1007

termination of services: of Henry Dangar, 835, 841; of Thomas Simes, 999; of William Wetherman, 881, 888; *see also* employment by A. A. Co., cancellation of agreement

termination payment: to Thomas Simes, 999; to John Stokes, 1097; to William Wetherman, 881, 888

Terry, Samuel: payment of account for stores by, 780

theodolite: return of by Henry Dangar, 947, 1023

Thomas Dent & Co: and order for Hyson Skin tea, and payment, 899

Thompson, Patrick (convict): medical treatment for, 716

Thorley, Philip (Richmond): and removal of stock from A. A. Co. land near 'Warrah,' 685

ticket of leave, 904, 923; alterations of, 638, 728, 860, 929, 1088, 1106; applications for, 645, 718, 719, 897; and compliance with regulations, 730; list of men holding, 763; list of men holding at Port Stephens, 762; muster of men holding, 763; petition for, 732a; request of men holding to receive small sums of money, 826

ticket of leave constables: salaries and allowances of, 644; transfer of one to Government service, 677

timber: cutting of on A. A. Co. land near Williams River, 1036a; saleability of, 809

tobacco: supply of, 656

Tozer, Thomas Norris (Company Farm Overseer).: and allowance on quitting employment of A. A. Co., 863; and cancellation of employment agreement with A. A. Co., 859

trades *see* agricultural labourers; bakers; blacksmiths; bricklayers; butchers; carpenters; farriers; gardeners; horseshoers; mechanics; miners; sawyers; shearers; stone-cutters; wheelwrights

trespassing, 647

Tulk, Thomas (former bricklayer, I.S.): and trespassing on A. A. Co. Estate, 647

Turnbull, Mr: and quality of casting work by James Rainey, 988

Under Secretary of State for the Colonies *see* Stanley, Right Honorable E. G.

unfurnished cottages to let: advertisement of, 864b

Note: References are to letter numbers not page numbers.

Van Diemen's Land, Government of: and account for supply of coal to, 1071, 1084
vessel: sale of, 679b; supply of coal to Colonial Government on board and 'at pit's mouth,' 949
vine-cuttings: for James King, 893
vinegar: deficiency in, 894
Vineyard Cottage, Patterson's River see Jones, Thomas
Viscount Goderich see Lord Goderich
wages see salaries and allowances
Walker, Mr: and John Blaxland being his agent, 827
Walker, Thomas: and stud service, 784, 811
Walleroba see Tulk, Thomas
Warlters, Jeremiah (King St): and cattle claimed by, 732
Warner JP, Mr (Lake Macquarie): and dumping of ballast in port of Newcastle, 902
'Warrah,' Liverpool Plains: advertisement for shearers at, 940c; offer to supply flour to, 1049, 1050; removal of cattle from A. A. Co. property at, 806a; removal of sheep from A. A. Co. property at, 806a; removal of stock from A. A. Co. property at, 684, 685, 686; request for extension of Scab Act to, 1042; request for Licence of Occupation of land near, 649 (para. 61); temporary occupation of land near, 683, 684, 685, 686, 841, 902a; and temporary occupation of land near, 683, 684, 685, 686, 841; tenders for supply of flour to, 738a, 765, 766, 767, 768, 1005a, 1049, 1050, 1053, 1054, 1055, 1056; see also Liverpool Plains; Telfer, William
warrant: for lands near Newcastle to be granted to A. A. Co., 922
water: importance of in supporting man, sheep and cattle, 49–50), 649 (paras 43–44, 841
Water, John (former convict): return to employment of A. A. Co., 705
water frontage and land grants, 764; custom governing, 50, 52), 649 (paras 46–48
Waterloo: convicts on, 706
Waters, John (convict): return of to A. A. Co. after punishment, 643
Watson, Joseph (sawyer, I. S.): and cancellation of agreement of employment, 955; and permission to go to Sydney, 937, 940 (a)
Welch ponies: servicing by stallions, 940d
Wells, James (convict): and ticket of leave, 923
Wetherman, William (Company Store Keeper): accounts with, 928; claim by, 711; and claim for extra allowance, 870; and deficiency in slop clothing, 928; and passage and outfit money, 888; and settlement of accounts, 917; termination of services of, 881, 888; and termination payment, 881, 888
Whalin, Robert (convict): transfer of to A. A. Co., 642

wheat: to be ground into flour, 651, 674, 753; order for, 1047; in payment for rams, 939; price of, 1047
wheelwrights: accidents to, 764a; application for assignment of, 764a, 958
White, George Boyle (Government Surveyor): and A. A. Co.'s Coal Works and proposed Town of Newcastle, 1069; and description of land grant at Newcastle, 998; and maps of land at Liverpool Plains and Peel's River, 1024; proposal of meeting with Dangar and party in Newcastle, 637; surveying and mapping of country adjacent to Newcastle for application for coal grant, 721; surveying and mapping of land between Peel's River and Dividing Range, 721
White, James Charles (Company Store Keeper): circumstance to be related to by Captain R. G. Moffatt, 1094; and collection of loan repayment of A. W. Scott, 731; and combination of Company Storekeeper with superintendence of another department, 881; and report of alleged drunkenness of Mr Price, 1091
William IV: transport of parcels for John Henderson and George Bunn on, 741
Williams, Henry (convict): and marriage to Lydia Quay, 1011
Williams River see Bench of Magistrates, District of Williams River; Mackenzie, George; Myles, L.:
 Singleton, B.; Yeoman, George
Wilson, Thomas Braidwood: and payment of account, 967
Wilson, William (convict): change of assignment of, 706
Wilton, Rev. Charles Pleydell Neale: and alleged prohibition of his coming on to A. A. Co. Estate, 1066; and marriage of two convicts, 1011; and performance of divine service at Carrington, 1040; and proposed visit to Port Stephens to conduct baptisms and divine service, 1029
Wimbourne, Penrith see Cox, George
Windsor see Feales, John
wool: price of shipment of on the *Arundel*, 746, 747; shipment of on *Craigievar*, 729; shipment of on the *Arundel*, 735; tender for transport of, 995a, 1006; tenders for transport of, 1007; transport of to London on the *Lochiel*, 1006
wool ships: and ballast, 901
Wylde, Sir John (Liverpool): and stud service, 787
Wynter, William: allegations by Henry Herring and against Sir Edward Parry and others in employ of A. A. Co. in relation to Aborigines, 989
Yeoman, George (Maitland): and order of flour and shipment of wheat to be ground, 753; and quality of flour and order of bran, 702; and transport of flour on the *Ellen*, 699

www.ingramcontent.com/pod-product-compliance
Lightning Source LLC
Chambersburg PA
CBHW040311240426
43666CB00022B/2923